Praise for the problem-space method

"Indi Young's approach to center understanding needs by deeply listening to others and framing people as multi-faceted beings using thinking styles, has completely changed the way I approach conducting design focused research.

"Currently, we are looking to increasingly augment humans with technology. We should have an intimate and deep understanding of people before we even think about doing any such thing. Indi's methods in deep listening go a long way to addressing how to do that understanding."
—Dawn Ahukanna, Digital Experience Designer

"Indi Young's method is a practical answer to healing the broken relationship between business and people. If you want to make equitable, inclusive design, pay attention."
—Yousef Kazerooni, Product Designer

"When we speak, we are not listening, which means we are not learning. Listening allows us to see challenges from a fresh perspective, and helps us uncover new insights we might not have considered before. Indi Young is the go-to expert when it comes to effective listening. *Time to Listen* will guide you through the process every step of the way."
—Maria Giudice, Leadership Coach, Co-author "Rise of the DEO"

"We rush from here to there, we rush from problem to solution, we rush from project kickoff to product release. But have we really understood the people whose problems we purport to solve? Have we truly listened to them in a deep way to understand their own experience of those problems? Indi Young has long considered and examined listening, and is a thoughtful and articulate guide through the ways in which we can listen more openly and effectively and why we should do so. Listen to her if designing experiences that are helpful and healing, rather than harmful, matters to you."
—Mark Connolly, Co-chair of Fluxible, Canada's UX Festival

"I've always secretly thought that I listen pretty well to others, whether at work or among my friends, until I attended Indi's course on Listening Deeply. What I thought was "listening" was really me trying to listen to find a solution for the person, and waiting for an opportune break to interrupt so that I can provide great advice or comments. What I didn't know is that listening deeply was never about me.... Applying [my new listening skills] to my work and personal life has had a transforming effect on my relationships, quality of work and empathy level. So thank you, Indi!"

—Pei Ling Chin, researcher in the problem space

"Qualitative researchers often learn, in graduate school, how to interview people. But learning how to listen is rarely addressed. My own personal copy of Indi's *Practical Empathy* is dog-eared and heavily highlighted. I can't wait to read about the evolution of Indi's listening lessons in *Time to Listen* and integrate them into my own practice."

—Marie Mika, PhD, Design Researcher

"Indi explains how to truly listen to what people are saying in order to strategize a solution that will have a positive impact (or will improve people's lives). Another game-changing book by Indi Young that even the most seasoned UX practitioners should read."

— Jaime Levy, Author of UX Strategy

"Healing our planet requires centering the connections across the human, technological, and natural worlds. Listening deeply to truly hear is essential toward building a flourishing future. *Time to Listen* provides actionable frameworks and insights to support people and organizations on this journey."

—Rainey Straus, Artist/Designer

"Real listening requires being open to learning something new and unexpected. And that often means admitting that we don't have the answers. Good listeners set aside their methods, frameworks, biases, and so-called expertise for a chance to glimpse the truth offered by someone else."

—Mark Hurst, founder, Creative Good

"I learned early on that listening is one of the greatest gifts we can give others. Deep listening without prejudice is hard. Learning from someone like Indi who has perfected it into an art form can go a long ways into understanding ourselves and others."

—Kelly Goto, Principal & CEO, gotomedia & gotoresearch

"Listening well means silencing our inner dialogue to focus on what the other person is actually saying. It's surprisingly difficult to do well, but Indi offers us a framework to improve our skills as well as strong arguments as to why it matters."

—Sara Cambridge, User Experience Research Consultant

"There is no more powerful question to learn about and from others than the question stem: "what was going through your mind..." I use this stem in my professional life working with research participants, stakeholders, and colleagues. I use it in my personal life to understand my mother, husband, and friends. After decades of conducting qualitative research, learning to learn using Indi's approach has been a game-changer."

—Kunyi Mangalam, Service Designer

"With growing interest in DEI, the idea of an average user is shifting. However, still, there is a considerable gap to fill. We need more and more businesses to invest in bringing all users, including those at the fringes, onboard and engage with them at every step of the product creation process. It's never late for the design teams to ask, 'who are we excluding?'"

—Renu Zunjawad, PhD, Sr. UX Research Consultant

"Learning to listen is basically learning how to care. Those who listen well also work well, collaborate well, and create well. Indi's book will give you the skills to improve your work, your partnerships, and even your life satisfaction because you will learn what triggers you not to care about yourself, your partners, or your world."

— Sam Ladner, Principal Researcher, Strategy, Workday, Inc. and Co-Chair EPIC 2021

"People never came with a 'how-to' manual. They figure things out themselves--in their own unique ways as they process their individual needs. This is what our ancestors did and something we continue to do today. So how do we design for people with agency? We can either be in awe of the diversity of thought and support them in their own approach or we can invalidate it and enforce our ways on them. The former makes us design to empower people. Getting stuck on ideas that we want to impose on others tempts us to average out everyone's needs, giving rise to a fictional hero in our product/service story - the average user. We don't find that kind of user in our own home, why are we looking for them outside?

"If we truly want to design for people, we need to acknowledge their sense of agency and practice deep empathy that considers the complexities and nuances of being human. There is enough evidence on WHY empathy is the future for all organizations. Indi's method does what many haven't been able to do - empower us with the HOW. Her approach isn't scientific; it's human, and it starts with listening."

—Zulaikha Rahman, Human-centered Design Practitioner, Empathy-Spark

"The nature of design practice is undergoing a fundamental change, with the makeup of design teams becoming more diverse, and the boundary between the 'team' and their 'audience' changing with it. The role of lived experience is taking a central place in the design process, but to truly unlock the potential for that experience to shape design practice, we need also to undertake a fundamental shift in the way we engage with people throughout the design process. One of those fundamental shifts, so brilliantly explored by Indi Young in this book, is to centre listening as a tool for understanding."

—Steve Baty, Director & Co-Founder, Meld Studios

Time to Listen

How Giving People Space to Speak
Drives Invention and Inclusion

by Indi Young

Foreword by Zulaikha Rahman
Visual explanations by Anna Iurchenko

Indi Young

Time to Listen:
How Giving People Space to Speak
Drives Invention and Inclusion
by Indi Young

Published by Indi Young Books

indiyoung.com

Cover and Visual Explanations by Anna Iurchenko, https://sketchit.co
Editing and Direction by Alex Hughes Capell and Nathan Boole
Book Design by Lovetree Creative

978-1-944627-11-9 (print)
978-1-944627-10-2 (ebook)

DISCLAIMERS:
This method is meant to produce a strategy for supporting more people
with the solutions you make. Results are not guaranteed.
All examples are either invented or used with permission from the
participants.

Dedicated to the memory of
Kevin Brooks,
who first opened my mind to rapt listening
during his workshop at UX Week 2008,
Storytelling for User Experience Design

Table of Contents

3   ASSUMPTION-WARY KNOWLEDGE   55

6 INSIDE THE LISTENING SESSION   145

7   ENSURING A SAFE SPACE   215

8   Handling Complexity Well   251

About This Book

This book about deep listening is intended for people directing or doing research for the purpose of designing and improving solutions. Those same people are also using deep listening to build stronger relationships and understanding with colleagues and with decision-makers at their organizations. Because of this focus, the examples will come mostly from the digital business world, but the principles of how to conduct effective listening sessions and what to do with the results should be applicable to a variety of product and service contexts.

When you are using deep listening to design and improve solutions, this book won't completely stand alone. Listening sessions exist as one step of a larger method: purpose-focused research in the problem space (concepts I'll explain later in this book). To get the most out of your listening, you'll then turn people's words into an opportunity map for your organization, a process which takes several steps. (This book does stand alone for building stronger relationships with colleagues.)

Here's a simplified summary of those steps. The two bolded steps are contained in this book.

1. Decide whether and when you want to build knowledge
2. **Frame the study – what purpose to understand and who to learn from**
3. **Build your understanding through listening sessions**
4. Summarize interior cognition concepts from transcripts
5. Cultivate patterns from these summaries, based on focus of mental attention

6. Find differences in people's approaches to the purpose, to define thinking styles
7. Lay out an opportunity map that shows gaps in how your solutions support these patterns and thinking styles
8. Prioritize and track over the years the new support you can provide for the gaps, and how well you help different thinking styles accomplish their purpose
9. Proceed with ideas, validation, design, and development for a priority area (via existing solution-space methods)
10. Decide whether and when to add more knowledge to the opportunity map

This book sits near the beginning of the method. In the courses I teach about the whole method, I always start with listening, because listening is the foundation. The purpose-focused philosophy of designing and improving solutions in support of thinking styles begins with realizing there is so much more beautiful human variation out there.

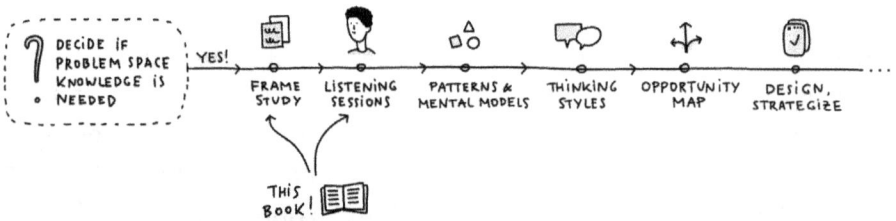

If you want to support a broader set of people, you need to think from their perspective. For that, it takes a human to understand another human. Listening is where you begin. That's what this book is about. You can take the concepts and mold them to your philosophies and help it take root in your organization. And share how you grow the practice, because you are going to take this work further than ever.

That Word 'Listen'

This book uses a word, "listen," that has a literal meaning implying that a person can hear audibly. That literal meaning excludes a lot of people who are our friends, family, co-workers, community members, and people whom we want to understand. I want to help everyone feel welcome, and give everyone access to everyone else, so I reached out to user-experience practitioners who are deaf to find out their thoughts on whether to use this word.

What I "heard" back (via written communication) is that the word "listen" is also used as a figure of speech in English. People can "listen" in various formats, like texting, chatting, and good video captioning. People can "listen" visually via drawing, sign language, facial expressions, and body movements. People can "hear" each other in these ways, too, and "speak" to each other. It's when the words are used as a command to do something that a person cannot ("go listen to my podcast!") that it causes frustration or offense.

In this book, I mean to help you "listen" deeply in any of these formats. I mean to help you help others feel affirmed and "heard" in all of those formats too.

I generally seek to use words that are inclusive, carrying a clearer meaning for a broader set of people. Language is imperfect. I will also introduce language that assists you as solution creators and as researchers in broadening the mindset at your organization. I also encourage you to reach for your own words, and existing words from other cultures and communities. Language is evolving. Ten years from now we will have a different set of words in use, so it will be interesting to see how quickly this book starts to feel outdated in terminology. (For example, three months after my first book, Mental Models, was published, the way I was using the word "task" became outdated. It's "concept" now.)

Each person has their own experience and their own way of thinking about and reacting to certain words and certain concepts. A word that is fine with one person may trigger another. I'm trying to welcome all thinking styles in the way I write this book—but I may fail in various respects, for various individuals. I believe and respect every person's approach. Every person also has agency and may change their approach from context to context, or as time goes by. People are complex and individual, and that's the beauty of it.

In this book, I intend to help you build a broader set of perspectives so that your organization can support a broader set of people. However, I am by no means an expert at design justice, so I will ask you to incorporate the work of people who are. The Design Justice Network and the Inclusive Design Principles are good foundations. As a community, we can together purposely break past the bounded and complacent way of thinking that exists at many organizations. It's a journey of creating an inclusive world that values plurality and every human.

—Indi

Additional Resources

The Design Justice Network - https://designjustice.org

The Inclusive Design Principles - https://inclusivedesignprinciples.org

Disability Language Style Guide | National Center on Disability and Journalism - https://ncdj.org/style-guide/

Foreword

"He is just a frustrated executive who can't meet his numbers," said my manager.

I disagreed, telling my manager about the challenges that had made it hard for the account executive we were discussing. I had just spoken with the account executive in a 30-minute conversation. There, I had heard stories about how he worked with customers on a day-to-day basis. These stories matched patterns from other account executives. There was evidence that clearly demanded the need for more capabilities to empower them. The manager, however, was quick to invalidate their need.

Three years later, the challenge became too damaging to ignore. It ran so deep that an entire team, with executive funding, needed to be put together to solve the problem. Resources were mobilized, processes were revamped, and investments were made—all in haste. The problem was so severe it was affecting the organisation as a whole.

Why? Because three years ago, the management felt powerful enough to not listen to what account executives were saying about their work, and years later, the business (literally) paid for it. As a person who was there listening to the account executives and as a person who was helping set up the new team—I was shocked at the power of the 30-minute conversation with the account executive. If we had listened, we would have had a beautiful opportunity to grow our business in a meaningful direction. Instead, we waited for the challenge to grow into a strategic issue. It took a crisis to get everyone to work on it. What a waste!

This is what is happening in organizations today. We are all surrounded by people with rich insights on what really matters. Instead of listening to them, we are talking amongst ourselves in closed rooms. Short-term validations are making us feel powerful enough to make decisions that impact others. As a result, assumptions & hunches—sometimes driven by biased data interpretations—start guiding product/service roadmaps instead of real needs. We end up creating broken—and sometimes harmful—systems. This has to stop.

In a world that's embracing inclusive design, listening to our people is a powerful way to build competitive advantage and this book may be the best way to learn how to do it right. Organisations often rely on focus groups, surveys, or interventions that try to average out people's needs. This book helps us understand why that doesn't work. To serve our people, we don't need to average out what everyone is saying but what we need to do is listen deeply, navigate conversations, and identify the non-obvious patterns in people's behaviour to find those rich insights that drive innovation.

Indi's approach to listening has been the most empowering tool for me as a designer. It helped me get past my own biases and take into account the nuances and complexities of being human. Her approach is honest, clear, and probably the only way we should be listening. I am fascinated by how she broke it down for us into concepts that we could quickly learn and adapt. I invite you all to be amazed by Indi's human approach to listening to people. This is empathy in its truest form—something we all need to get better at.

—Zulaikha Rahman, Human-centered Design Practitioner, EmpathySpark

CHAPTER 1

CHAPTER 1

What's Wrong with Average

Average solutions aren't just average as in "meh." They often cause harm to the people who weren't considered in the design. In the design field, there is an oft-repeated story about how a solution designed to support the average person actually killed people. In case you haven't read the story, I'll recount it here. In the late 1940s, the United States Air Force had a problem. A new generation of Air Force jets were flying dramatically faster. The original cockpit had been designed in 1926. The jet manufacturers had taken a series of measurements of 1926 pilots' bodies at that time. They had averaged out all their measurements and designed a helmet to fit the average measured head, a seat to fit the average rear end, and cockpit distances to fit the average arm length. They designed for ten key dimensions, to fit the average (1926 male pilot's) body. Unfortunately, by the 1940s, the cockpit design was absolutely not working.

Pilots were crashing, again and again.

The Air Force needed its military suppliers to redesign the cockpit so that the pilots would survive. So, in 1950 they put a newly graduated twenty-three-year-old, Lt. Gilbert S. Daniels, on the task. And his first idea was to check the math, which meant measuring 4,000 pilots in the Wright Air Force Base.

After the measurements were taken, Lt. Daniels sat down to look at the data. Of the thousands of pilots measured, literally zero were average in all ten dimensions. Even more interestingly, only 3.5 percent would be average-sized in three dimensions. "It can be seen that the 'average man' is a misleading and illusory concept as a basis for design criteria, and is particularly so when more than one dimension is being considered," Lt. Daniels said.[1] (He must have had a good mentor to be able to speak so decisively in his conclusions.)

As a result of Lt. Daniels' work, the Air Force asked the jet manufacturers to change their design. Those engineers figured out how to make fighter jet helmets, cockpit seats, and floor pedals adjustable. The pilots were more able to handle the planes while under G forces, pilot performance soared, and many fewer people died.[2] Physical product manufacturers responded, *changing* many things in the decades since, understanding that *one size really doesn't fit all* in many circumstances. The innovation also led directly to the adjustable seats we have in modern cars, adjustable medical equipment, adjustable desks, and so on.

The Air Force cockpit story is the story of an inflection point, a moment that changed everything. Or not. There are limits to how adjustable any particular design is. Every manufacturer puts limits on how much they are willing to spend on setting up factory production. There are thousands of people who still have to make do with one extreme or the other of the adjustment. Plenty of people still add cushions to their desk chairs. We may not fully design to the average in every physical product anymore, but we certainly don't design for everyone.

Access for People with Disabilities

After the end of the second World War, many soldiers came back to their countries with mobility-related injuries, needing canes and wheelchairs to get around. The battles, weapons, and chemicals had blasted their hearing and sight. Former soldiers with these kinds of disabilities, in fact, joined society in such vocal numbers in the late 1940s and 1950s that accessibility issues finally began reaching the public awareness.[3] The world at that time was not built for wheelchair users; deaf and blind people were not supported. Most buildings—even public buildings— relied on stairs or had other architectural issues that prevented people with disabilities from accessing them without assistance.

Over time, activists with disabilities fought worldwide to create environments that could include wheelchair users. The American experience illustrates the trend. In the 1960s, American protestors took to the streets, smashing curbs to create their own accessible ramps. In the 1970s, founders of the Independent Living Movement established a wheelchair route through the University of California campus, even "covertly laying asphalt in the middle of the night."[4] By 1973, the first American law was passed banning discrimination on the basis of disability. Sit ins and protests continued.

Meanwhile, individuals with hearing and vision impairments were making strides toward better access to technology. The hearing impaired gained greater access in the U.S. in 1972, when Julia Child's "The French Chef" was broadcast with captions, and by 1982, ABC's World News Tonight was broadcast with captions in real-time.[5] People with visual impairments were able to access computers more easily with the development of the first Braille translator in the early 1960s[6] and the first refreshable Braille display in 1975.[7] As a result of the tireless efforts of activists and lawmakers with disabilities, laws about providing access for people with disabilities slowly passed all over the world. Japan's passed in 1970, and it was revised and expanded several times until it became the "Fundamental Law for Disabled Persons," mandating social support, welfare, healthcare, community services, and work opportunities for people with disabilities[8]. In 2007 to 2008 over 100 countries signed the UN treaty "Convention on the Rights of Persons with Disabilities".[9] Everywhere, Braille began appearing on public keypads and elevator controls, in airplanes, and on building signage.

This decades-long inflection point changed everything. A little bit. There are still online resources, buildings, and transit systems without accommodations for people with disabilities. Adjustment remains an ongoing struggle.

Designing for Access, Not Average

Today, there are still organizations that don't spend much budget or attention on designing support for people with disabilities into their products. Even technologists think that machine-driven support such as automated video captions "work well enough." They don't invest in improving the experience, remaining oblivious to how frustrating automated captions can be for the people who have no choice but to rely on them.

Even when they do design for support, they approach everyone with a disability with the same average solution. Svetlana Kouznetsova, an independent consultant and accessibility trailblazer, has spent her career educating professionals about accessible on-screen design. She explains that all deaf people are not alike, not all blind people have the same thinking style, and you can't treat a large group as if everyone in it has all the same needs, experiences, and desires. Yet technology companies do just that.

The Average Does Harm

Designing to an average user was lethal in aviation. Similarly, designing to an average user in other contexts also hurts people. Without accommodations, the built environment does tremendous harm to wheelchair users, the blind, sight impaired, deaf, and hard of hearing. Since 2016, when books, articles, and talks all over the design community began to tell the adjustable cockpit story, everyone has been repeating "We can't design for the average." It's been a refrain in education, healthcare, and government circles as well. The digital and service industry, unrestricted by the same limitations of physical space and materials, can incorporate adjustability and customization so much more easily than the designers of cockpit seats or the built environment.

Why, then, does solution design *still* revolve around the average, especially in the technology world where there seems to be budget and awareness?

What drives the problem is the mindset organizations use. Traditionally, organizations build one solution for one market. They target single solutions to the largest part of the bell curve of people, not understanding that even those people don't all think the same. In business, government, and even the non-profit sector, organizations define the people they serve by addressing an avatar, a citizen, an average user, a job title. People act as if there are only enough resources for one approach in the digital world, as if they were building physical things. This isn't true.

Another thing driving the problem is the "market curve" and market segment approach that businesses and their financers still unquestioningly believe. The market curve, the high place in the bell curve with the most people beneath it, is the belief that the laws of math predict what people are thinking and how they are making decisions. The market curve equates demographics to thought and behavior. The market curve is an argument to minimize effort and maximize profit by supporting only the people under the high point of the bell curve—people who think like the employees of the organization. The only way to get organizations with this mindset to support people under the low ends of their curve is to make laws, try to enforce them, and charge penalties. Which means those organizations don't lift a finger until, or even when, they are caught.

The low ends of the bell curve are not actually low at all when you look at it from the person's perspective instead of the organization's perspective. Each person is addressing a purpose, or a part of a purpose, and does a lot of thinking and decision-making toward that purpose. Each person applies a variety of solutions (mental, social, manual, mechanical, and digital) that serve that purpose. Instead of using a bell curve, depict the parts of the purpose, and people's thinking and decisions therein, as a better way to segment the market.

For example, flying to a different city to attend a conference involves deciding how to get there, getting a ticket, arriving at the airport, boarding the flight, enduring the flight, arriving at the other end, and making adjustments for the new location. These are all parts of the purpose. Airlines often focus only on "business travelers" and "vacation goers," the highest points of their bell curve. But a business or vacation destination doesn't really affect the way an individual thinks and makes decisions about getting to the airport gate and boarding the plane, for instance. There are different thinking styles with regard to getting to the gate and boarding the plane. There are some people who focus on doing things correctly, to make the process smooth. Others focus on using their time wisely. Some maintain a peaceful bubble around them to keep the stress out (or to keep their stress from affecting others). And a few focus on making a positive experience for everyone, including other passengers and flight staff. People switch between these thinking styles from trip to trip, depending on who is with them and what's happening.[10]

If you look from the passengers' perspective, there is no bell curve. It's a set of different approaches to the different parts of the purpose. Airlines can measure themselves by how well they are supporting each thinking style, in each part of the passengers' purpose. People who are deaf are a part of each of the thinking styles and have additional thinking that surfaces in this perspective. People who are neurodiverse are a part of each of the thinking styles, and also have additional thinking that surfaces. Airlines will see the gaps where they are failing to support this thinking and decision-making. Airlines will see that a large portion of the thinking is ignored. In this way, when you look from the passenger perspective, it's utterly evident that the market curve is false.

AVERAGE USER
(FLATTENED PERSONA)

VS.

PEOPLE IN DIFFERENT CONTEXTS, WITH DIFFERENT PURPOSES

BIASES
ASSUMPTIONS

YOUR OWN PERSPECTIVE
SHAPES SOLUTION

SOLUTIONS THAT TRULY
SERVE PEOPLE

DESIGNING FOR AVERAGE VS. REAL PEOPLE

This problem is fixable, especially in technology. All digital experiences and lots of services are, in fact, driven by a "back end" of software, databases, networks, and humans—a back-end that can support several different front-end experiences. Organizations are not actually in the position of having to multiply costs to build multiple physical products—if they will design for that ability. Granted, there is thirty-year-old software architecture still in service, which breaks at the slightest touch. There are debates in the board room whether to pitch the old back-end into the bit-bucket and start fresh. There are cost tradeoffs, and the balance is increasingly tipped toward starting fresh. A well designed back-end can interface with several different user experiences for a comparatively nominal extra cost. The design will then lead to more people experiencing support instead of harm, and more people reaching for that experience, knowing that it was designed with them in mind.

No one has the time or money to make 1,000,000,000 custom-tailored user experiences for each individual. Users also do not have time and motivation to adapt solutions to their own needs. But you *can* go from designing one average experience to two or three excellent experiences that solve for the thinking and decision-making of people with different thinking styles. You can look from the perspective of the people's purpose. You can support people in an inclusive, positive, powerful way. With a little extra work, you can effectively support *people,* and break the mindset of the average.

It's that or fall back into the habit of creating harm.

The Real Harms We Do

The news is full of stories about software that is failing in ways that harm people. The harm may be mild or systemic, accidental or deliberate in practice, but it is all harm. You have likely experienced this harm yourself.

The mildest harm looks like the simple frustration of someone being forced to repeat their actions, waste time dismissing ads, or spend a moment wondering if they've made the right decision with every gaslighting "reminder" from an app. Another user might find that their needs are simply neglected, such as when the original iPhone health app failed to include menstrual cycle tracking, a major component of health for a large portion of the globe. This harm is real, but it gets far worse.

More serious examples of harm are making people feel unwelcome, causing them to fall victim to scammers, or allowing them to be harassed by trolls because of ineffective online protections. It has even led to people being jailed because of biased facial recognition software. The most severe harm can mean injury or death—and it can happen from something as apparently minor as momentarily taking your eyes off the road to understand details on a navigation screen. Few of these harms can be completely mended after they occur, and some cause serious lasting injury. All of them can be prevented if enough attention is paid when the experience is designed.

Harm is not distributed equally; the same solution can cause mild harm to some users and serious harm to others. In an interview for The Markup's *Hello World* newsletter, Professor Brooke Erin Duffy talked about how the constantly changing nature of algorithms affects content producers in the gig economy. Duffy said, "If you use Instagram, you may recall that a few years ago they changed the algorithm ... Instagram replaced its chronological feed with an algorithmically curated one. It was frustrating for [regular] users, but our livelihoods are not dependent on it. For media and creative workers, their entire job is structured by the command to be visible—and the algorithm comes in and suddenly renders their content invisible."

When the algorithm changes, content producers have to spend time developing theories about how it works so they can get back to earning what they were earning before. They are never told the explicit rules through which they can succeed. Similarly, when the behavior of other kinds of software (such as Gmail, or Word) changes, there is no person to talk to about how to adjust to or combat the change. The team designing the software is not accountable to users in this way.

There is also systemic harm baked into most software, just by the nature of how it has been made. Systemic harm is when you don't realize that bias shaped a strategic decision, because it's part of society. You accept a "way of doing things" as given because that is what you grew up with.

It doesn't seem hurtful until suddenly you realize the history of where a social norm came from, and the very real stories of pain and death in that history. This is the water everyone is swimming in. Each society has this kind of history, this kind of water. You and I didn't *make* the water, but if we continue to make decisions without realizing the water is there, then we are perpetuating the harm. This is the way we are culpable.

It's hard to know the water is there. Fortunately, many voices are helping us discover its presence.

In Cathy O'Neil's book *Weapons of Math Destruction,* she gives many examples of systemic bias directly coded into algorithms. Algorithms look at the data associated with a person and make a decision: richer people are seen as more credit-worthy, have more stable employment and housing, and therefore due to a multitude of factors their car insurance costs less. The result is every bit as pernicious as if the software were designed intentionally to make life harder for people who are already ignored or repressed by the system.

Facial recognition technology often fails to accurately identify people with dark skin or female features, leading directly to systemic harm. Joy Buolamwini's definitive work and documentary[11] on the subject has resulted in several cities disconnecting facial recognition from their CCTV networks—and this is a good thing. Already three people in the United States have been falsely arrested based solely on faulty software identifications. Lawsuits are pending.[12]

You might say, "But my product isn't anything like these!" Even if your product is aimed at a professional process, like data warehousing, content management, hiring and supporting employees, or maintaining enterprise software, you are harming people with different philosophies, different speeds of working, who have ADD/ADHD,[13] who had a bad experience that shaped their own approach, who had mentors who laid different foundations of thinking.

How do you as a researcher, designer, or product manager help avoid this cascade of harm? Spread the word that the experiences and thinking of the people with your organization is not universal.

Organizations cannot continue to shape solutions according to an average user, because there is no such perspective. There is no average thinking and decision-making style. By considering and planning to support everyone affected by your solutions, you can act to prevent harm.[14]

Why We Listen

It's not enough merely to have solutions that don't harm. That is only the foundation, the minimum, the basic requirement. Most designers, researchers, and product designers want more. You want to be proud of the solutions you make. You want to support people in ways that match the way they think. You want to see the people using your solutions feel respected and enabled.

Yet it's common to feel stuck, serving users exactly the way you served them seven years ago. You may feel constrained at work, hands tied. You may have limited resources and decision-making power. Your organization rolls out new features and you may have little faith that those features will make a difference. Your team adds features for personas, but the personas are actually unconscious copies of one "average user" archetype. Users leave even after the organization gives them what the data models imply they want.

How can you shift this ineffective cycle? How can you build relationships with users, deliver solutions that recognize their different approaches, and truly help them succeed?

Changing the cycle requires making space to listen, and it requires listening to more than just the answers to a preset list of solution-related questions. You must listen *deeply* so that your organization can support peoples' real purpose.

Listening Sessions

This is a book about listening, but not just any listening. Here I am talking about **listening deeply,** listening to understand another perspective and challenge your assumptions. Specifically, this book will talk about this kind of listening in the context of a **listening session.**

Listening sessions put a person and that person's purpose at the center. This is by design. When an organization puts resources toward "user research," "usability," and "big data," they are only covering their own perspective. They are looking at people through the lens of their products and services, and distorting reality to suit the organization's perspective.

Communicating and listening deeply with actual people in listening sessions, by contrast, focuses on the person's purpose. Any useful solution must support that purpose. (I will explain more about purpose in Chapter Four.) Deeply understanding the person's approach to the purpose, therefore, allows you to see additional ways of helping people within the framework of your solutions. Most importantly, conducting listening sessions enables you to see other people accurately, without assumptions or bias. And in so doing, you will be able to see opportunities to connect the strategic direction of your solutions with the mission of supporting more people in radically better ways.

If you want to build solutions you are proud of, things that help people and do not harm them, you cannot do it without listening deeply. It is time to be intentional about confronting your assumptions, and about listening to people to get beyond those assumptions.

Feeling Understood

It is a rare moment when any of us feels truly understood. Most interactions with others happen mostly on the surface. If you make a statement like, "Everyone on this project feels overwhelmed," it is often met with comparisons or solutions. "It's not as bad as x," or "Well, if you scheduled better and spent less time getting coffee …" Immediately offered solutions tend to make people feel rejected and managed.

What is it like to make someone feel understood? Avoid offering the comparisons and solutions. Give someone attention; ask questions that help you understand their perspective: "What made you feel overwhelmed this week?" and "At a moment when you were really feeling overwhelmed, what went through your mind?"

These are how you open a deeper conversation and help someone unpack what is going on internally for them. These kinds of questions help someone explain their interior cognition and go beyond opinions, preferences, explanations or perceptions.

Recognizing how much of our communication skims across the surface, speeding along too fast to build understanding, is revelatory. It is very hard to slow down enough to ask questions that reach for depth and wait for someone to explain their thinking—without interrupting or pulling them into your own framework. It takes effort, and skill. And yet, paying rapt attention to another person's words is incredibly rich for both people.

Deep communication is powerful. It builds relationships and connects people, even across the gulfs of distance and difference. It allows for new perspectives and builds new understanding that is impossible to get any other way. And the good news is that listening deeply is also a skill, a skill nearly everyone can improve.

In this book, I'll teach you listening principles that will be useful in nearly every context where you interact with people. You can use them with your peers, your bosses, and your stakeholders. You can use them in your personal life, with the people close to you. Everyone wants to feel understood, in work and outside of work.

However, it's important that you never lose sight of the real purpose for learning these methods: to understand deeply the people who will use your products. These people are not averages. They are not flat personas defined only by demographics. They are people with lived experiences. Understanding them in both their differences and their similarities is how you create the next-level products you want to make.

You cannot design outside the average if you do not understand how your perspective shapes your solutions, and how other perspectives may offer other, better approaches for you to use. You cannot make great products until you can lay your assumptions aside.

Actionable Data

I recently heard from a man whose music streaming organization wanted to know why its customers were leaving. He went through all the data he had and made a decent model of what was happening. He told the executives that customers left after about two and a half years. The executives said, "Okay, but what type of people are leaving exactly?"

The man looked at them, surprised that the executives wondered *what type* instead of *why*. After further study, he came back to say, "It's young people. The young adults are leaving."

That demographic answer sounds nice, and it lulls colleagues into thinking they've isolated the issue and can easily come up with a solution. But they are probably solving the wrong problem. Instead, what if they'd set up a study to listen to people who had left? The company would have discovered valuable information about why attrition had happened. "Oh, you know, I wondered why I couldn't log in." "I lost that phone and couldn't find the password, so I'm just using my flat mate's account." "I'm now into vinyl, so I turned it off." Or perhaps the person faced a month when bill collectors confronted them, and in an effort to regain control of their life, canceled all the subscription accounts that had built up over the years.

All of those conversations would have led to deeper understanding of the user's purpose, of the context they are in, of the lack of priority the solution had in their lives—real, actionable data. The company could then use the patterns that show up as guides to help prioritize where to focus first, and to bring up new, different questions about people's purposes. They could see who they were harming, and who they were supporting. Choosing a priority to pursue first, they could roll out a smoother password recovery system, then roll out a more affordable service tier, and keep following the steps pointed out by the data they gathered from real people's thinking. No more choosing the ideas of the highest-paid person in the room, spending resources to make that idea, and then launching it at the "market" to see if it "sticks."

This is just one of many cases where demographics didn't illuminate the problem. **Research founded on listening would.**

The Shift Starts Now

This book will teach you how to start creating better solutions by understanding the way people approach a purpose or goal. That may, eventually, lead to those people becoming your users and customers.

Note that this is the last time that I will use the words "users" and "customers" in this book. I begin with the framing that is commonly used, in order to connect to *your* purpose and ground you in why you may find this book useful. Throughout the entire rest of the book, I will use the word "people" instead.

I do this because a "user" (or any other similar noun, like "customer," "member," "merchant," "passenger," etc.) is someone with a relationship or potential relationship to your organization. It is how you refer to people when your mind is in the solution space: thinking about your existing solution, fixes to the solution, ideas you can try out, and thoughts about how to solve the problem. This wording pulls attention away from a person's purpose. People exist apart from your organization, within their own framework, and our language throughout this process must reflect that.

People exist in their own context. They are centered in their own worlds. Your product, if it appears in their world at all, is one of the tools they are using to make progress on their own purpose.

Listening to people and understanding them requires putting them back at the center. It allows for you to see opportunities and insights you would never have seen any other way. This is a tool you can use to contend with the way things have always been done at your organization—to help your organization realize that it has been seeing itself as "the expert" rather than as a student of the people it serves.

In this book you will learn how to stop being the expert, how to stop being the colonial explorer intent on "discovery" and "utilization." Instead, you'll learn to draw on your human connectedness. You'll embody respect and curiosity and support. By doing so, you can get beyond the broken assumptions and the "average user" fallacy, to create things that truly serve people.

Now is the time for another inflection point in history—to remove the "average user" mindset from solutions and organizations. Now is the time to listen.

Endnotes

1   United States Air Force, The "Average Man"? by Gilbert S. Daniels, Technical Note WCRD 53-7, Wright-Patterson Air Force Base, Ohio: Wright Air Development Center, Air Research and Development Command, 1952, https://apps.dtic.mil/sti/pdfs/AD0010203.pdf.

2   Todd Rose, "When U.S. Air Force Discovered the Flaw of Averages," Toronto Star, January 16, 2016, https://www.thestar.com/news/insight/2016/01/16/when-us-air-force-discovered-the-flaw-of-averages.html.

3   "The History of the Wheelchair Ramps," MedPlus, October 29, 2019, https://www.medplushealth.ca/blog/the-history-of-the-wheelchair-ramps/.

4   Emily Nonko, "How Wheelchair Accessibility Ramped Up," The Atlantic, June 22, 2017, https://www.theatlantic.com/technology/archive/2017/06/ramps-disability-activism/531273/.

5   Olivia B. Waxman, "How Deaf Advocates Won the Battle for Closed Captioning," Time, March 16, 2020, https://time.com/5797491/closed-captioning-captions-history/.

6   Joe Sullivan and David Holladay, "Early History of Braille Translators and Embossers," Duxbury Systems, August 12, 2021, https://www.duxburysystems.com/bthist.asp.

7   "History," HelpTech, accessed November 22, 2021, https://helptech.de/en/info/help-tech/history.

8   The 38 Selected Japanese Laws Related to Persons with Disabilities, (Tokyo: Japanese Society for Rehabilitation of Persons with Disabilities, 2004), 2-4, https://www.dinf.ne.jp/doc/english/law/japan/selected38/index.html.

9   "Convention on the Rights of Persons with Disabilities," opened for signature March 30, 2007, Treaty Series: Treaties and International Agreements Registered or Filed and Recorded with the Secretariat of the United Nations, vol. 2515, no. 44910 (2008): 3, https://treaties.un.org/doc/Publication/UNTS/Volume%202515/v2515.pdf.

10 Thinking styles synthesized from a series of eight studies that Indi lead from 2011-2013.

11 Coded Bias, directed by Shalini Kantayya (2020; Brooklyn, NY: 7th Empire Media), https://www.netflix.com/title/81328723.

12 The work that Joy, Cathy, and the Algorithmic Justice League are doing to stop the use of facial recognition software is detailed in the documentary Coded Bias.

13 Conversations with actual people with attention deficit diagnoses show that different parts of the country and/or different age groups of people prefer ADD or ADHD for the general term; there does not seem to be a consensus, so we use both here.

14 There are many books that provide examples of the harm. However, I'm writing this series because there are no books I'm aware of that offer how to undo and avoid the harm in the digital world. There is the method "design thinking" and the method JTBD that purport to design better, but they don't pay any explicit attention to harm or to how real people use products. That attention has defaulted, so far, to the designers and researchers themselves, who may or may not understand the perspective of the people they hope to support.

LISTENING TO BUILD KNOWLEDGE 20

CHAPTER 2

Listening to Build Knowledge

art of the reason some company leaders are paid mind-bending amounts of money is that the wrong strategy—the wrong decision—can cause a lot of harm. These leaders could harm their organization's future, their employees, the people that the organization supports, the community, the environment, and the economy. Oh, and the shareholders and the board. So, leaders need to be well-informed and *careful* with the direction they choose.

We in the product field are responsible for providing some of the information that keeps the leaders well-informed—information that can help reduce harms. We can make different solutions that match more people and create less harm. We as researchers can reject the idea of "the average user" and build knowledge from different perspectives.

We can do *careful*. We can identify where we are making assumptions, what knowledge we have, and what knowledge is missing. Depending on what knowledge we want to create, we can choose the research method best suited to make that knowledge. We can mix methods and layer data together to form a bigger picture. We can create knowledge about the future paths to bring support to more people effectively. We can even push our assumptions aside by *carefully* looking at our way of seeing things as we collect and analyze data. It takes time, though.

We can do *careful* but mostly we do shortcuts. Our leaders urge us to speed on. Product owners request "quick insights." We complain that they don't understand the power of knowledge-creation—when we should instead be building deeper trust relationships with them. We hold ourselves back because there is general *dis*trust of certain knowledge-making methods. Namely, qualitative data.

Most leaders and most product owners distrust listening as a data-collection method.

Here's why: there are many *types* of listening, and some *are* less informative or less reliable. The leaders and product owners are not wrong to distrust those types of listening.

As knowledge-providers, we know that empirical[1] qualitative data[2] is just as valid as empirical quantitative data.[3] But trying to convince our leaders to trust qualitative data is difficult because many of them have already learned to mistrust unhelpful knowledge based on less-systematic types of listening. And since only a few top organizations leverage listening deeply for knowledge-making, leaders may be unwilling to be early adopters.

I'm about to give you, in this chapter, the ability to recognize the kinds of listening that do *not* make for good data. And I'll give you the reasons why deep listening works. But this is for *you*; it's *your* tool. It's for building trust. **Your leaders don't need to know how the tool works to be able to trust it. They need to trust *you*.**

You can create knowledge carefully. You can focus your energy on developing interpersonal trust with leaders. You can push back against requests for incomplete, single-perspective, assumption-laden knowledge. You can carefully build knowledge that leaders can trust and stake the organization's future on.

You gather that knowledge in the same way you build trust with leadership—through deep listening.

Preoccupied Listening

Conversational listening is usually distracted listening. Mostly, you let your mind think while half-hearing the other person. But even when you try hard to listen to someone, you are actually doing something other than listening. Even in many professional roles, people who are supposed to be listening are actually busy with something else. After I point these dynamics out, you'll start seeing them everywhere in your life.

THE WAY WE ALREADY LISTEN

Conversational Listening

Conversations are personal, and they evolve as they go. We all feel our way through conversations. We connect. We get to know one another. We share our backgrounds. Advice flies back and forth between friends. We might reassure, sympathize, distract, or even analyze what each other has said. We depend upon body language, tone of voice, and the other person's reaction to our input to let us know where we should take the conversation next.

No one formally teaches us how to have conversations. Adults model it for kids. There are few rules. Sometimes people are taught *not to speak on top of others*, but they think nothing of *thinking* on top of what another person is saying.

In fact, in western culture people are habituated to solving things. "Solving" can sometimes mean offering advice to a friend who needs to complain. Maybe your friend wants to talk about how much work she has to do or how she can't cover all the bills with what she earns, and feel understood. You might "solve" the problem by explaining how budgeting works, as if she didn't know. Perhaps you've known this person forever, and your connection is based on making her laugh, to ease the tension, cheer her up, or change the subject. *None of these responses is listening.*

In this example, you aren't trying to understand what's going through your friend's mind about her work and her bills. You are trying to *change* what's in her mind, or to *escape* from it.

It's important to become aware of the *reasons* you say what you say. If you can work on recognizing your own conscious or sub-conscious reasons for saying things, then you can start to recognize the reasons someone else has for saying something to you. And as a listener, this is the foundation. William Miller is a psychology professor at the University of New Mexico, and as an expert therapist, he has written many psychology texts. In 2018, he published a slim book for lay people called **Listening Well.**[4] The early part of the book highlights what the mind is doing *instead* of actually listening to the other person.

Examples of NOT Listening, by William Miller

1. Give direction, like orders or commands
2. Warn of risks or dangers
3. Advise about what to do
4. Persuade to convince someone
5. Moralize what someone should do
6. Judge, blame, criticize
7. Agree, approve, praise
8. Shame someone or their ideas
9. Analyze to explain meaning of words, actions
10. Probe to press for more information
11. Reassure, sympathize, console
12. Distract someone from their emotions

You recognize these kinds of goals. These goals are about *what you want, or about changing the other person's thinking.* There are other goals to add, like **planning an exit strategy, showing someone how funny or entertaining you are** or **impressing them** with something you know or can do. There's even **trying to make that person understand you**, which happens when you're not feeling heard. It's a partial list. If your own life experience spans multiple cultures and languages, you can probably think of additional intentions to add to this list.

IF YOU ARE DOING ANY OF THIS
YOU ARE NOT LISTENING

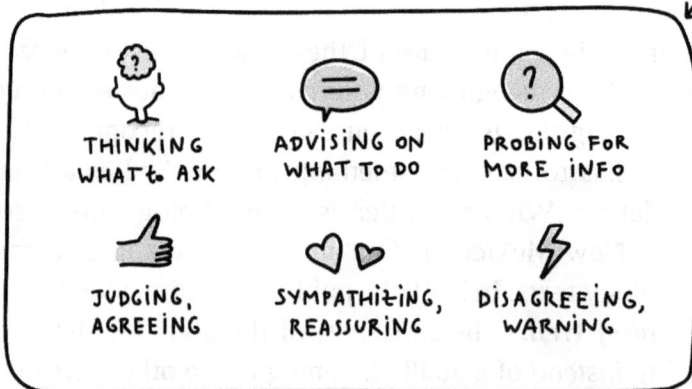

THINKING WHAT to ASK	ADVISING ON WHAT TO DO	PROBING FOR MORE INFO
JUDGING, AGREEING	SYMPATHIZING, REASSURING	DISAGREEING, WARNING

These goals and intentions exist. Noticing when they are present is part of the foundation for your practice. Here is a quick reference list of examples. Try covering up the column on the right to see if you recognize what is going on.

Examples of Conversational Listening

Example	Goal
Someone's talking about something you're an expert at, so you think about what you want to say in response to show how they're wrong.	Impressing someone
When your director says, "We're going to need a high ROI in the next two quarters" in the strategy meeting, you think to yourself, "That's the weak point. That's what I'll bring up next."	Persuading
One of your new team members is mouthing off, so you tell her, "That's not how we act around here."	Ordering, or shaming
"Wow, that was amazing. You unloaded the dishwasher; thank you!" You smile encouragement to your son.	Approving or praising
You're at one of those endless company parties, talking to someone very uninteresting. Instead of listening, you think about how you can get out of the conversation politely.	Planning an exit strategy
"Be careful. There's a blind corner on the left side of the street. There've been six accidents in the last year. They really need to put a mirror up."	Warning of danger
The person substituting for your boss on maternity leave sits you down and says, "I can't believe that you went ahead with such a stupid design on the last project."	Shaming or judging
"So you think aiming for higher ROI is a weak point?"	Probing for more information

Your friend texts you: "Hang in there!!! If anyone can do it, it's YOU!!!"	Comforting, reassuring
"You really should give the product managers credit for some intelligence."	Moralizing

---

Professional Listening

The professional host role, whether it takes place on tv, radio, or podcast, involves listening to a guest and shaping a conversation for the benefit of the audience. Some show hosts are skilled at listening for entry points the guest brings up for deeper conversation, letting the concepts unfold in an unplanned and enlightening direction.

Other hosts are less attuned. Instead, they focus on pre-planned points that have the most entertainment value for the audience. Some of them prod the guest to say something outrageous or memorable that will get their show high ratings. Higher ratings attract more money, in terms of sponsors, advertisers, and media hubs that pick up the show. It's all about **entertaining or captivating the audience**.

Many show hosts abhor silence. "Dead air" is anathema. When there's a lull in the conversation, they fire off a random question from the list. Avoiding silences is a goal that takes up space in their minds. Listening, or understanding the guest's perspective, isn't the point. They'd rather avoid silence and use questions to show how smart they are, or what they have researched. They may even try to increase the intensity of their show by challenging their guest, saying something like, "But that's not what the report implies."

Other show hosts, in contrast, focus on exploring what people are saying in the moment (listening). When there is a lull, they go back to ask deeper follow-up questions on interesting topics that came up earlier. They're not concerned with seeming smart or being a strong presence in the conversation at all. They're there to bring out the other person's experience, to the benefit of the audience.

Maybe you've had a chance to attend an event with a set of speakers and a master of ceremonies (emcee). This emcee is concerned with creating smooth transitions between presenters, and focuses on avoiding "dead air," keeping things moving along, and not delaying the event. Making sure speakers transition quickly, an emcee might say, "Okay, great, Ian. Next we have Pauli here to talk about ..." It is especially jarring if Ian just finished talking about the sudden death of his child.

Not every emcee does this, however. Some are as just skilled at facilitating as good podcast hosts. I have proudly watched my co-founder at Adaptive Path, Jesse James Garret, mature as an emcee at the now-defunct UX Week conference. As the yearly conference grew, he too grew in his ability to turn the intense points the presenters made into little comments after each talk. By 2017 Jesse was having a ten-minute chat with each presenter, keeping them on stage to explore more detail about a few of their points. He focused on the presenter and helped them say more about their thinking. This was also to the benefit of the audience.

Here's an example of the contrast between the emotion of a guest and the mechanical response from a radio host. The example is based on a real conversation from a real radio station's AIDS Memorial event, with details changed to protect the identity of the station and the caller.

During the memorial event, people called in to tell stories of loved ones they lost to AIDS. This particular caller was talking about her stepbrother, who was diagnosed with the condition in the mid-80s.

Radio Host:	Could you give us one sentence that describes <person's name>? What was he like?
Caller:	(crying) I'm sorry, I just miss him.
Radio Host:	Take your time. (but in an impatient tone)
Caller:	(sniffs, stops crying) He was an extraordinary person. He would make these beautiful cakes. You couldn't just frost them, he had to go and make flowers one by one with a bag, you know? He was kind to everybody, even people who were foolish to him. When he was sick, really sick, my grandfather was also sick, and he called me up, the nicest phone call, saying how much he hoped my grandfather would get better.

> Then, a couple of weeks before he died—<person's name>, I mean—he was so out of it. His mom was in Savannah with us, because his brother on his other side was getting married, you know.
>
> And <person's name> ended up coming all the way out to Savannah, sick as a dog. He was dying, but he didn't want his mom to have to choose between them, but he wanted his mom with him, you know, when...

Radio Host: (trying to cut in): Well...

Caller: ...he died. Anyway, it's just so great that, you know, it's not like that for...

Radio Host: (interrupting/talking over) <caller's name> ...

Caller: ... gay men anymore, or I guess anybody LGBTQ, not like it was. Not like it was.

Radio Host: (continuing on) ... thank you so much for telling us about <person's name>. Next up, we have a message here from <a different person's name> about her best friend who was diagnosed in 1998 ...

Notice the lack of sympathetic words on the host's part. They were more focused on controlling how many words each caller could convey than on the callers' experience. A simple word or two about the pain being expressed would have made the radio program a better experience for everyone.

Debates, especially political debates, are great venues for you to practice goal identification. The next time you see a debate, see if you can discover the agenda behind the debaters' words. You may expect them to *disagree,* but you may also find them **shaming** each other, **judging** people, **moralizing, warning,** or **blaming**.

But what's interesting is when you notice one debater **distracting** the other away from a particular topic that might put them in a bad light. Stay alert for those. You can even make a game out of it with friends, noting down as many types of goals as possible. A debater is sharply focused on achieving a clear win over the others, and they use every tactic and goal in the lists above to do it.

There are other professional roles where people are listening for particular points in order to respond with particular solutions. Molding the conversation in a shape and direction that meets a goal is different than a listening session.

Think about the kinds of listening and the goals of listening in these situations and jobs.

Trained to Listen	Typically Untrained, Learned on the Job
Customer service	Team meeting facilitator
Social Work	Employee performance evaluations
Mediation	Design collaboration
Courtroom professionals	Collecting feedback from a group
IT helpdesk support	Team managers

Interviews Aren't Listening Sessions

Interviews and listening sessions are different enough that I wouldn't even call them siblings. Cousins, maybe. Each tool has its place in our work. If you are an experienced user interviewer, you have probably developed specific skills that help you listen, like not asking leading questions and exploring a participant's context. In fact, many user experience researchers pride themselves in their ability to **analyze** on the fly or **probe** to get more information. Interestingly, look at number 10 on William Miller's list above: probing. When I saw that in his book, I thought, "What? Wait a minute."

Isn't it a researcher's superpower to probe and dig deeper?

It took me a couple of weeks to figure out what he meant.

Most product research interviews are either evaluative or generative. This means most interviews either aim to (1) evaluate an existing solution against a real person and tally what the gaps are, or (2) to generate solution ideas based on how a real person is trying to get their task done. In this context, when interacting with the participant, a researcher's mind is busy with these other agendas. They are considering the process, goals, and steps the participant is following—not always what the participant is thinking or what their decision-making process is. I have encountered interviewers who rarely explore further than the participant's explanations, opinions, preferences and attitudes. Teams put confidence in observing behaviors. Researchers often listen to analyze, and they interpret their analysis through the lens of the organization's needs. User research interviewers mostly listen to *see how to improve the product or service*. Market research interviewers mostly listen to *see how the brand could improve*.

That is why probing is not listening. It's digging for information in service to these other goals. These are fine goals to have, and we need these kinds of research, but they should not be mistaken for deep listening.

Other Professional Interviewers

Journalists interview experts, witnesses, and those involved in an event. You can probably guess why this is not listening; they are trying to create a story. Journalists need details, facts, and quotes that will back up a point their story touches on. They want to **reassure**, **persuade**, **advise**, **warn**, and **criticize**, all with the audience in mind. They are not listening to understand an individual, but what an individual knows. Journalists aim to gather what they need to create the story.

Hiring managers interview job applicants. They want to see if the applicant has the skills for the job, so that's where their cognition is. Simultaneously, most hiring managers are also looking for "personality fit" or "culture fit," which is a way of filtering out people who are not already similar to them in philosophy, without actually exploring anyone's guiding principles. There are rare hiring managers who are actively looking for applicants with *different* philosophies, which is a recent, inclusive development, and here deep listening can help.

When you see the word "interview," now you can begin to recognize that something other than listening is going on.

Deep Listening

So what is deep listening? You may have heard of active listening. Deep listening is a form of active listening, honed for people making supportive things for others. If you were to listen deeply to your friend who needs to complain about her workload and how she still can't cover the bills, you would seek to *understand what has gone through her mind*. A therapist does this to help their patients become more familiar with themselves, and recognize what is driving their behavior in order to change it.

A deep listener is not a therapist, of course. They are not trying to help a patient (and are not licensed to do so), but a deep listener does help the other person express what has gone through their mind already. The goal is to *understand the other person's way of thinking*—not to change it … not to escape it; not to move them along or persuade an audience. It's just to really grasp their approach.

A deep listener only seeks understanding.

An organization benefits greatly from understanding different ways of thinking, and making wise decisions about whether, or how, to support those different ways of thinking with solutions. Every different solution represents a potential new "market." Supporting some of these "markets" strategically can be economically valuable and also brand-enhancing. When the organization understands the landscape in which it operates and how people think, it leads to clear direction on what to prioritize, and it leads to whole new landscapes to work in. The organization can combine this understanding with other metrics. And it can create new metrics that measure how well the person can address their purpose their way. These new metrics are your organization's key to doing less harm. Listening deeply leads to understanding of the market and of people in a way that is very powerful for organizations.

Notice the word "support" in the paragraph above. Some kinds of research seek to *change* a person's buying decisions, or to *manipulate* a person's behavior, to their benefit or not. Deep listening does not seek to change or manipulate the participant. If anything, the deep understanding that results from listening is used to support someone in accomplishing the purpose they already have in a way that matches their way of thinking better. It does not attempt to change their purpose or way of thinking.

Feeling understood is a rare, cherished thing. Many of us are subject to power dynamics that leave us misunderstood or ignored. And many people never find out what it is like to feel understood for who they are on the inside. A deep listener acts as a witness to another human, to acknowledge that they exist, that they have valid emotions and thoughts, that they are part of the human community. Your act of listening helps that person describe their inner landscape, sometimes for the first time. Here is a second goal for deep listening: to help the person feel understood.

A deep listener only seeks understanding … and to help a person feel understood.

- DROP YOUR ORGANIZATION'S GOAL FOR NOW
- REVERT TO A BEGINNER'S MIND
- FOLLOW THE PERSON RATHER THAN LEAD
- PAY RAPT ATTENTION

DEEP LISTENING

Interviewers often view themselves as explorers. It sounds useful and innocent, but explorers in world history are not innocent. They explore to gain resources, spread their way of thinking, or make a name for themselves as "the first one there." As a researcher, none of these goals serves the person being "explored." If you want to distance yourself from these exploits, stop thinking of yourself as an explorer. Stop using that word. Your role is not the point at all. Start thinking of yourself as a witness. You are merely a listener, there to witness the participant and make them feel understood, accepted, and justified.

To help you step away from that identity, in these kinds of interactions, call yourself a listener. These are listening sessions, where you seek only understanding and to help the person feel understood, accepted, and justified.

Your organization's goals do not matter during this period. They matter before and after, but not while you are growing your understanding of each participant in each listening session.

But how can you just drop your organization's goals?

The Beginner's Mind

Usually when people talk about "the beginner's mind" they talk about going back to being a blank slate. They talk about becoming curious about everything and anything. It's like when you are around a toddler. Isn't it amazing how much they ask, "Why?"

Parent:	It's now time to go to bed.
Toddler:	Why?
Parent:	Because... (looks around, points to window) It is dark outside. People sleep when it is dark outside.
Toddler:	Why?
Parent:	Otherwise we will be tired in the morning.
Toddler:	Why?
Parent:	People need sleep. I'm sorry, I don't make the rules, that's how it is.

Toddler:	I not sleepy.
Parent:	I am sleepy. I don't get to sleep until you sleep.
Toddler:	(with genuine curiosity) Why?
Parent:	(considers explaining the full answer, developmental psychology, relative danger, culturally acceptable child rearing practices and so on, decides it is too much) It is now time for bed.

The toddler is asking "why?" to fill up their sponge-brain and gain understanding of the world around them. Toddlers are not embarrassed about not knowing something. They're *not worried that you'll think less of them* if they ask "why" about everything and anything.

That lack of embarrassment is key.

THEY ARE NOT EMBARRASSED

NOT KNOWING!

BEGINNER'S MIND

It can be difficult for us, as adults with years of schooling and possibly years of experience working in teams, to openly display a lack of knowledge. It has been driven into our brains that we should bring answers to the questions, come up with solutions to the challenges, and contribute somehow. So when we are faced with a situation where we don't know an answer, our initial response is to hide it. We try not to let anyone know we're out of our depth. We keep quiet, or at least come up with some guesses or assumptions.

A deep listener must get past this habit and ask the participant about things that seem obvious.

Remind yourself that *there is no way to understand someone's mind in advance.* You are conducting a listening session for the express purpose of understanding how their mind works and to help them feel understood. There is no possible way to know what they were thinking, short of telepathy. So you will ask questions about some things that may appear simple and obvious, but which might be hiding a different way of thinking. It's okay; it's your job. Yes, the participant might think less of you. Yes, you will feel a bit vulnerable. But if you don't ask, you won't understand their thinking, and that's the entire point.

Channel that toddler's lack of embarrassment.

Here's an example:

Listener:	How do you use the three laundry baskets?
Person:	What do you mean? (pause) They sit there on the floor. And (slows down, sweet voice) I put the dirty clothes in them.
Listener:	Over the week?
Person:	Yeah, on a daily basis.
Listener:	Some people use baskets differently. So, when you're done with something you go put it into the proper basket.
Person:	Correct. And at other times I've had one basket and I've thrown everything in the one basket. Then I had to sort it out, so I didn't like that.

At the end of this example, we finally reach the point in time where the listener has enough information to go to depth. Finally, the listener is equipped to ask what went through the participant's mind when they used just the one basket, and how they decided to use three baskets instead.

Be prepared to accept the participant's unspoken derision over the course of doing your job.

Transform from Interviewer to Follower

So, if you're going to (1) drop your organization's goal for now, and (2) focus on understanding the other person's way of thinking from non-embarrassed blank slate, then this requires that you (3) enter into a different relationship with the idea of interviewing.

Within both applied research and academic research, there is a history of considering the researcher the authority, instead of considering the person providing the information to be the authority. To get the most out of deep listening, the traditional research study hierarchy needs to shift.

For example, I have sometimes heard study participants referred to as "subjects." That word implies a power structure in which the subjects have no agency; they are controlled by the researcher or studied like a specimen. This mindset clearly leads the researcher towards another goal (controlling or studying) rather than deep listening.

The word "participant" isn't quite perfect, although it's a neutral word to use for the person's role in research. "Participant" may lead your mind astray because it puts the emphasis on the role rather than the person. Moreover, it isn't the right word when you are listening deeply for relationship-building. So I try to vary between "participant" and "person." When you are entering into a listening session, use words that help you put the person at the center in your thoughts and in your communication (and later in transcripts). It will help you keep your mindset in the space of deep listening.

Additionally, probably half the contexts you will be listening in will be outside of a research study. You can listen deeply to your colleagues, to your boss, to the people that you manage, and to people on other teams.

Outside of work, you can listen deeply to friends and family, and to new people you meet while running errands or pursuing a hobby.

There are two primary modes in a listening session, an interview, and even in many everyday conversations.

1. **Session mode:** When the participant's focus of attention is in the present, on the listener, on what the listener wants, and on the session itself. In session mode, the listener outlines how the session works and builds a safe space for the person to express themselves. The participant may describe things the listener needs to know before diving into their memory. They might talk about how the session makes them feel or relate some inner thinking that the session is currently setting off in their mind.

2. **Memory mode:** When the participant's mind has gone back to a past place and time, recounting their context and thoughts back then. In memory mode, the participant is in the lead, going back to a *strong* memory. They describe the context of the memory, their opinions about it, and what passed through their mind at the time.

Memory mode is like a TV show where a character goes back in memory: chimes sound, the screen fuzzes out, and the scene focuses on that character's memory of the past. Like a TV character relating a flashback, the participant in memory mode is not really present in the listening session anymore—they've temporarily gone back to a strong memory. You can still reach them in their memory mode to ask questions about that scene they are in. But they are much less focused on the session or on you.

I've read too many interview transcripts that spend most of time in the session mode. The participant is focused on trying to give the interviewer what they need. Any trips back in memory are curtailed. Many researchers believe they are legitimately cutting off the memory mode because of the belief that a person can't or won't reliably tell you what actually happened. **This belief has its roots in observation-prioritized**

research, when researchers seek to evaluate how well a solution works for a "user." The interviewer is focused on the participant's current emotions and inner thinking regarding the use of that solution. The participant follows where the interviewer indicates, answers what the interviewer asks, and waits to see where the interviewer will take them next. The traditional power hierarchy of an interview is very much in evidence here.

Instead, in a listening session you want to spend as much time as possible in memory mode. You seek not to evaluate a solution, but to understand a person's thinking in past situations where they used all sorts of solutions, including mental and social solutions. (I explain more in Chapter Four.) The person you are listening to is no longer in the traditional researcher-subject relationship with you. Instead, with your support, they have transformed into your partner in the session, guiding you through their interior cognition. **To build knowledge about how another person thinks, you have to give that person control of what topics to bring up.**

Now they are in control, and you are following them.

Following Their Lead

Here is the most critical difference between user interviews and listening sessions: in a listening session, you don't introduce topics. You follow along. You listen to understand, wherever the participant takes the conversation. They will tell you everything that went through their mind at certain points in the past. Give them the space to unfold their own perspective.

A listening session, where you are not in control, not guiding the other person through topics, is a very different approach for many. To some listeners, it feels terrifying. There are big differences from other listening approaches. Some of your familiar research techniques will be set aside. It's so much change that some people cling harder to those familiar techniques and argue against the logic of deep listening itself out of fear of that change. Every technique has a place in knowledge-building, and I'm not asking you to forsake these other techniques completely. Instead, I am introducing another form of valuable knowledge

DROP YOUR
ORGANIZATION'S
GOALS

FOCUS ON UNDERSTANDING
PERSON'S WAY OF THINKING
(FROM THE BLANK SLATE)

FOLLOW THEIR THINKING.
THEY ARE IN CONTROL
OF WHAT TOPIC TO BRING UP

Listeners tell me they look forward to listening sessions much more than their user interviews. After some practice, the depth of the conversation and the richness of the human connection are often relaxing or energizing for listeners. Listening sessions can be both more helpful and less stressful for you than user interviews because you are not expected to analyze and probe when you are together with the participant. As a way of creating knowledge for your organization, listening sessions can break past traditional boundaries of understanding people. But the transition can be frightening.

Listening Sessions Free You

Listening deeply truly does open up some of the constraints you may have been working under. Freedom from these constraints helps you develop a deeper understanding of that person's interior cognition. Here is a summary list of your new freedoms, for reference. The rest of this chapter (and book) will expand on the items in this list.

1. Communicate remotely or in-person, by any method
2. Skip the list of questions
3. Skip writing notes
4. Focus on the person, not the session
5. Follow their topics
6. Ignore traditional time limits, focus on theirs
7. Schedule one session per day, or at intervals across days
8. Focus on interior cognition

1. Communicate Remotely or In-Person, by Any Method

Because you will be observing memories, not observing how someone uses your solution, you have the option of communicating remotely. Let the other person choose the method of communication that they prefer: writing, audio, video, in-person, sign language, etc. You may also have the option of conducting listening sessions in the format you are more comfortable with, if that method works for the participant. I will cover this in more depth in Chapter Five.

2. Skip the List of Questions

You can't possibly know what has gone through a person's mind in the past, and you can't guess what similarities in thinking exist between people. So it's pointless to try to list questions, in advance, about someone's inner thinking and regarding their purpose.

Not having a list of questions is often the scariest thing to new listeners. In their first practice session, new listeners tell me, "I kept thinking about what I should ask next!" And *that is not listening*; that is trying to formulate new questions in your head while the participant talks in the background.

If you pay rapt attention to what the other person is saying, you will notice places where there could be more depth to ask about. These are your questions. There will be plenty of them, so don't panic. If you create trust for communicating, the participant will be comfortable diving deep into their thinking, and their topics will flow. In the next chapters, I'll show you what these opportunities for more depth look like.

If your organization has requirements about getting your list of questions (the protocol) approved by an ethics review board in advance, then do so. Make a list of concepts that you guess might come up. Get it approved. Then ignore the list during the listening sessions. Stay completely within the bounds of ethics, but don't follow a list of questions that does not apply to your participant. Follow what they say instead.

Here are some other general guidelines for sessions.

3. Skip Writing Notes

The chief rejection I hear about this idea is, "But writing notes is how I make sense of what I'm hearing!" Making sense of what you are hearing *is not listening.* If you bring your focus back to the participants words, rather than trying to "make sense" of them, you can stop that cognition in your mind, and you can pay better attention to the person.

Some people truly can focus on a participant's words *better* when their hands are busy with an activity that does not require conscious attention. For example, someone like this might doodle, color, or use a fidget cube. This is fine if it facilitates focus and allows for the listener to listen raptly. I will emphasize that the activity must be silent, so that it cannot be perceived by the other person, and the activity *must require no conscious attention from the listener.*

Do what enables you to listen with as much cognition as possible—which in neither case is note-taking.

4. Focus on the Person, Not the Session

The listening session is the time to pay attention to the other human—to really pay attention. To do this, you need to feel reassured about a few things, all of which are covered in this book.

One thing that's fairly common among interviewers, who are used to taking notes and doing a bit of analysis work as the session unfurls, is the strangeness of letting these go. For some people, it feels like abandoning their work. This work feels necessary in order to analyze what you're hearing, recognize patterns, compare perspectives, and tell your boss some insights. But for listening sessions, all that happens during synthesis, long after the listening session. You're on a different schedule here than with solution-space research.

So, to feel reassured about letting go of this work while listening deeply, you will need a record of the session. Specifically, you need a record of the person's words.

If you and the participant have chosen audio, in-person, sign language, or drawing as a method of communication, you may need an audio or video recording of the session, depending on how you plan to synthesize the data. If you use a written format instead, then the text of the conversation is the record—the transcript. This will be your account of what the person has communicated, in their voice. It is not filtered through your writing of what concepts you thought were being expressed.

It is best to pay to have an audio or video recording transcribed by a human. Yes, there are apps that make transcripts, but they are never perfect. A human has to go over them in detail to make corrections and annotations, so I like to pay a human to make the transcript in the first place. I ask them to put in notations like [laughter] and [long pause].

A human transcriber can look up acronyms and figure out if "AC" means "alternating current" or refers to the local public transit system. It also gives someone a reasonably pleasant job.

Can't make a record? There are lots of valid scenarios where an audio or video recording isn't plausible. (Or a recording fails.) In these scenarios, here's what to do: *don't take notes*. Pay rapt attention. After the session is over, you can then capture the concepts that came up and write them in the participant's voice.

Later you or a teammate will go through the record in detail to synthesize patterns across participants. Insights come even later, after your organization's solutions are deconstructed and aligned beneath these patterns, to see what gaps are there.

5. Follow Their Topics

It is of utmost importance to let the participant bring up the concepts and topics to be discussed. Except for the germinal question at the start (which I cover in Chapter Six), never introduce a concept or topic that hasn't previously been spoken about. The participant will feel obliged to talk about the concept you bring up, and if it's not a concept they've done much thinking about, they will have to invent what to say to you. Not only does it pull the other person back into session mode (because there is no past memory of the concept to draw on), but it also opens the door for make-believe.

In qualitative research, there is always the worry that a participant will tell you what they think you want to hear. There is always the worry that they will say things that cast them in a better light for you. These stories mainly happen when the participant is in the session mode of the session, present with you as the researcher. They also happen when you have attracted participants based on payment, rather than attracting them based on a chance to feel understood about a particular purpose they have done a lot of deep thinking about. (I will cover recruiting in this book in Chapter Five.)

Following a participant means following where their mind has gone at particular points in the past as they addressed the particular purpose you are studying. It means letting them unfold the concepts that actually did go through their minds in the past, patiently, without adding any concepts of your own.

6. Ignore Traditional Time Limits, Focus on Theirs

A listening session is over when it is over. Only pay attention to the clock if the participant has a hard stop.

Some research techniques depend upon setting a specific period of time, say 30 or 60 minutes, within which to gather data. The researcher watches the clock and starts wrapping things up when the time limit approaches. If the participant seems like they've run out of things to say, I've seen researchers try to draw the session out to meet the time limit, instead of ending early. Neither of these habits belong in a listening session. (There is more on ending a listening session in Chapter Six.)

In a listening session, you are paying rapt attention to the other person. You know the topics they are unfolding, and what they've already told you. You can sense what sub-topics still need to be resolved. Don't look at a clock. Only pay attention to the participant's concepts and pathways. You will know when they are winding up, and you will end the session when they are finished.

A listening session is over when the participant has told you about all their past thinking with regard to addressing their specific purpose.

7. Schedule One Session Per Day, or at intervals across days

There seems to be an applied research tradition of doing a set of day(s) or week(s) of interviews. Pack it together, do it fast, get it all done at once. If you have experienced this kind of scenario, where you have scheduled seven different participants in one day, you know what this is like. You start the day fresh, and have a "productive" first interview, then you hurry to the next participant, then another, and another, until your mind can't remember which person went with which topics. By the last two sessions your mind drifts. You end the day feeling drained and exhausted.

This exhaustion leads to the common understanding that "the hardest part is over." The intense day(s) of interviews with participants has been conquered. Your mind can stop forging connections and high-lighting anecdotes. More times than not, I hear about researchers feeling so overwhelmed that they put off the data synthesis, or try to do it all in one painfully intense day. And what happens is that the *otherness* of people's perspectives get translated into concepts the organization is comfortable with. Basically, little knowledge gets built about how others think about and address the purpose.

I've even heard of organizations having "mountains of data" yet to be synthesized.

To avoid this result, make sure you don't overwhelm and exhaust yourself:

(1) Separate data collection from knowledge creation, so that the latter step gets much more emphasis and energy than it has historically at your organization.

(2) Slow down so you can develop a solid understanding of how each person thinks. Bury yourself in the participant's mind for the sessions, and let that new perspective stay with you for the rest of the day. If you are engaged in a multi-day text chat with someone, try not to multi-task while they are communicating. Don't immediately overwrite the person's concepts with another's. Avoid the embarrass-ment of asking about something a different person brought up.

So, limit yourself to one listening session per day. In an emergency, you can do two, but make sure they are scheduled four or five hours apart. Seriously.

Make sure you don't overwhelm and exhaust your mind.

Conserve some energy for the important task of accurate data synthesis later.

8. Focus on Interior Cognition

Stick to questions about what went through a participant's mind at a past point in time. Any other questions will result in answers that are not about the participant's interior cognition. Avoid questions like, "How is that typically done?" "Do you like the wine and cheese nights?" "When you looked online, what information did you find?"

These may strike you as common questions in other types of research, so you may be surprised by this restriction. I will clarify what I mean by exterior versus interior cognition and how to avoid exterior-level questions in Chapters Three and Six.

Summing Up

In this chapter, we covered:

+ Examples of NOT listening
+ Following a participant's lead with a beginner's mind
+ How a listening session differs from an interview; how terrifying and freeing it is

It's key to your skills as a human to be able to recognize what you are doing when you are communicating with another person. If this book teaches you one thing, it's to begin a practice of **building your awareness of why people say what they say**. Work on your awareness until you can eventually spot some different conversational goals; even harder, try to pinpoint the goals of your own words.

Second, remember what I said in the beginning of this chapter about building trust with your leaders. If you haven't already been developing strong relationships with your direct leaders, and theirs, begin that work now. It's urgent. Use deep listening itself to learn how to trust them. If you don't understand and trust them, then they will not understand and trust you. Trust is key.

Knowing the difference between preoccupied and deep listening will help you decide when to employ each. **Deep listening means you're listening raptly, with your full attention. Deep listening is building cognitive empathy.** Deep listening means that we are building knowledge by listening, knowledge that aims to help a person and their purpose, knowledge that helps our organization, knowledge that supports our community.

The people in organizational leadership who distrust listening have never built awareness about these different kinds of listening.

You can use the deep listening methods taught in this book to build trust with them, and to help them understand.

Additional Resources

Listen Like You Mean It: Reclaiming the Lost Art of True Connection, Ximena Vengoechea, March 2021.

Empathy for Change: How to Create a More Empathetic World, Amy J. Wilson, January 2021. https://www.amyjwilson.com/empathyforchange

Empathy-Driven Software Development, Andrea Goulet and Carmen Shirkey Collins (coming mid-2022 through Pearson/Addison-Wesley) https://empathyintech.com

Endnotes

1   Empirical: verifiably observed (as opposed to subjective or perceived).
2   Qualitative data: producing knowledge based on patterns, regularities, difference (of thinking, in our case).
3   Quantitative data: producing knowledge based on quantity, amount, scale.
4   William R. Miller, Listening Well: The Art of Empathic Understanding (Eugene, OR: Wipf & Stock, 2018).

Endnotes

1. [illegible]
2. [illegible]

CHAPTER 3

CHAPTER 3

Assumption-Wary Knowledge

Much of our current data about how people think is riddled with assumptions. Assumptions become part of the data because they are part of us, and part of the data collection processes that organizations use. So how can you become aware of your own assumptions (on both a personal and organizational level) and start creating "assumption-wary knowledge"?

It begins with addressing the potentially harmful assumptions that all of us accidentally perpetuate. This is where the idea behind "assumption-wary knowledge" comes in: most of our current knowledge-generation techniques do not take our own perspectives and assumptions into account. Deep listening does.

In this system, rooting out assumptions and accurately understanding a person's thinking starts right away in the Listening Session. In fact, a major part of the researcher's role is getting their own mind and assumptions out of the way so they can make room for understanding.

Now I'm going to dive into the role that the listener plays during the listening session, how to approach the role, and why it's important. Along the way I'll also discuss the reasons that this system of deep listening is scalable, and some of the ways it can be valuable for your organization.

As a listener you will:

- Shrink your own thinking down to a bare minimum
- Monitor what type of thing is being said
- Focus on the subset of types that build cognitive empathy

However, paying attention to the participant is the highest priority. Approximately 90 percent of your cognition should be focused on paying rapt attention to the other person.

With the remaining 10 percent of your mind, you can learn to recognize the types of things being said and identify opportunities to encourage the participant to unfold their inner thoughts. It takes work and practice, but once you can easily identify when the participant's interior cognition is coming through, you can more effectively gather knowledge that comes directly from the participant's world.

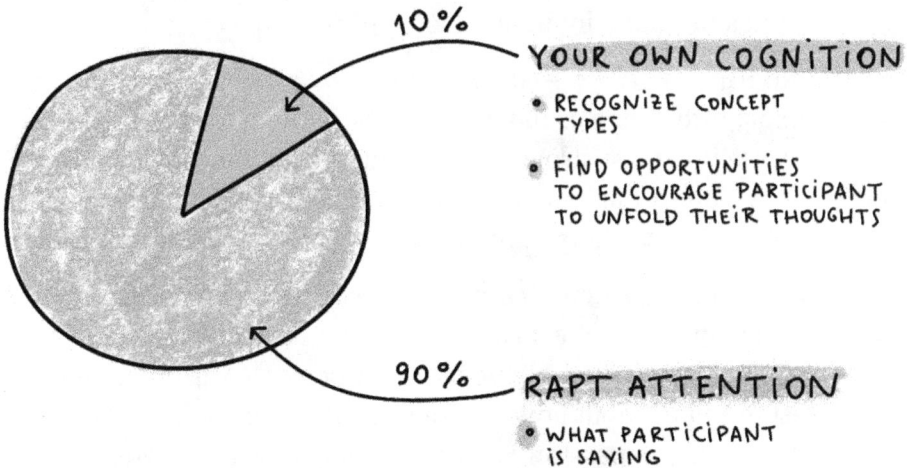

10%

YOUR OWN COGNITION

- RECOGNIZE CONCEPT TYPES
- FIND OPPORTUNITIES TO ENCOURAGE PARTICIPANT TO UNFOLD THEIR THOUGHTS

90%

RAPT ATTENTION

- WHAT PARTICIPANT IS SAYING

This 90/10 split is important because immersing yourself in someone else's perspective is the best way to build cognitive empathy with that person. And developing cognitive empathy with someone is the best way to undermine your assumptions about them.

But to build cognitive empathy, you first need to know what it is, what it is not, and why it is the key to creating assumption-wary knowledge.

Types of Empathy

Empathy has many faces and many types.[1] All of them are valid and accorded different names in the psychology field. (Dictionaries parade out an "average definition" of empathy, so don't rely on the dictionary for your understanding.) Empathy has a long history which other writers have covered in great detail. I've included a few excellent books in the endnotes to this chapter, in case you want to read more. For our purposes, just knowing and embracing that there are different, valid types of empathy is enough.

A. **Emotional contagion** – catching an emotion from a person or external source; causing someone to feel an emotion; often used in advertising, engagement algorithms, and behavioral economics; the primary kind of empathy referred to in the writings of Paul Bloom and Don Norman[2]

B. **Empathic distress** – feeling upset by the state of another person; often cited as the dishonorable sibling to compassion—because you have strong feelings but are not motivated to help that person (if that person wants your help); nonetheless, it is a common and valid type of empathy

C. **Empathic concern (commonly called "compassion")** – feeling upset by the heavier, negative emotions of another person *and* trying to relieve the other person's suffering—or at least thinking about how to relieve it (if that person wants your help). Yes, compassion is a type of empathy, according to the psychology field.

D. **Empathic listening (commonly called "empathy")** – *provide support* for another person *in the moment* about their negative *or positive* mental situation; this is the type of empathy referred to by the majority of speakers and writers, although they usually refer to *emotions*, not the person's whole mental situation. It includes inner thinking, too. When you recognize somebody has *something going on*—when somebody has

paused or seems distracted, glowing, agitated, bouncy, etc.—
it's an opportunity to listen and support that person, right then
in that moment. After a person has shared their *something* and
feels understood, they feel connected and validated. If the
something was heavy before, it is lightened. If the *something*
was light before, that lightness is reflected more broadly. The
goal of empathic listening, to make someone feel understood
and supported, can be a secondary goal of deep listening.

E. **Cognitive empathy** – consciously cultivating an understanding
    of a person's inner voice: the inner thinking, emotional
    reactions, and guiding principles running through their mind;
    this is a long form of empathy, one that can be developed
    further over days, months, and years after your interaction with
    someone. The goal of cognitive empathy is the same as that of
    deep listening: to understand another person's approach. This
    is different than the goal of empathic listening, although it still
    often results in a person feeling understood and knowing that
    you "get" their way of thinking.

F. **Facial or posture empathy** – subconsciously mimicking or
    interpreting the expression of someone's face or body; the
    source of the human ability to believe you understand what's
    going through the mind of a pet or wild animal (anthropomor-
    phize), or to see #faceseverywhere.

The above list includes just a few of the different types of empathy; there
are more. There is a deeper history about how the types were defined
over time, if you want to know more.[3] The overall takeaway here is
that one type is *not better* than another. However, there is one type of
empathy that is a perfect fit for building assumption-wary knowledge
for your organization: Cognitive Empathy.

Cognitive Empathy

Although both empathy types D and E from the list above require deep listening, their functions are actually very different. Empathic listening is *supporting* someone in their positive or negative moment of "something going on." Cognitive empathy is building an *understanding* of another person's approach over time.

In listening sessions, cognitive empathy is the tool that unlocks the knowledge you'll build for your organization. You will employ this tool with the participants in a study, and as you do, you'll start to notice patterns of thinking emerging from their different approaches. These patterns are your knowledge.

The chief complaint I hear from organizations that are resistant to applying empathy in their work is that it's not scalable. This complaint is rooted in a misunderstanding about which type of empathy they should apply. Many organizations get stuck in the belief that type D, empathic listening, is the only type of empathy. But empathic listening is about supporting a person in the moment they are having an experience. It's a time-sensitive, one-on-one, human-to-human interaction. It's not clear how to scale the use of empathic listening across an organization, and so it gets relegated to the realms of customer retention, public relations, social marketing, etc.

Empathic listening doesn't provide the scalable knowledge that organizations need to make decisions. Mostly because it's done *in the moment* when *something is going on* for a person. It does not lend itself to long-term knowledge-building about a particular purpose. Also, it's typically only focused on a person's emotions, not their whole mental situation.

Cognitive empathy (type E), in contrast, scales beautifully. Cognitive empathy scales because you are seeking to *understand* a person first, and then to find patterns across larger groups about the way they address their purpose. The patterns allow you to develop cognitive empathy with a "thinking style": an approach to a problem or purpose that many different people have in common. This is why cognitive empathy works at the organizational level. It informs a broad perspective that is actionable at scale, allowing the organization to *support* more people with less harm.

UNDERSTAND PERSON → FIND PATTERNS ACROSS LARGER GROUPS → CREATE SOLUTIONS TO SUPPORT THEIR DIFFERENT APPROACHES

Moreover, because cognitive empathy is about how people *think,* it can provide a much-needed understanding of how discrimination, culture, and physiology affect people's approaches. Rather than assuming that all people think the same, it can give your organization the knowledge it needs to provide nuanced support for the people it has previously ignored.

Developing Cognitive Empathy

Understanding another person's perspective *requires* that you drop your own perspective. A great way to make this happen is to get up close to the details of the other person's interior cognition. It will be different than your own, even if you have a lot in common with the person. This interior cognition (a person's inner thinking, emotional reactions, and guiding principles) is the foundation of cognitive empathy.

Every person has a way of showing up in the world and expressing themselves. This expression, across different topics, takes the form of preferences, attitudes, etc. The preferences and attitudes are a shorthand to represent interior cognition to people. However, the preferences and attitudes don't actually reveal the reasoning behind them, or what went through the person's head when they formed the preferences and attitudes in question.

From the outside, you can only interpret and make assumptions about what went through the person's mind to build the opinions and perceptions they're expressing. When someone tells you what went through their mind, they invite you inside their thinking for a moment.

Developing cognitive empathy with someone means learning to get out of your own thinking and into theirs, bit by bit. It takes time, effort, and, most importantly, it takes repeated journeys into their interior cognition.

Develop Empathy Before Applying It

Leadership has made "go fast" a cultural mindset. So is it any wonder that teams leap to the conclusion without taking time to find patterns based on cognitive empathy? The "go fast" culture has almost forced teams to rely on their imaginations—to rely on assumptions and bias.

I watch teams reach for empathy but try to apply understanding before they develop it. They imagine scenarios and characters to create solutions for, then put themselves in these characters' shoes. The scenarios and characters are based on examples from movies, tv shows, and articles, rather than on primary or even secondary research.

Without taking time to develop cognitive empathy and find patterns, it's all a guess.

What is a Concept?

People think and speak in concepts, so I will need to define what I mean by "concepts" before moving on. Concepts are the various discrete ideas or notions that a participant brings up about a topic. Any conversation or listening session will be full of many concepts. And, each concept can be tagged with a concept type. The concept types group into different layers.

Let me start by giving you some examples of concepts that a single participant brought up during a tiny part of one listening session, covering two topics.

	Concept	Topic
1.	Have groceries delivered when the pandemic starts, instead of going to the store	Grocery delivery
2.	Re-start grocery delivery at the start of the pandemic, after having stopped when I retired because it felt too decadent at the time for a person who could go to the store	Grocery delivery
3.	Recognize that my cough could be more than just allergies, because I had been out where there were people who could have had Covid	My cough
4.	Quarantine myself for two weeks to see what's going on with my cough	My cough
5.	Get my computer out to make an order	Grocery delivery
6.	Feel confident setting up a grocery order with Giant Delivery because I have done it before	Grocery delivery
7.	Love having groceries delivered	Grocery delivery
8.	Feel pleasure that Covid gave me the excuse to let someone deliver my groceries right to my kitchen again	Grocery delivery

See if you can spot the above concepts in the listening excerpt below. You'll notice that the second and the sixth concepts above are expressed in a few places in the text. That's because the way people naturally unfold concepts is not always linear, and repetition can be normal. I only list a repeated concept once.

Person: Well when the pandemic first started, I did grocery delivery only. I actually didn't go to the store. And that was not unusual for me because I've been doing delivery in the past when I worked, before when I was too busy. And I thought well, I know how to do that, I can just do that.

Listener: What led to that decision? What was going through your mind when you decided at that time to do delivery only?

Person: I had a cough early on in March that turned out to probably be more related to allergies, but it made me feel cognizant of my health and just thought well I had been out somewhere where there could have been people before we knew what this was, and I wanted to give it at least 2 weeks to find out what was going on. So, I just got my computer out. I hadn't ordered with the Giant delivery for a while and just went ahead and did it.

Listener: How was that?

Person: Oh, it's great. I love it. I feel a little bit decadent doing it because they bring it right to your kitchen. I've always loved doing it, but once I retired, I taught myself how to shop again because I thought, "I have time. I don't need someone to deliver my food." So, COVID gave me the excuse to let someone deliver my food again.

During the listening session, you will follow the participant, and let them take you to various past times and places when they were addressing the purpose you are studying. You will primarily pay attention to the concepts the participant is saying, but you will also monitor the layers of the concept types. Why? To make sure that they go fully into their interior cognition of what happened in that past time and place. You want to make sure you can develop cognitive empathy—an understanding of their inner landscape. You want to zoom past your own assumptions and interpretations of what the person might express or present to understand what is really there.

Here are the *types* for the concepts I listed above:

	Concept	Concept Type
1.	Have groceries delivered when the pandemic starts, instead of going to the store	Explanation
2.	Re-start grocery delivery at the start of the pandemic, after having stopped when I retired because it felt too decadent at the time for a person who could go to the store	Inner thinking
3.	Recognize that my cough could be more than just allergies, because I had been out where there were people who could have had COVID	Inner thinking
4.	Quarantine myself for two weeks to see what's going on with my cough	Inner thinking
5.	Get my computer out to make an order	Explanation

6.	Feel confident setting up a grocery order with Giant Delivery because I have done it before	Emotional reaction
7.	Love having groceries delivered	Preference
8.	Feel pleasure that COVID gave me the excuse to let someone deliver my groceries right to my kitchen again	Emotional reaction

Monitor Concept Types & Layers

Concept types and layers make it simpler to minimize your cognition in a listening session.

Here's how. The key is NOT to correctly identify each topic, concept, or concept type. You don't want to put that much of your processing power there. Instead, monitor the *flavor* (or *sense*) of what's being said, and only take action if it's staying too much in the exterior layers.

Having an idea of what concept layers the person is conveying to you is one way to reduce your conscious thinking. Rather than spend a listening session worrying whether you are correctly identifying the type of each concept, using your sense of whether the person is dwelling in the exterior layers versus the interior layers is good enough. You can use the tool of concepts layers to know if you are getting close to the right stuff for developing cognitive empathy.

At first, the idea of monitoring concept layers will seem a little daunting, like learning to spell English words. But there is a technique for monitoring concept types, and it is simple and reliable. There are only twelve concept types that you need to recognize for listening sessions. Each type is distinct. Better yet, you don't have to stay alert for all twelve types, but instead only the ones belonging to interior cognition. There are only ***three*** interior cognition types. It requires practice to be able to recognize these three while in a listening session, but listeners I have trained have found the technique straightforward to grasp.

You can practice this technique in a variety of ways.

At the end of this chapter, I help you think about how to practice in a way that suits your personal contexts. I also include a little example quiz at the end of the next section.

So, keep your cognition light. There are only a few things to think about during a listening session.

A listener's three cognitive activities:

1. Pay rapt attention
2. Monitor whether the concept type is exterior or interior
3. Be aware if the person has popped back into the session mode of the listening session

---

The third point above comes from Chapter Two. Maintain a thin awareness of when the participant is in session mode and when they go to the memory mode. Session mode is when the participant's focus of attention is on you and on the listening session itself. Memory mode is when the participant is focused on a past time and place. You can effectively build cognitive empathy when a person is speaking about their interior cognition—and that can happen in both modes, but is more likely in memory mode.

The second bullet point above is where I want to focus now. I'll walk you through the twelve concept types and show you how they separate out into subsets or layers.

The Concept Layers

The twelve concept types fall into distinctly layered categories. You can picture the categories like the spherical jawbreaker/gobstopper/pachicleta type of candy. **Each candy represents one topic**, and at the end of a listening session the person will have mentioned twenty or thirty topics. It's like they laid that many jawbreaker candies out on a table for you to understand.

Each candy—each topic—has a few concepts associated with it, stored at one of the four layers of the candy. The sphere at the center of the candy is the layer where cognitive empathy can be formed. You will want to help the person communicate as many concepts from this center layer as they can, for as many of the topics/candies as possible. Wrapping that center is a candy layer, then another different layer, and another layer beyond that. Let me describe each layer, starting at the outside and working toward the center.

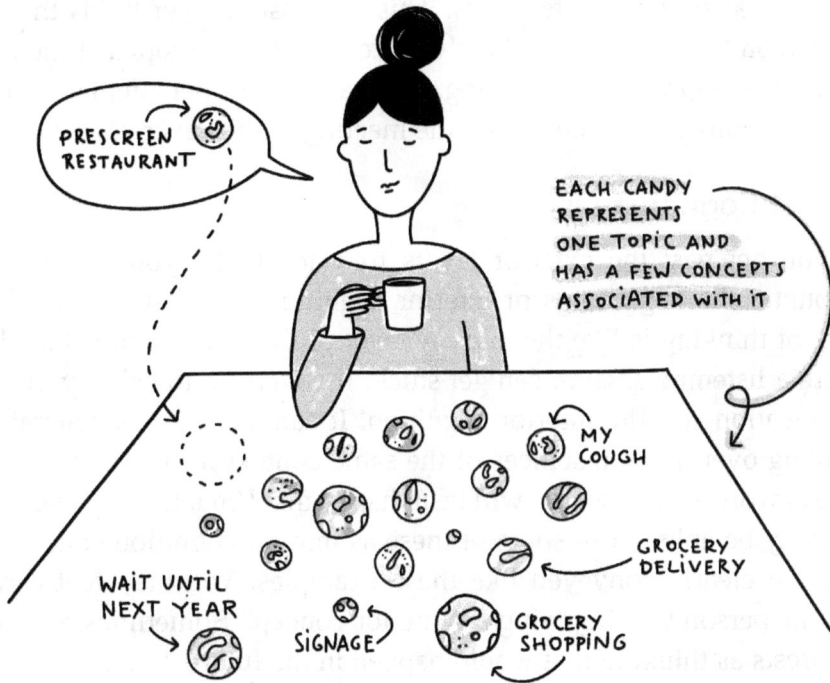

Description Layer

The outermost layer consists of descriptions of the how the topic works from this person's perspective. (It includes not only the aspects of the actual physical world, but also the societal, collaborative, process, strategy, and configuration aspects, and any systems etc.) When a person first brings up a topic, they are likely to start by describing their understanding of the topic and its context with concepts that live in this thick outermost layer. When they bring up another topic, it is a separate jawbreaker candy, and they will express other concepts in the outer layer of that candy. They want you, as the listener, to understand what each topic is.

Expression Layer

The next layer inward is the candy "flavor" a person presents to other people about the topic. It includes things like opinions and attitudes. People are often inclined to tell you about this next layer because that is what they expect you want to know. It's what surveys ask and what people hear on news interviews. This expression layer holds the way the person "shows up" to others with respect to each topic. If the topic is about an unproductive meeting, for example, the person may express their opinions or attitudes about the meeting in this layer of that topic.

Almost Cognition Layer

As you get past the exterior layers for each topic, you will start to encounter the beginnings of interior cognition. This almost cognition layer of thinking is like the gummy layer of the candy, and is the place where a listening session can get stuck. It covers up the clarity of time- and location-specific interior cognition. It can manifest as generalized thinking over many instances of the same context for that topic. "I am always worried that people will be unhappy that I'm late to the meeting." You may be able to use some of these as interior cognition concepts, if they are clearly conveyed like these examples. You may feel certain that the person was implying an interior concept. Sometimes this layer manifests as thinking that would happen in the future. "I am sure I will refuse when my boss tries to assign me the task in the meeting." Market research asks people to imagine using a product or service in the future, but that approach is not viable here. The thoughts have not been thought yet, nor the reactions felt. You will build more stable knowledge if you get past this layer to the clarity of candy's center for the topic.

Interior Cognition Core

At the center of the topic-candy is the crystalline space containing the person's inner thinking, emotional reactions, and guiding principles regarding the topic. The participant reconstructs their cognition from a past point in time. Their *inner thinking, emotional reactions,* and *guiding principles* are clear, discrete, and easily recognized. Those three concept types are the same components of cognitive empathy that you are after. For example, "Last Tuesday I felt stressed about my back-to-back video meetings. [emotional reaction] I worried about showing up late for the second call. [emotional reaction] But then I realized I could drop out of the first meeting early because I'm not the one presenting; no one will miss me. [inner thinking] Then I can be on time for the second meeting, where I do have some things to say. It's best to be on time for meetings where I want people to hear my ideas. [guiding principle]"

Next, I'll describe the concept types within the separate layers.

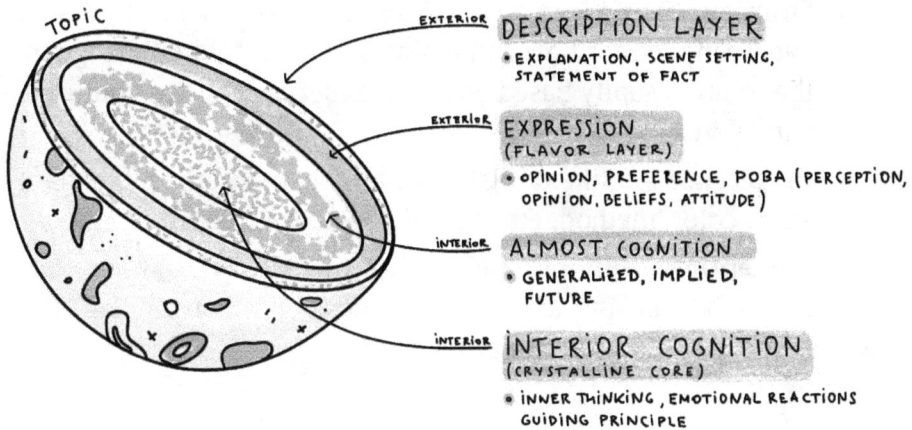

DESCRIPTION LAYER
• EXPLANATION, SCENE SETTING, STATEMENT OF FACT

EXPRESSION (FLAVOR LAYER)
• OPINION, PREFERENCE, POBA (PERCEPTION, OPINION, BELIEFS, ATTITUDE)

ALMOST COGNITION
• GENERALIZED, IMPLIED, FUTURE

INTERIOR COGNITION (CRYSTALLINE CORE)
• INNER THINKING, EMOTIONAL REACTIONS GUIDING PRINCIPLE

Description Layer

These three concept types give context and allow the participant to communicate to you their understanding of the situation around this topic.

→ **Explanation** – an account of how or why something works or is done, especially with regard to systems and methods, but also software, mechanisms, physics, biology, mathematics, etc.; usually conveyed in session mode so the listener understands

- **Scene setting** – laying out the context of where a person was, or what had happened, who was there, etc.; usually done in session mode so the listener understands; similar to what appears at the start of a scene in a written play

- **Statement of fact** – description using numbers, time, qualities of an entity, placement, etc.; usually stated in session mode so the listener understands

Expression Layer

These three concept types signal a person's way of presenting their relationship to a topic.

- **Opinion** – an approval or disapproval of an idea, person, event; an idea for how something should unfold or change in the future; usually based on a past experience; often confused with advice

- **Preference** – a like or dislike of a food, environment, experience, color, method, etc.; usually based on a past experience

- **Perceptions, opinions, beliefs & attitudes (POBA)** – market research concepts to understand how a person thinks of a brand, person/group, or product

Almost Cognition Layer

These three easily masquerade as interior concept types about the topic, but they are unpinned from a past event. Sometimes you can use them as placeholders for interior cognition.

- **Generalized** – any concept (description, expression, or cognition) representing several instances of what is being described; the typical manifestation of a concept over the course of time and experiences; a concept that is not tied to a place and time

- **Implied** – an interior cognition concept (inner thinking, emotional reaction, guiding principle) that seems to be what the person meant, but wasn't conveyed explicitly

+ **Future** – imagining any future concept type (description, expression, or cognition)

Interior Cognition Core

This is the person's interior cognition about the topic. These three concept types together produce cognitive empathy. They are made clear by being tied to a past point in time.

+ **Inner thinking** – active thought process at a specific time and place, including whys and wherefores, decision-making, indecision, intent, procrastination, motivation, that little voice inside your head

+ **Emotional reaction** – emotion, feeling; might cause an action or decision, inner thinking or another emotional reaction

+ **Guiding principle** – a personal rule or instruction for actions or decisions

Since these three concept types are particularly important for listening sessions, I will explain them at more length below.

Inner Thinking

Inner thinking includes a few states of mind that are called out in other research techniques, such as a person's intent and motivation. These are part of inner thinking, but the category also includes states of mind which are less certain, like indecision and procrastination. Inner thinking can also include more than just what is listed.

Often your inner thinking operates so fast that it doesn't even form words in your head. Sometimes thoughts are like sparks in linear succession; sometimes they are a cloud of sparks flickering around a single concept. Translating it into words to tell a listener requires a little instant replay of the past moment. That's why I ask participants to talk about a specific date and time; it helps them translate interior cognition to words. (I talk more about this in Chapter Six).

Here again I want to highlight the difference between a listening session and a conversation. Thinking about what you want to say to a person in conversation is usually not inner thinking. Instead it's usually a manifestation of the conversational goals listed in Chapter Two.

Emotional Reactions

Emotions are an important part of anyone's inner landscape and are a part of understanding someone's perspective. Emotions are feelings; they arise because of thoughts, memory, stories, a preceding emotion, smells, etc. Here are some example emotions: worried, frustrated, hopeful, pleased.[4] Some cultures think of emotions as controllable, while other cultures think of them like weather, beyond anyone's control. Cultural attitudes toward emotions also shift over time.[5]

What's important for listening sessions is that you treat a participant's emotion as valid. You may hear them bring up an emotion they had in reaction to something, and you may think to yourself, "that's a silly reaction," or "why get emotional over that?" These are judgements, and you are supposed to avoid judging the participant in order to develop cognitive empathy. Moreover, judgements take up your cognition, when you should be paying rapt attention. Let it go and get back to deep listening.

If you work in an atmosphere where the idea of emotions or feelings is laughed off, try calling them "reactions." Often team members will ascribe value to "reactions."

In English, people use the word "feel" to introduce an emotion. "I feel reassured by the ideas I'm reading." But people also use the word "feel" to introduce a physical sensation. "The weather changed and now I feel cold when I go out." Cold is not an emotion. However, there is a gray area in between physical sensations and actual emotions that you will need to use your best judgment to unpack. One person describing the cold weather might be using a description layer concept; a different person using the same words might be describing the emotion of feeling chilled and horrified. "I feel cold as I read her xenophobic tweet." So be careful to note whether "feel" is used as an emotion or a description. You can usually tell, in

English, by the preposition that comes right after the adjective. For example, "feel fatigued by the endless lecture" versus "feel fatigued after babysitting the toddler all day." The "by" in the first example indicates it's an emotion and the "after" in the second example means it is a physical condition.

Additionally, the verb "feel" is used colloquially in English to indicate things that aren't emotions or physical conditions at all. "I feel like he shouldn't be so upset by my decision" is an *opinion* about another person's reaction. "I feel that it isn't right to give a CEO an extra bonus on top of the huge salary they already earn" could be a *guiding principle* if the person saying it is a director on a bunch of corporate boards. Usually when I hear people saying "I feel" in spoken conversation, they are using it in these ways, to preface an opinion or a guiding principle. So, it's yet another nuance to be aware of with the word "feel" in English.

Guiding Principles

Guiding principles deserve a closer look. Unlike values, they are more particular to a person. Values are broader, existing at the community or culture level. Values shift across time. Different communities and cultures espouse different values. For example, one community might believe in "patience," "growth," and "forgiveness," while another might emphasize "self-discipline," "respect," and "authority." Unlike values, guiding principles are smaller and often unique to an individual. Guiding principles can be *based* on values. For example, a value like "family" may inform a guiding principle like "turn down invitations that don't include my family." A value like "caring" may inform a guiding principle like "take time to say a kind word to the airport gate agents."

But guiding principles are just as likely to be based on superstition, expediency, lack of resources, discrimination, or other lived experiences. This is one reason why guiding principles are valuable to building knowledge for an organization that wants to support people of different thinking styles. Here's an example of a guiding principle based on discrimination: "Every time someone asks me "where are you from" I just change the subject, asking them a different question in return, just ignoring their question. Why? That's my defense mechanism. I am a second generation American, and just because my last name is Latinx, they assume I'm an immigrant, or worse, undocumented. I get treated to commands instead of respect. And even though this is painful, I still want to model respect for them, so I just change the subject."

Guiding principles are personal rules. They help a person act or decide. As such, they can range in size and specificity. For example, "Allow myself to nap when I feel the need." "Stay focused until I finish the thing I intended." "Avoid visiting anyone in the hospital." "Never leave open cans of cat food where my cat can cut her tongue on the sharp edges." Some of these are common across people, and some of these are more unique.

In deep listening, you will sometimes hear people expressing their guiding principles using the words "I believe." *"I believe in building a workplace where each employee feels welcome."* Or people use "make sure" or "avoid" to introduce guiding principles. *"I make sure my daughters know that texting while driving is forbidden." "I avoid making restaurant servers mad at me."* Usually, though, guiding principles are *hidden* in what people say. You will sense there is a guiding principle there, and may encourage the participant to describe it more specifically. (I will cover how to do this in Chapter Six.)

What's interesting is that people occasionally decide to go *against* one of their own guiding principles. It might be for the duration of a context, like being pregnant. Or maybe it's momentary, like when a person is late for a medical appointment and decides that texting the doctor's office is okay while waiting in line at a stop light. If it comes up this way in the listening session, you will sense it as a hidden guiding principle and perhaps ask about it. Even if the person has reversed or ignored their guiding principle for this particular time frame, it is still a guiding principle.

Inner thinking and **emotional reactions** are time-bound events. They occur in a person's mind during a particular point in the past. **Guiding principles** will be invoked at a particular point in time to make a decision or guide an action, and that's usually how you will hear about them.

Guiding principles come up much less frequently than inner thinking or emotional reactions. They are fun to recognize and explore because of this rarity.

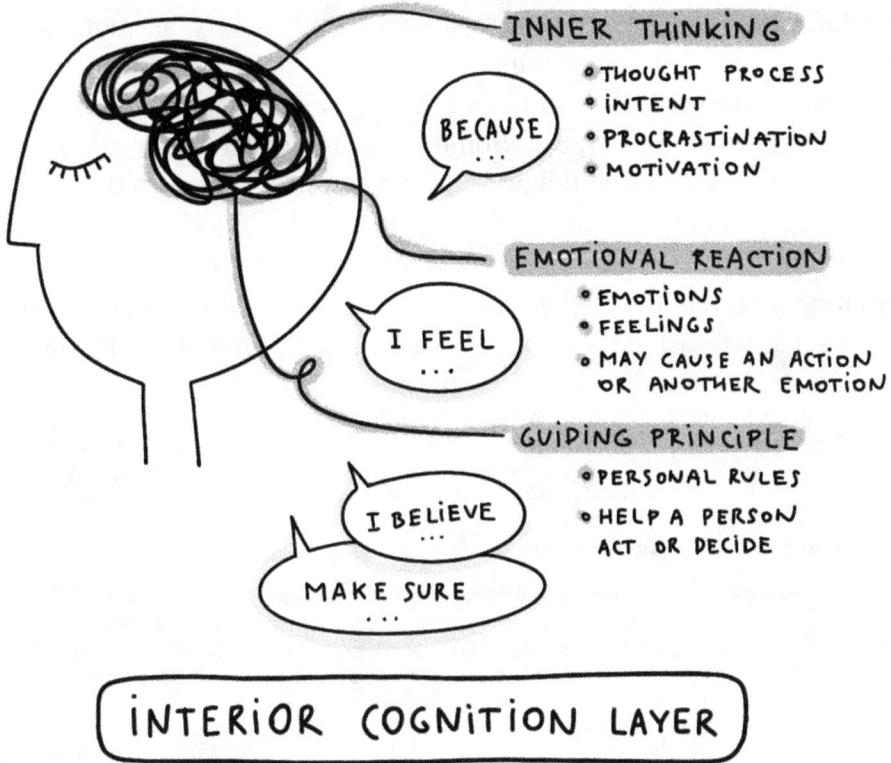

INNER THINKING
- THOUGHT PROCESS
- INTENT
- PROCRASTINATION
- MOTIVATION

BECAUSE ...

EMOTIONAL REACTION
- EMOTIONS
- FEELINGS
- MAY CAUSE AN ACTION OR ANOTHER EMOTION

I FEEL ...

GUIDING PRINCIPLE
- PERSONAL RULES
- HELP A PERSON ACT OR DECIDE

I BELIEVE ...

MAKE SURE ...

INTERIOR COGNITION LAYER

A Note on Formatting

In this chapter and throughout the rest of the book, I will be using many examples to help clarify techniques you can use as a listener to help participants express their interior cognition. Sometimes these examples are direct quotes (when I had permission) and other times the example is based on real listening sessions but changed for privacy reasons. I'll also be using inline comments in the form [comment] to identify concepts and concept types the participant brings up. If you see a technique mentioned that I have not explained yet, rest assured that I will cover it at a later point in the book.

Aren't Preferences and Opinions Important?

It may seem like some description or expression concept types, like **explanation**, **preference**, and **opinion** could qualify as motivations, which are part of inner thinking. But not quite. **Preferences** and **opinions** have their *roots* in inner thinking. These two are each formed by experiences in the past. Some of those experiences are simply something from your childhood that an authority figure told you, like "if you grow your own vegetables and cook them for dinner, they taste better" [opinion]. Other past experiences have inner thinking and emotional reactions attached, like how you learned that not everyone is as sensitive to loud sounds as you are. *That's* the part you want to understand. That past interior cognition.

Person: Unfortunately they were serving stuffed peppers. [implied emotional reaction] I hate stuffed peppers. [preference]

Listener: Where did that come from?

Person: I remember hating them as a kid. [session mode] There was this one dinner I remember well. I did not want to eat the stuffed pepper because it tasted bad, but Mom made me sit at the dining table until I had eaten half of it. [scene setting or explanation]

That took two hours, [statement of fact] and I remember the trembling fork as I put another small bite of pepper in my mouth and began to chew the acrid, unpleasant thing. [implied emotional reaction]

I remember Mom checking on my progress and telling me to keep going until it was half gone, [scene setting or explanation] even though I felt desperate to quit. [emotional reaction] I remember feeling anguished that it was still light out and I couldn't go outside and play, [emotional reaction] but I had to sit at the table slowly forcing myself to take bite after bite as the light outside got dimmer and dimmer. [explanation or implied inner thinking]

Listener: How did you force yourself to eat bite after bite? Or do you even remember? (laughs)

Person: (laughs) I have no idea. The power of Mom Authority? [session mode] (laughs)

Listener:	So what did you do at the dinner party where they served stuffed peppers?
Person:	Ah! I have always felt judged when I say I don't like a certain food, [generalized emotional reaction], so over time I learned to say I am allergic to it. [guiding principle] People respect allergies. I figured that out when I saw a friend mentioning an allergy at a restaurant, and I decided to copy them. [inner thinking]

This description is full of emotional reaction as well as scene setting, statement of fact, and explanation. The listener notices the flavor and pulls back to the dinner party where the stuffed pepper was served. At that point, the almost cognition and interior cognition come out.

Substitute "bitcoin" or "ELISA assays" for "stuffed peppers," and you see how this could work to create deeper knowledge for your organization.

Concept Types with Colleagues

When I work with teams who are having collaboration issues, discovering the conversational goals and the concept types is an epiphany for them. Often they've never considered what is actually being exchanged in conversation. It's surprising to realize the team members are lobbing commands at each other or speaking at the description and expression layers rather than sharing their interior cognition. I have worked with teams to help them learn how to get to the center, to reach for the layer where team members speak about their inner thinking, emotional reactions, and guiding principles with each other.

Speaking from this interior cognition layer really helps with collaboration, and it all starts with noticing the concept types of what is being said. Recognizing these concept types and understanding what layer collaborators are communicating in gives the team structure to reach past assumptions and heal past harms.

Diving from Exterior to Interior

Notice when a participant mentions concepts that are tangled or not entirely clear. If you think they may be hinting at interior cognition by saying something as an explanation, or if they are implying an emotion they had, you may want to ask about it. I will explain how in Chapter Six.

Each time you ask about something at the outer layers to get down to the crystalline interior cognition, the participant picks up on what layer you are after. As the listening session gets going, the participant will learn to dive into hints and implied concepts on their own. They might even get really good at it, which is fun, because then you can notice when they bring up several implied concepts and then they dive into each concept on their own. If they are on a roll, let them roll. I will return to this in Chapter Six to cover what to do if the participant hasn't quite picked up on when to dive in.

Knowing which concept types your participant is using will help you orient during the session and encourage depth. Without concept types at the interior, you can't form cognitive empathy. With description and expression concept types, you are apt to misshape the participant's thinking to fit the container of your expectations. This is how you accidentally introduce assumptions and bias that you cannot remove later.

Instead of assuming, encourage the participant go into to their past interior cognition. I'll show you how in Chapter Six.

Examples

Here is a breakdown of the concept types in the recounting of the long-past stuffed pepper dinner. That's the topic. You can cover up the right columns to see if you can identify each concept type.

Concept	Concept Type	Layer
Unfortunately they were serving stuffed peppers	Implied emotional reaction (unhappy)	Almost cognition
I hate stuffed peppers	Preference	Expression
I remember hating them as a kid	Session mode (commentary that can be ignored)	Almost Interior
Mom made me sit at the dining table until I had eaten half of it	Scene setting or explanation	Description
that took two hours	Statement of fact	Description
I remember the trembling fork as I put another small bite of pepper in my mouth and began to chew the acrid, unpleasant thing.	Implied emotional reaction (disgust)	Almost cognition
I remember Mom checking on my progress, telling me to keep going until it was half gone	Scene setting or explanation	Description
even though I felt desperate to quit	Emotional reaction (desperation)	Interior cognition
I remember feeling anguished that it was still light out and I couldn't go outside and play	Emotional reaction (anguish)	Interior cognition
but I had to sit at the table slowly forcing myself to take bite after bite as the light outside got dimmer and dimmer	Explanation or inner thinking	Description or Almost cognition
I have always felt judged when I say I don't like a certain food	Generalized emotional reaction	Almost cognition
I learned to say I'm allergic to it	Guiding principle	Interior cognition
People respect allergies. I figured that out when I saw a friend mentioning an allergy at a restaurant, and I decided to copy them	Inner thinking	Interior cognition

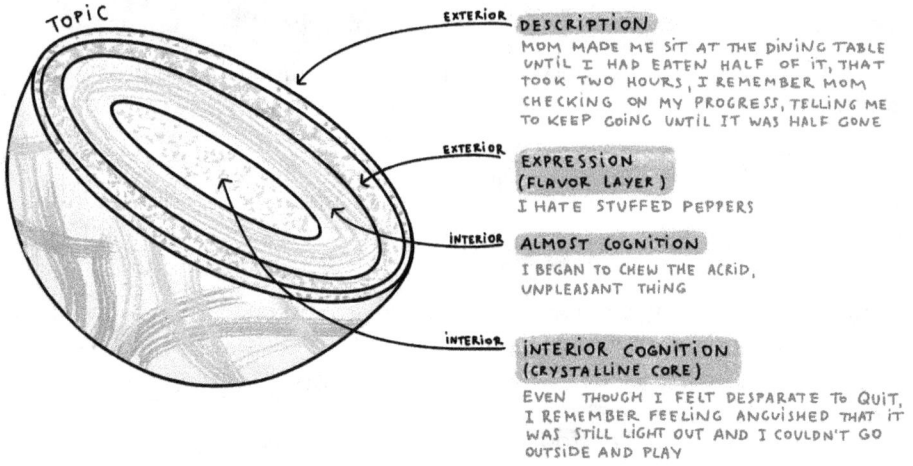

TOPIC

EXTERIOR DESCRIPTION
MOM MADE ME SIT AT THE DINING TABLE UNTIL I HAD EATEN HALF OF IT, THAT TOOK TWO HOURS, I REMEMBER MOM CHECKING ON MY PROGRESS, TELLING ME TO KEEP GOING UNTIL IT WAS HALF GONE

EXTERIOR EXPRESSION (FLAVOR LAYER)
I HATE STUFFED PEPPERS

INTERIOR ALMOST COGNITION
I BEGAN TO CHEW THE ACRID, UNPLEASANT THING

INTERIOR INTERIOR COGNITION (CRYSTALLINE CORE)
EVEN THOUGH I FELT DESPARATE TO QUIT, I REMEMBER FEELING ANGUISHED THAT IT WAS STILL LIGHT OUT AND I COULDN'T GO OUTSIDE AND PLAY

What if your organization would never hear about people's food preferences? Here is another example from the workplace. Here, a preference is stated, the listener notices, and they dive into the roots of that preference to understand the interior cognition when the preference began.

Person: So I put that off for a whole two weeks. [explanation or statement of fact] I hate making estimates how long a project will take. [preference]

Listener: How did this hatred form in the first place?

Person: How? Hmm ... that's a good question. I don't think— wait. I remember the time I was working for a company that had six big clients. [session mode] I was helping the customization team roll out one of the packages in our software, and it had some components that were fairly generic. You wouldn't really change the settings for anyone. [explanation or scene setting]

When my boss at the time asked me how long it would take me to get that component ready for each client, I figured I could make an estimate for one and multiplied that by six. [inner thinking] I think it was a total of four days that I estimated. [statement of fact]

Little did we know that two of the clients actually wanted that component changed! [implied emotional reaction] And it was a bit of code-level change, not just setup. So I worked until 1:00 am for three nights, [explanation or scene setting] and on the fourth day I had to tell my boss there was no way I could finish by the end of the day. [implied inner thinking]

And that boss was inflexible. [opinion or implied emotional reaction] She told me I had to stick to my estimate. I was a bit shocked by that. [emotional reaction]

So I figured I'd pull an all-nighter and see what I could do. [inner thinking] Ugh, I remember that night. [session mode] I was worried that I would make mistakes since I was already tired. [emotional reaction] I was also really angry at my boss. [emotional reaction] She had no right to take my whole night away. What if I had kids? Why did she assume I had no other responsibilities? [inner thinking] I was so mad. [emotional reaction]

That's when I swore not to make estimates again without really spending four hours at it, [guiding principle] listing every little task, everything that could go wrong, every mistake I might have to fix ... [explanation] and I am not thrilled about the idea of sitting down for four hours racking my brain for all these possibilities. [emotional reaction] But now I make myself do it. Because, you know what? [session mode] The boss comes in the next morning and I'm wearing the same clothes as the day before, and she just ignores it and asks if I finished on time. [guiding principle and emotional reaction, tangled together]

Listener: Arg! That *is* shocking.

Here is the breakdown of that example. You will notice that the participant doesn't stay at the interior cognition layer much—just a sentence here or there. In Chapter Six you will see how to recognize these hints and barely-there references, and how to help the participant unpack the ones that are important to them.

Concept	Concept Type	Layer
I put that off for a whole two weeks	Explanation or statement of fact	Description
I hate making estimates	Preference	Expression
I was working for a company that had six big clients. I was helping the customization team roll out one of the packages in the our software, and it had some components that were fairly generic. You wouldn't really change the settings for anyone.	Explanation and scene setting	Description

I figured I could make an esti-mate for one and multiplied that by six	Inner thinking	Interior cognition
it was a total of four days that I estimated	Statement of fact	Description
Little did we know that two of the clients actually wanted that component changed!	Implied emotional reaction (surprise)	Almost cognition
it was a bit of code-level change, not just setup. So I worked until 1am for three nights,	Explanation and scene setting	Description
and on the fourth day I had to tell my boss there was no way I could finish by the end of the day.	Implied inner thinking	Almost cognition
And boss was inflexible.	Opinion or implied emotional reaction	Expression or almost cognition
She told me I had to stick to my estimate. I was a bit shocked by that.	Emotional reaction (shocked)	Interior cognition
I figured I'd pull an all-nighter and see what I could do.	Inner thinking	Interior cognition
I was worried that I would make mistakes since I was already tired.	Emotional reaction (worried)	Interior cognition
I was also really angry at my boss.	Emotional reaction (angry)	Interior cognition
She had no right to take my whole night away. What if I had kids? Why did she assume I had no other responsibilities?	Inner thinking	Interior cognition
I was so mad.	Emotional reaction (mad)	Interior cognition
I swore not to make estimates again without really spending four hours at it	Guiding principle	Interior cognition
listing every little task, every-thing that could go wrong, every mistake I might have to fix	Explanation	Description

I am not thrilled about the idea of sitting down for four hours wracking my brain for all these possibilities.	Emotional reaction	Interior cognition
But now I make myself do it. Because, you know what?	Session mode (commentary that can be ignored)	
The boss comes in the next morning and I'm wearing the same clothes as the day before, and she just ignores it and asks if I finished on time.	Guiding principle and emotional reaction, tangled together	Interior cognition

---

Deep Listening Is for Short Periods

Deep listening depends upon minimizing your cognition. You must seek to fully comprehend the other person's perspective while losing your own. At the same time, you monitor the topics to see if the person is unfolding their interior cognition, and if not, you might help them. Concentrating on the person, minimizing your cognition, and monitoring for interior cognition takes effort. It feels overwhelming at first.

In comparison, having a list of interview questions asking the person to explain, compare, run through, and imagine is easy. But part of learning to listen deeply is letting go. Let go of getting it right. Let go of chastising yourself. Let go of watching the clock. Let go of being an expert. Let go of everything except paying rapt attention and monitoring what layers the person is unfolding.

There is an analogy I like to use. A listening session is like putting on a very heavy hat. You cannot wear this hat for long without giving yourself a neck ache. Even the most experienced listeners can only keep the focus and balance of a listening session going for about two hours. New listeners can maintain it for less time, since they have yet to build up the mental muscle.

You will want to work up to wearing the heavy hat of deep listening little by little, to build your ability. In the beginning, **develop an awareness of when your mind wanders away** from these three things.

A listener's three cognitive activities:

1. Pay rapt attention
2. Monitor whether the concept type is exterior or interior
3. Be aware if the person has popped back into the session mode of the listening session

---

This awareness is a little like meditation, where you begin to notice the thoughts floating across your empty mind. In meditation, the idea is not to banish those thoughts, but to accept that they will always come floating in, notice what happens, and let the thoughts dissipate. Likewise, in a listening session, it's not "bad" to find your mind thinking about what to ask the participant next, getting caught up in the emotion of the participant's experience, or comparing what the participant is saying to something similar from your own past. Just notice that your cognition has shifted. And let those thoughts go. Return to paying rapt attention to the participant.

You can lose the value of a listening session if you cannot focus on the other person. You might imagine you know what emotion is implied without actually asking them. You could accept their exterior concepts and miss asking for interior concepts. You might assume what they said matches your own approach to the purpose. The whole idea is to allow someone else's perspective to be clearly, deeply understood, so that your organization can make strategic decisions based on patterns in these perspectives. That takes listening at depth, which requires your rapt attention.

You will want to notice your mood, and if you are tired. Even when you desperately *want* to listen, your focus may repeatedly slip away from the participant and back to your own inner cognition. Support yourself. Allow yourself more time to collect your focus. Maybe even tell the participant you are a little slower than usual, to see if they will relax the pace for you. If you encounter an opportunity to practice but are not in the right frame of mind, skip it. Take care of yourself. Mental muscles take time to build just as physical ones do. I will cover more about this in Chapter Seven.

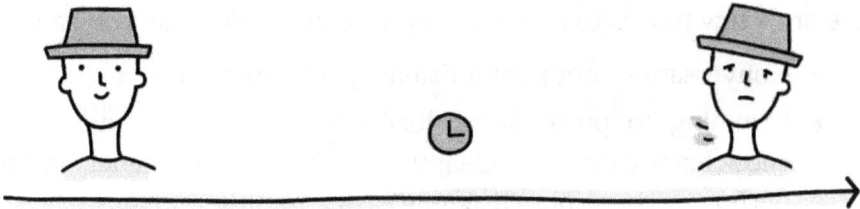

DEEP LISTENING IS A REALLY HEAVY HAT!

☑ PAY RAPT ATTENTION
☑ MONITOR CONCEPT TYPES
☑ SESSION OR MEMORY MODE?

Don't let your manager force you to work past your ability. At the same time, reassure yourself that when you feel in focus, a listening session is so much more relaxing than any other form of knowledge creation. You can work up to longer listening in a few weeks.

As an analogy, don't try to run the 50k trail run until you have built your endurance. Don't try heavy weightlifting without beginning with light weights. Listening is the same. Practice listening with little increments you can easily handle at first. Skill, confidence, and enjoyment will come over time.

Beginning Your Practice

The kind of listening in this book may not be something you can master immediately. It takes practice, and it is also a practice. It's a thing you do a lot, maybe daily, in order to feel confident with the technique and relaxed when you get to a formal listening session. Here's a way to get started.

Begin with a basic understanding of the twelve concept types. Focus on the three concept types in the subset of interior cognition. Work on your **awareness of whether someone's words represent the exterior or interior layers of their topic**.

Here are a few places to practice. Try as many of these as you can.

- Conversation (not a mini listening session, yet)
- Listening to professional listeners like podcast and radio show hosts (review in Chapter Two how these listeners often perform preoccupied listening)
- Reviewing your team's past interviews (recordings or transcripts)
- Reviewing the concept types that show up in a team conversation

When practicing listening in conversation, it's usually easier to start with people who do not have a lot of history with you. Instead, start with "familiar strangers." These are people who you don't have a lot of background with, but who have a certain amount of trust that you are not trying to manipulate them or get something out of them. (For example, a fellow volunteer worker, another parent at the playground, or someone waiting in line next to you at a store.) Ask a question and see how the person responds. See if you can take them to depth, even if in just a small way. This kind of conversation will only last 1-3 minutes, so treat it very lightly.

When practicing with a person, there are ethics involved. You will want to make sure they want to chat with you—don't just drag them into conversation. Make sure they seem like they're in the mood for it and be sensitive to signals that indicate they want to stop.

Be patient as you practice. It usually takes weeks of daily practice to consistently become aware of what someone's words represent—where they are in the layers of the candy jawbreaker. At that point your mental skill will be strong enough to get started with real listening sessions. You'll be ready to use that skill in listening sessions, tracking whether you are getting to cognitive empathy with your participant.

Summing Up

Deep listening is about gathering different cognitive approaches to a purpose, and turning those into strategic paths for your organization— paths that support a broader and broader variety of humans, not a mythical "average user." By creating space for people to speak in safety, you will be able to get past your assumptions about how other people think.

Follow the technique of recognizing what layer the participant is in and aim for the interior cognition crystalline center. This will reliably build cognitive empathy, providing the raw data that helps your organization see patterns and shapes through the fog of the uncertain future.

Listen raptly. Pay attention to the concept-type layer the participant is in. The participant will lead you where you need to be.

Also, take the time to build trust with your leadership and decision makers by listening deeply to them. Do the labor of building those relationships. Decision makers do not need to fully understand the techniques if they trust you. They do not have to worry as much about the details if they see who you are and feel listened to and supported by you as a human.

To get to a point where you can run a listening session, there are two additional concepts you'll need to understand in this method: patterns and purpose. Let's take a look at these in the next chapter.

Additional Resources

Empathy for Change: How to Create a More Empathetic World, Amy J. Wilson, January 2021. https://www.amyjwilson.com/empathy-forchange.

Empathy-Driven Software Development: Practical Advice for Coding with Compassion, Andrea Goulet and Carmen Shirkey Collins (Fall 2022 through Pearson/Addison-Wesley) https://empathyintech.com.

Vocabulary List

Concept: the various discrete ideas or notions that a participant brings up about a topic (e.g. deciding to stop grocery delivery because I'm retired and have time to shop now; feeling joy to restart grocery delivery during COVID).

Concept type: a way of categorizing concepts.

Concept layers:

Description layer: contains these concept types:
- Explanation
- Scene setting
- Fact

Expression layer: contains the concept types that the person uses to summarize how they see something or how they show up in relation to it:
- Opinion
- Preference
- POBA (perceptions, opinions, beliefs, attitudes)

Almost cognition layer: contains these concept types:
- Generalized (about description, expression, or interior cognition concepts)
- Implied (about interior cognition concepts)
- Future (about description, expression, or interior cognition concepts)

Interior cognition core: contains these concept types:
- Inner thinking
- Emotional reaction
- Guiding principle

Session mode: there are two mental focuses for the participant of the listening session; session mode is where the person is focused on the listener and their current session together.

Memory mode: the second mode of the listening session is where the person is focused on relating a memory of theirs.

Topic: the subject a person is communicating about (e.g. grocery delivery); each topic is like a jawbreaker candy, with four layers and several concepts mentioned at different layers.

Endnotes

1   Be reassured that within the psychology field, even the names used for each different type of empathy vary. They appear differently in different researchers' reports, but generally people in that field recognize this variation and group them together to indicate certain faces of empathy. For a more detailed list of the types of empathy, see C. Daniel Batson, "These Things Called Empathy," in The Social Neuroscience of Empathy, ed. Jean Decety and William Ickes (Cambridge, MA: The MIT Press, 2009), pp. 3-15.

2   These authors write against the use of empathy in product and service development. Both authors insist that compassion is a nobler goal to aim for than the type of empathy they chose to write about. Compassion is one of the types of empathy. See Paul Bloom, *Against Empathy: The Case for Rational Compassion* (New York, NY: Ecco, 2018), and Don Norman, "Why I Don't Believe in Empathic Design," XD Ideas (Adobe, May 8, 2019), https://xd.adobe.com/ideas/perspectives/leadership-insights/why-i-dont-believe-in-empathic-design-don-norman/.

3   Here is an excellent article written for the technology field that traces the history of empathy: Andrea Goulet, "Defining Empathy is Like Nailing Jell-o to a Wall," *Empathy in Tech* (monthly newsletter), LinkedIn, August, 4, 2021, https://www.linkedin.com/pulse/defining-empathy-like-nailing-jell-o-wall-andrea-goulet/.

4   If you want to explore more, there are two good places to find lists of emotions: Center for Nonviolent Communication - Feelings Inventory (https://www.cnvc.org/training/resource/feelings-inventory); and "wheel of emotions," which is derived from Dr. Robert Plutchik's work; Hokuma Karimova, "The Emotion Wheel: What It Is and How to Use It," Positive Psychology, May 20, 2021, https://positivepsychology.com/emotion-wheel/. The anthropologist who did forty years of research to show that eight basic emotions are universal across cultures is Paul Ekman. One of his books is **Emotions Revealed**.

5   Joseph Lee, "Mental Healthiness Science Fiction & Science Fact: What They Tell Us about Our Emotions," Mental Healthiness, March 28, 2016, https://mentalhealthiness.com/2016/03/29/science-fiction-science-fact-what-they-tell-us-about-our-emotions/.

CHAPTER 4

CHAPTER 4

Setting the Purpose

Building knowledge wary of assumptions is not usually an activity that fits within a discovery-design-develop cycle. That cycle lives within what's called the "solution space," where you come up with, test, and implement solutions to support people. Our more thoughtful process of building long-term knowledge is separate. It is about understanding how a person addresses their purpose, regardless of the tools they use.

You'll probably do this more thoughtful study of "the problem space" only once every year or two, and you'll want the knowledge you build to last. So, it makes sense to spend time framing what kind of knowledge you need and how you will get it. Careful knowledge-building begins with thoughtful choices. These choices take time.

Before you even schedule the first listening session, you want to have several thoughtful discussions with your team and decision makers. You'll want to discuss what to study, which stakeholders and teams should be involved, who to recruit as participants, and what tools to use in this effort to find knowledge. You will also want to consider whether a study is even the right thing for your organization right now. These discussions usually take a few weeks; they cannot be decided in an hour meeting.

If you decide to use listening sessions in your research, then you'll need to decide what purpose you are studying. The first question is not, "How can our solution help?" But rather, "How do people address their purpose?"

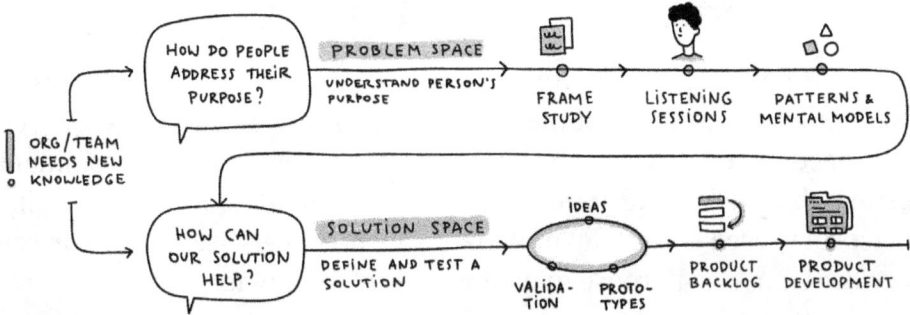

I have heard stories from people practicing their listening that it was a struggle to keep the session going, that they had to cast about for topics to bring up or questions to ask. They were upset because they knew neither of these things belong in a listening session. The one thing they were missing was this: the person's purpose. This chapter is about setting that purpose so that a listening session can unfurl smoothly. This chapter covers *what* a person's purpose is, how to *establish* it, and what you need to be thoughtful about as you plan how to build knowledge based on deep listening.

Looking for Patterns

When you do qualitative research, you end up with one of two kinds of results. If you see strong patterns in the data, you'll have valid, reliable, empirical results. Without patterns, you'll have a pile of disconnected anecdotes. So, you'll want to set up a study that has a good chance to result in patterns.

On the other hand, when you are building relationships, you might look for patterns over time. For instance, if you use deep listening with people you are mentoring, you can keep annotations of people's purposes and changing approaches to them over many months and years. Or, you might not need to look for patterns—as in relationship-building with the goal of developing deeper understanding and trust.

Research vs. Relationship-Building

You will have many opportunities to use your deep listening skills in your connections and relationships outside of research. In this case, you still need to identify what purpose the person is or will be communicating about. You still need to focus your listening on a purpose that person has been doing a lot of thinking about. Otherwise, the person can wander from one purpose to another, wondering where to stop or what you are interested in.

Sometimes wandering will be fine, especially when building relationships by deep listening with colleagues, stakeholders, or friends and family. Other times it annoys people, who will expect you be efficient with their time: when holding a listening session with a stakeholder, for instance. For this, you need to keep the focus of the session within the frame of the purpose that you want the person to communicate about.

Purpose is an excellent focus.

In a listening session, focusing on a specific purpose will help the other person express their interior cognition, rather than skipping across the exterior from topic to topic. In the context of research, maintaining the listening session's focus on the purpose is how you find patterns between different people's thinking about that purpose.

Without the focus, patterns can't emerge.

If you are going to do a research study, though, a quick refresher (or introduction) will help clarify why patterns are important in this context.

Applied Research: A Flawed Approach

You may or may not be familiar with the academic field of knowledge-creation: epistemology. There are clearly defined methods and terminology for building knowledge across various fields such as sociology, statistics, and biology, each with different approaches. But the business world does not seem aware of more than a few epistemological tools. The business world seems to limit knowledge creation to methods that *feel like* the scientific method in the natural sciences (e.g., chemistry, biology, and physics).[1] This is odd.

Businesses tend to approach research *as if* they are using the scientific method. In other words, they try to create a hypothesis or theory based on an idea or some reasoning. Then they create a "test" based on observation to prove or disprove the hypothesis.

The scientific method is meant to apply to the directly observable physical universe. And it works because *the hypothesis is about things that don't have agency or consciousness*. Most businesses are trying to build knowledge about the behavior of people, who *do* have agency and consciousness. It is much harder to design a "test" that will "prove or disprove" a hypothesis in this context. Even the design of the hypothesis, and the test itself, are subject to assumptions and bias based on the designer's worldview.

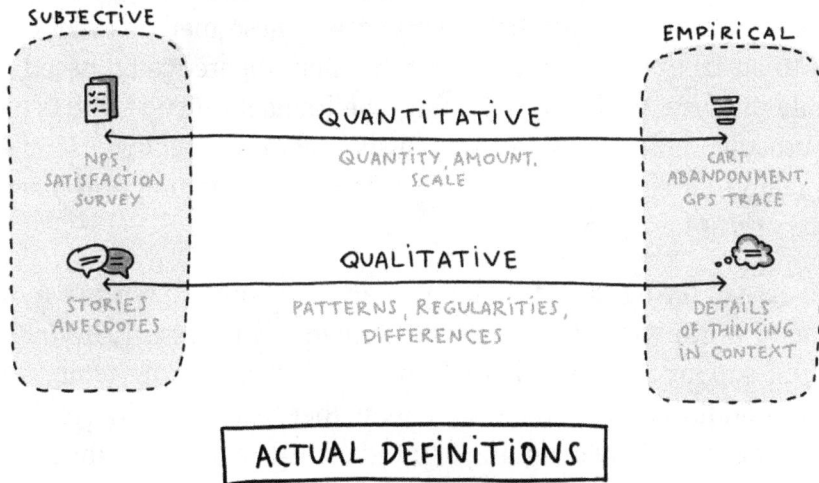

SUBJECTIVE

EMPIRICAL

QUANTITATIVE
QUANTITY, AMOUNT, SCALE

NPS, SATISFACTION SURVEY

CART ABANDONMENT, GPS TRACE

QUALITATIVE
PATTERNS, REGULARITIES, DIFFERENCES

STORIES ANECDOTES

DETAILS OF THINKING IN CONTEXT

ACTUAL DEFINITIONS

Here's the problem. Businesses tend to veil the fact that they are operating in the world of humans, and they try to equate human-created processes and systems with things that follow rigid laws. This veil lets organizations feel comfortable avoiding the epistemological methods that are meant for building knowledge about people. Sociology is one of several fields where research methods have been developed to understand human behavior—specifically for groups of people. A lot of the tools in sociology fall into the category of qualitative research.

Unfortunately, a whole lot of people in the business world don't believe there is a reliable way to build qualitative knowledge about people. Often, they aren't aware of the tools of sociology, or epistemology in general. Or they see those tools as "squishy" or too complicated to use.

Not only that, the business world seems unaware of methods other than the deductive approach: starting with a guess about an observation or idea and testing whether that guess is false or true.

Instead of Starting with a Hypothesis

A deductive research study that starts with a hypothesis is not the only method of study. There are *inductive* and *abductive*[2] research studies, as well. Inductive and abductive methods seek to build enough knowledge to become the *foundation* of a hypothesis. These methods require patterns to surface first. The hypothesis is then, theoretically, based on a reliable premise. With deep listening, the foundation you build is based on a broader, more intentionally inclusive set of perspectives. It enables your team to create solutions that go beyond the assumption that they are experts at how people think.

In the case of trying to understand humans and build supportive systems for them, waiting to see what patterns emerge is necessary. If you want to build supportive systems for a broader set of people, you will be building additional parts of the systems that match the different ways people operate. If you are going to build additional parts for the systems, you will be investing resources, and to invest resources wisely, you don't want to build anything based on the way just one or two people think. That's just going back to the old "average solution" mindset. So, patterns must emerge first, before you choose where to invest your resources for the next five or ten years.

You are *not* the expert at the thinking people use to pursue their purpose. Therefore, you do not make hypotheses to test. You *can* make hypotheses about something you are expert at, like the *solution* your organization produces. But it's unprofessional, not to mention unethical, to make hypotheses about another person's inner world.

Instead, you go and listen, and you see patterns. Those patterns can *become* good hypotheses, based on first-hand knowledge rather than assumptions, later.

Listening sessions are mostly used for inductive and abductive research, the foundation for hypotheses and strategy down the line. You can apply deep listening in evaluative and generative studies, as well. Most of the studies I have done with deep listening have to do with creating the foundations for strategy.

A Widespread Misunderstanding

Journalists also share this misunderstanding about qualitative data. The media covers an experiment and gets excited about an intriguing deduction but covers it in a way that fails to deliver the insight it might. You'll frequently encounter stories about studies where people are observed but not asked what went through their minds. Popular studies treat people's cognition as if it isn't important—that the resulting patterns of behavior are all that matter. This leads to odd results.

For example, there are many versions of a study about how much women are interrupted by men, with guesses about how women, as a demographic, handle it. Versions of this study have shown up in many fields, studying businesswomen, academic professors, and even women on the U.S. Supreme Court.[3] These studies used automation to parse transcripts for an indicator, such as "--", where one person interrupts another person. Automation counts how many times a gender interrupts another, showing that most interruptions are a man interrupting a woman. When human researchers look at these interruption counts over time, they begin to see changes in how the women they are studying interact with the people who interrupt them.

At the end of the study, the researchers make deductions about what the changes mean. These kinds of studies imply that all members of the demographic cope the same way. The way the researchers framed their study presumes that interruption behavior is tied to gender, when it could be driven by something else entirely, like power dynamics.

Researchers somehow never asked those women, "What went through your mind as you handled interruptions at first, and as you spent more time with the interrupters?" People's answers would shed light on different approaches to coping with interruptions. The answers would also be likely to uncover some surprising new understanding of the cognition patterns driving the social relationships studied. Those patterns would then be much more reliable than any guesses the researchers could make.

Patterns

For qualitative data to be valid, *patterns* must emerge within the framework of a study.

Patterns.

Patterns.

Patterns.

With respect to listening sessions, then, what are patterns?

Each participant in a listening session will bring up many different concepts during the session. Some of them will be interior cognition concepts.

When you do synthesis across different participants, you look for what interior cognition concepts are similar and make piles of those similar concepts. Each pile is a pattern. Each pile represents a concept that several participants brought up. There will inevitably be some concepts that don't fit into a pile, but if you've framed the study well and listened well, there will be a lot of piles. That's what I mean by patterns.

On the other hand, if you end up with different concepts from each person, then all you have is a table full of lonely concepts all spread out, with no similarities. No patterns.

So, how do you set up a study to result in these piles—patterns—of concepts? And how do you do it without artificially influencing what patterns show up?

Framing So That Patterns Emerge

To answer the first question, you set conditions so patterns are likely to arise by making sure that all the people participating have done a lot of interior cognition about the same thing.

But, the "thing" that everyone has been thinking about **is not** "using a solution."

The "thing" that everyone has done lots of interior cognition about is their "purpose." I use "purpose" here (rather than "goal" or "task" or "job," for instance) to help you shift your mind away from typically solution-focused thinking. Traditionally, teams might say, "The customer's goal is to sign up and get that first meal kit box delivered this week," when that person actually has a different purpose. Those different purposes vary. Perhaps it's, "try to make healthier meals for myself," or, "cook dinner faster given the increased demands on my time." That last purpose is probably being applied to other areas of that person's life, as well, like "give up on cleaning the kids' room because there's not enough time these days."

Signing up for a meal kit is *using that solution*. That's not any person's purpose.

Solution Space vs. Problem Space

Before I go further into "purpose," you might be wondering about how you would research how people are using the meal kit in their home. That is also important knowledge to have. To capture that data, you would employ *evaluative* research methods. You would ask questions like: are people able to understand directions, recognize ingredients, and create the meal? Evaluative research helps your team fix what is already part of the solution, based on observed patterns.

Or you might use *generative* research methods to create knowledge about how people use the ingredients to create customized meals for their context, or how they adapt the instructions to the kitchen tools that they have at hand. Generative research helps your team create new ideas to serve the patterns they find.

You can use deep listening for both generative and evaluative research. In both cases, you aim to let patterns emerge. But these kinds of research are in the "solution space," by which I mean that they revolve around a solution, the meal kit in this case. You would frame these kinds of studies differently than you would a problem space study. For problem space research, you frame by the person's purpose, not by the features of a solution.

In other words, research that is in the "solution space" is focused on a solution, creating one, making it better, understanding how people use it now, etc. Research in the "problem space" is interested not in any particular solution, but instead seeks to deeply understand the people.

A person's purpose plays a large role in problem space research because a person's purpose **is what they already are addressing**, when and if they reach for any tools or solutions. A purpose **can be anything a person is addressing, doing, pursuing, making progress on, deciding, planning, or even putting off**. It's their aim, intent, objective, what they want to accomplish or achieve.

A purpose is something like, "try to make healthier meals for myself," or, "learn how to cook in a non-intimidating way." If you think for a moment, you can already recognize that someone who is searching for a meal solution would approach that search differently depending on their purpose.

Purpose can be a measurable goal, "task," or "job," but a purpose also goes beyond goals like "find a comfortable pair of running shoes" to include the *reasoning and guiding principles behind that goal*. A purpose in this case might be something like, "make sure I'm comfortable exercising and don't injure myself."

Purpose is a level or two up from a solution like "use the meal kit website to sign up" or "use a shopping app to find good running shoes."

A Purpose Can Be Large or Small

The person's purpose **can range in size**.

Let me continue with the meal kit example, where the person's purpose is "to cook dinner faster, given the increased demands on my time." If you take a step back, it is actually a sub-level of a larger purpose. The larger purpose is "adjust my activities based on the increased demands on my time," and it has probably been in that person's awareness for a while now. But "adjust activities" has such a broad landscape that it will take hundreds of people telling you their thinking before you start to see patterns form. Fifty people could tell you fifty stories about fifty different things they have been doing to make room for other demands on their time. Quit the gym, hire a housecleaner, do errands only once a week, get medicine delivered, sleep less, find someone to drive them between jobs, postpone doctor appointments, pray for a break, wash the sheets every other week, ask the kids for help with chores, etc. No two people talk about the same approach.

This purpose is extremely broad. While patterns of guiding principles, inner thinking, and emotional reactions *will* form, your team may not have the resources or desire to harness such a broad landscape quite yet.

So, if you step closer again, you can state the person's purpose differently to make it narrower, yet slightly broader than the original. You could say, "get dinner on the table faster," rather than "cook dinner faster." Any person with the purpose "get dinner on the table faster" might use another solution than a meal kit to serve this purpose. Buying take-out meals serves that same purpose. So does frozen pizza. So does visiting parents or friends once a week and making a big enough meal to take home leftovers. Same with just cooking the same meal every night, and so on. Still, your team may not be inclined to even work with that larger frame.

And that's fine. You, your team, and your organization get to pick what breadth you want to work with. If you work for a meal kit company, maybe the knowledge you need most right now is a deeper understanding of people who *cook*. The purpose as originally stated is fine, in this case: "cook dinner faster, given the increased demands on my time."

Even within this *cooking* purpose there are several contexts to frame by:

- people cooking most nights, or only one or two nights a week
- people cooking for themselves or for one other person, or for larger groups
- people who like to cook versus those who see it as a chore
- people cooking for specialized nutritional needs, allergies, or strong preferences
- people with confidence or uncertainty about cooking, etc.

Your team will use these kinds of contexts to help frame a study that results in the knowledge you need.

A Purpose Can Take a Lot of Time or a Little

A person's purpose **can also range in length of time**. A purpose could be something like "cook dinner" and be accomplished within an hour or two. A longer purpose could be "make sure I've got ingredients for dinners for the week." A purpose could be something that takes decades, like "keep my household nourished" or "make space in my life for people and activities that I enjoy."

Purposes aren't restricted to a solution. They can be large or small, take a long time to accomplish or be very quick. So, picking the right purpose to study requires discussion and careful thought.

Fortunately, purposes can be very specific and still be a purpose that many different people have interior cognition about.

A Purchase Decision Can Be a Purpose

A purchase decision can be a purpose. Signing up for a meal kit comes *after* a decision-making process. The sign-up action itself is *using the solution*, but any decision-making process can be a purpose. Many organizations are keenly interested in the purchase decision, so I want to reassure you that purchase decision-making counts as problem space research. It counts as a sub-level of a larger purpose.

If you were on the meal-kit team, you might want to study what went through people's minds as they decided to, or decided *not* to, sign up for any type of meal kit. Both outcomes of the decision need to be understood. You will miss half the interior cognition if you only study decisions in favor of the purchase of a meal kit. Likewise, if you only study the purchase of your own meal kit, and not other types of meal kits, then you will only understand a fraction of the interior cognition. People could be thinking about concepts you had not considered, such as who is behind the organization, where the profits are going, where the ingredients and recipes are sourced, who is the apparent audience, etc. Push beyond your own solution to find the broader perspectives people have.

There are many opportunities for improving your solution that only become available to you when you can ask about the *purpose* without including your solution in the question.

Not the Perspective of the Solution

The person's purpose can be the same as a goal or a task. If "goal" and "task" are words that your organization understands as something the person has in mind, then go ahead and use the vocabulary your team is already using. However, if your organization tends to think of "goal" and "task" as something accomplished using your solution, then using "purpose" may help people understand how to switch perspective away from the solution and to the problem space.

For example, the way some teams typically use the word "task" has to do with the small steps associated with using an interface or a service. That's *using the solution*, not a person's purpose. And yes, a person might actually say to you, "Well, now I'm going to log in and enter these payments as received in the accounting system," but their purpose is always something else like, "Take care of the invoicing." That purpose is part of their larger job or role, in this example.

Why is it so important to move away from describing their purpose in terms of your solution? Because your organization needs to understand a broader perspective. Organizations tend to look at the person through the lens of their own solution—to only examine the 10 percent that they think is important. **Looking at people only as users of your solution blocks 90 percent of your vision.**

Let's return to the meal kit organization. This organization looks at the person through the aperture of the meal kit—a thin slice of knowledge about the person's behavior that has to do with their own solution. This narrow "lens of the solution" prevents the organization from considering other approaches to support people with the same purpose.

Instead, consider the person through the lens of their purpose, to "get dinner on the table faster, given the increased demands on my time." From that perspective, the person has many options they could use to fulfill their purpose. You can imagine those options in a kind of ring or dial of solutions surrounding them. (Represented in the image below.) One of the solutions is meal kits, of which the organization's solution is one type. Other options for the person's purpose could be making big dinners once a week with friends or family, or asking their social network for help. These examples fall into the category of "social" solutions or tools.

Social solutions aren't the only option to solve a person's purpose. There are other categories, too. There are digital apps for ordering take-out, there are physical calendars and schedules of places to grab a church meal. The person might review their memories of how their grandmother handled a similar overwhelming situation.

Your solution is one of many, many, *many* options.

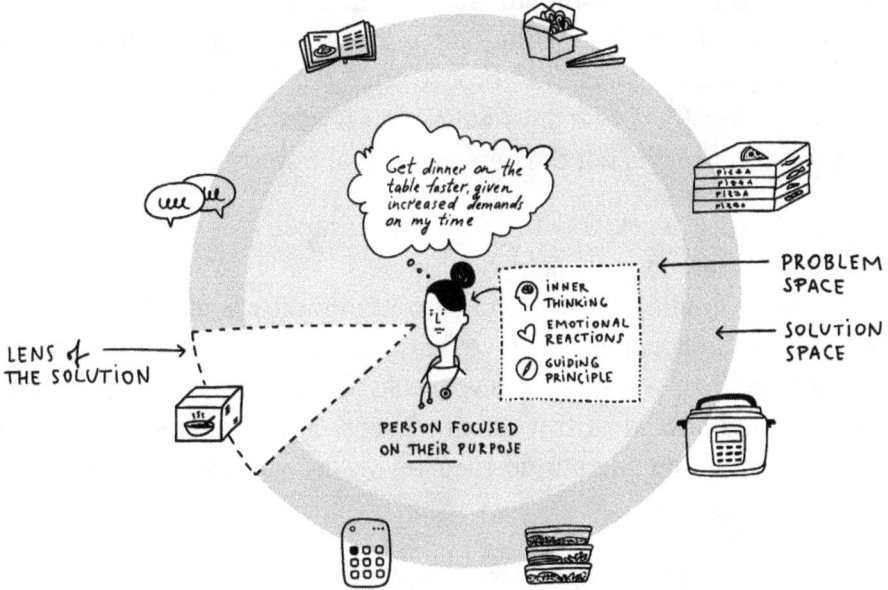

LOOKING THROUGH THE LENS OF YOUR SOLUTION
PREVENTS UNDERSTANDING ALL THE APPROACHES PEOPLE HAVE TO THE PURPOSE

Think outside of your solution by considering these possible tools and solutions categories:

+ Mental
+ Social
+ Manual
+ Mechanical
+ Digital

If you take all those solutions away, that person would still pursue their purpose, finding additional means. In other words, how the person thinks about your solution (if they think about it) has very little to do with their approach to their purpose, because the person's approach does not depend on your solution at all.

This is why it's so important to shift away from the narrow lens of the solution, and to understand the person's perspective, and *their approach to their purpose*, instead.

Centering a Person's Purpose

It can be a big mental shift to frame with a person's purpose. We're so used to thinking about solutions and processes and systems that it traps us. To shift to a person's purpose often requires great mental effort, going in circles for a few days while you try to convince yourself that "using the solution" is not the person's actual purpose.

For example, I worked with Alexandra Jacoby, a community and gathering researcher,[4] to help her frame a study to understand what women were thinking with regard to community and gathering. But "community" and "gathering" were both *solutions* to the larger purposes women have. So, we spent a few weeks discussing how to approach this study, and how to narrow down what "women" she meant. The first study Alexandra decided to do focused on the purpose of "combat the feeling of isolation."

Another mental pitfall is that you might get trapped in thinking that your own purpose is the person's purpose. For example, if you want to "support your employees and keep them from wanting to leave," that is your purpose, not theirs. Their purposes vary widely, from complaints about managers to figuring out the best way to commute, yet none of their purposes is "make sure I don't want to leave this company."

As a field, product creators have been trying to get organizations to focus on being human-centered, but this effort has always faced pushback from business leaders who are aiming for more growth, more market, more "users," more profit each year. The two goals clash. Re-centering on the purposes is a way to actually serve these business leaders—to give them an opportunity map that shows current gaps to fill in over the coming years. Filling in gaps provides paths toward growth.

At the same time, the opportunity map is organized by patterns in people's thinking as they address their purposes, which achieves the goals of being human-centered. Re-centering on people's purposes bridges the two clashing goals. Understanding a person's purposes clearly will get easier as you practice it over time.

Framing Your Study

Framing a study requires a lot of discussion with your team, even if you are all experienced with framing problem space research. Each time I frame a study, it takes anything from a week to two months of back-and-forth, as the team and I explore what knowledge we need right now, and how to frame it in a way that encourages patterns to arise across the study participants.

Usually, this back-and-forth includes a lot of thinking and discussion around how narrow the purpose that we study should be. Too broad of a purpose would result in a study that has too large of a scope. Too narrow of a purpose, and there will likely be few or no patterns to show for it at the end.

Collaborate with your team (and stakeholders if possible) to decide on what purpose makes the most sense to try to understand with this study. You can use the ideas about purpose laid out in this chapter to help you find the right balance of breadth and specificity.

Size of a Study

To set conditions for patterns to arise, you must frame your study in such a way that each participant brings up 50-100 potentially related concepts. For problem space research, you frame your study using the person's purpose—the same purpose for each participant. And if each person brings up many different, unrelated concepts, then there is a good chance that at the end of your study, not enough of the concepts will be about the same focus. Patterns won't arise. If this happens, you can go back and choose a frame that is narrower, a frame that will produce patterns, and invite more people to participate in the study.

You can go broader or narrower with the purpose, and it can be over different timespans. You choose which magnitude makes sense for the knowledge you need to create, and which makes sense for allowing patterns to arise from an achievable study of 10-40 people.

Yes, if your framing is precise enough, you can do a valid study that results in patterns with just 10 people participating.

You can only *approximate* in advance how many people you will need to include in your study. You then adjust the total as you see patterns forming, or not. In my courses I teach how to calculate this initial approximation based on three variables. I'll explain the variables briefly later in this book, in Chapter Five.

Once you have the purpose, and have approximated the size of your study, there's one thing left to do before you begin inviting people to participate: ***Write the germinal question.***

The Germinal Question

The germinal question directly represents the person's purpose. For the example of the meal-kit team, the germinal question will represent the purpose of "get dinner on the table faster, given the increased demands on my time."

> **Listener:** What went through your mind as you tried a few ways to get dinner on the table faster, given the increased demands on your time?

The germinal question asks the person about their thinking as they addressed their purpose. The germinal question is called "germinal" because it is the first question of a listening session, and from it the rest of the topics grow. It is like a seed.

THE GERMINAL QUESTION STRUCTURE

REFER TO INNER COGNITION + SPECIFY POINT IN THE PAST + INDICATE THEIR PURPOSE

It is asked of the participant in past tense, taking them back to a memorable time they were addressing their purpose. The past tense helps the person start out with a particular memory, rather than with generalizations about their interior cognition.

You can change the wording of the germinal question however you like, as long as you include these three components, in any order:

- a reference to their interior cognition, using past tense
- at a point in the past
- the purpose they were addressing

Listener: <reference to interior cognition> <at a point in the past> <the purpose they were addressing>?"

Listener: <What went through your mind> <as you tried a few ways to> <get dinner on the table faster, given the increased demands on your time>?

You don't have to say it exactly the same way for each germinal question. Use language that makes sense to the participant.

Listener: What was your thinking the past few months as you tried different ways to get dinner on the table faster?

Listener: As you have been trying ways to get dinner on the table faster, what came up in your mind and your heart these past few months?

Listener: What thoughts have gone through your mind these past few months as you tried different ways to get dinner on the table faster?

Germinal Questions to Build a Relationship

If you are doing a listening session to build a relationship, then your germinal question will be different. It will depend upon the circumstance of the person's purpose. Here are a few examples.

If you are trying to get a better sense of your manager's or leadership's approach to a project or strategy:

Listener: What's been on your mind this past <time frame> about <purpose>?

If you notice that a person had strong inner thinking or emotion, or hesitated over a decision as if their guiding principle was at stake: (This is an empathic listening example.)

Listener: There was something going on for you <in that room/meeting/etc>. I'd love to hear what went through your mind (and heart) then.

If you are trying to understand someone's decision or reaction that surprised you:

Listener: What went through your mind that time you <addressed your purpose>?

The above examples will give you ideas about how to shape a germinal question, both for a formal study and for less formal listening situations.

The germinal question is also the question that you will use to invite people to participate in the study. The next chapter will cover who to invite, and how.

You Want to Do This, But

Here's the point where you might have thought, "I'd love to build this kind of knowledge for my organization, but there is just no time." Hopefully ten or twenty years from now, we will have reversed the trend of cost-cutting via layoffs, with its subsequent doubling and tripling of workloads for the remaining people. In the meantime, it is a reality that many employees live with. There is often simply too much work to be done, so lots of folks are doing it in the spare corners of their lives, if there are any spare corners left. You may not be in a situation that allows you to do this knowledge creation.

Unless your organization hires more people to shoulder the workload, unless your manager re-assesses what really belongs in that workload, unless you want to jettison some of the work that you don't think is productive—these are all reasons to skip this knowledge-building. When I work with teams, the manager has typically already decided this knowledge is important to create; I get to skip past all those reasons you will fight. Maybe building trust relationships with managers and stakeholders is the place to start.

The other thing I do when working with teams is to assume only 10 or fewer hours will be available per week for any one team member to work on this project. I allow the project to stretch out over many weeks—I've frequently seen projects that span six months or more, simply because there's not a ton of time available from each team member. But we still keep working on it. One of the team members holds the center of the process together and keeps track of what we are doing, what we've done, and where we're heading next.

So possibly, in that stretched out way, you can make this happen. Especially if some level of leadership sees value in creating the knowledge.

Practice Setting the Purpose

Getting out of the solution mindset is hard, even when you intentionally set it as a goal. Therefore, it benefits you to practice. Don't just wait until the next study you and your team want to do.

Here's a game:

As a team, or with colleagues at a meetup, take a feature from one of your solutions, and shift it incrementally back to the person's purpose. This will probably take the form of a series of questions, as you start with the solution and get further and further away until you're finally looking at the person's real purpose.

For instance, someone is using the meal-kit website to choose meals for a week. Ask the team "why?" Then ask "why" again. Keep asking why until the answer no longer has anything to do with the website or the meal-kit company or the meal-kit itself, but only has to do with what the person wants to accomplish. Something like "put food on my table quickly that I know my family will enjoy."

Discuss whether you are still stating the person's purpose as a *use of the solution*. If you're still on something like, "I'm *navigating this website to find* the right meals for my family," then you need to go further. Ask yourself (or the team) why again. Additionally, there will almost always be more than one purpose that can lead to the same behavior or use of the feature you're examining. See how many of them you can list for each feature.

Do it again with another feature, just for fun. Or do it again on another day. Time spent practicing here will make it easier and easier for you to see the purposes that people have, without letting your solutions get in the way.

Summing Up

I often describe my method of research as "purpose-focused." Centering the person's purpose focuses a listening session. It creates deep understanding of how someone approaches the topic of study. It allows for a listening session that follows participants into their interior cognition where cognitive empathy can thrive. Without that guiding purpose, a session wanders, and provides little information your organization can use. With purpose, you can build deep understanding that will last for years.

Just as understanding the purpose and germinal question is critical for a successful study (and productive listening sessions), so is choosing your participants carefully. You want people who have already considered the topic you want to study in some depth.

We'll discuss how to recruit the right participants in the next chapter.

Additional Resources

Mixed Methods: *A Short Guide to Applied Mixed Methods Research,* Sam Ladner, PhD.

Freakonomics Radio, Episode 481, "Is the U.S. Really Less Corrupt Than China?" with guest Yuen Yuen Ang, 03-Nov-2021 (includes a part about how research is often driven by "how easy it is to get the data").

Vocabulary List

Address: (in this context) a more inclusive verb to use to describe how a person does their purpose, since it's possible to actively "not do" (postpone) it.

Approach: how a person does the thing that they are occupied with (their purpose), which is often different from how another person does that same thing, and is also defined by people's different guiding principles.

Centering: (in this context) to focus on peoples' purposes rather than focusing on your organization's solution and features.

Framing: defining or setting the scope of a study based on an existing purpose people are addressing.

Germinal question: the one question that a listener poses to the person at the beginning of a listening session; basically, "what went through your mind the last few times you were addressing your purpose?"

Purpose: a purpose can be anything a person is addressing, doing, pursuing, making progress on, deciding, planning, or even putting off. It's their aim, intent, objective, what they want to accomplish or achieve.

Endnotes

1   Maybe: It's possibly because capitalism evolved at about the same time as the scientific method, or possibly not. I'm not sure if there is a similar reverence for "scientific-feeling" methods in socialism or communism.

2   Inductive and abductive studies both seek to form a plausible, best available conclusion. This conclusion can later become a hypothesis.

3   "Justice, Interrupted," *More Perfect*, Jad Abumrad, host, WNYC, December 18, 2017, https://www.wnycstudios.org/podcasts/radiolabmoreperfect/episodes/justice-interrupted.

4   The study built knowledge for the community Alexandra Jacoby supports at https://UNDERMININGnormal.com. Example used here with permission.

CHAPTER 5

CHAPTER 5

Recruiting for Research

For listening to bring the most good to your organization and your study, the participants you listen to must be chosen carefully. (You must also have determined a specific purpose you are studying and chosen a germinal question; see the previous chapter.)

Choosing participants carefully is necessary because, for a listening session, you need to connect with the person's interior cognition. You want to follow *their* topics rather than introduce anything new. This means that the participants must have done a lot of thinking about that purpose. If they are just beginning to address that purpose, they may or may not have done enough thinking about it to tell you. They may not have experienced enough of their purpose to talk for more than a few minutes. Or they may not be used to reflecting about past experiences, or at least not enough to be clear about what went through their minds at the time. If someone is unclear in this way, it's an indication that they are not a good choice for the study. You want to choose people who can be clear, who have reflected about their past experiences and can share their interior cognition about those experiences.

In this chapter, I'll cover how to define who you want to choose, and how to include a broader set of people than your organization may have listened to before.

Always keep in mind that this particular study is one of many that you will conduct in the problem space, which together accumulate broader knowledge and clearer destinations for the direction of your organization. Problem space research happens maybe once a year, and it is done separately from the solution space work. Design the study you need for your organization's immediate needs, but also keep an eye on how this work interlocks with other knowledge over time.

PARTICIPANTS MUST HAVE DONE A LOT OF THINKING ABOUT THE PURPOSE

Once you know what you are studying, what the person's purpose is, and what your germinal question should be, you must go and *find* the people who have thought about that purpose in depth.

Who Has This Purpose?

Spend some time to consider who has done a lot of thinking about this purpose, and where you might find them. You can do a series of thought exercises to brainstorm who might qualify as someone to recruit.

I like to use the following list to help me think broadly about people who might meet the criteria of this particular purpose.

People who act to address this purpose

- Whose work includes this purpose
- Who are members of associations, groups, clubs, communities
- Who have taken classes or studied toward this purpose
- Who make purchases or sales toward this purpose
- Who are members of a team related to this purpose
- Who are *near these people*, to be able to relay the invitation

People with expertise/deep interest (paid or unpaid) in this purpose

- Instructors, authors, known for their expertise
- Attendees of a conference, event, meeting
- Innovators related to this purpose

A broader category of people (here are some examples)

- Government service users
- Have a medical condition
- Do certain tasks (like get dinner on the table)
- General public (also known as: no criteria defined)

Try to avoid listing roles, titles, user types, and traditional demographic assumptions. "Get dinner on the table" is not carried out only by "women," or even "parents," for example. Many people from the old to the young (and over many other demographic categories) pursue this exact purpose.

But there is more to picking the right people to recruit than just going through this brainstorm list. You also want to consider what you already know from the research you've already done and models you've already built from data. You want to consider research from the academic or public sphere about who has this purpose. Depending on what you're trying to study, you may want to supplement the brainstorming phase with some research, digging to find out who has thinking on the topic. Defining who has thought about this purpose is how you set up a study without *artificially influencing* what patterns show up.

The Limitations of Recruiters

The recruiting requirements for problem space research are unique. It's difficult to convey to a recruiter how to look for people who have done a lot of thinking about the purpose, and it can be difficult to find recruiters who are able to recruit with that much nuance.

Market research recruiters, especially, have established practices and methods that may not be conducive to recruiting based on a person's purpose. They typically maintain databases of people categorized by demographic and other characteristics. And, if they have not done a lot of thinking about the purpose, those people the recruiter selects will be more inclined to hide that fact so that they can earn money in your study.

Because of this, finding people who have done a lot of thinking about the purpose you have set is never going to be as easy as calling up a recruiter and giving them the number of people you need.

You may find that you can work with recruiters to make some parts of the process easier, but do so with care. You will need to work with a recruiter who can provide you with a list of the people they are recommending so that you can communicate with the people directly. You'll need to determine whether the people have done thinking about the purpose, and whether they are able to communicate their interior cognition clearly enough. A recruiter will not have time to gain a deep enough understanding of the nuances of the purpose to do this part for you.

Center the Person, Not Your Organization

For evaluative and generative research, you want to interact with *people who really do have the purpose* that your solution supports. So, you will need to do the work to decide who has the purpose, who has done some thinking about it, and recruit in a nuanced, intentional way. Speaking with a group of random people will not provide the same results.

There are still organizations who are so caught up in their solution that they think everyone has the purpose they think it solves. Some of them still do the classic "café visit" with their mock-ups, asking people on-site to react to the solution they've come up with. Faced with this, people in the café (who were in the middle of something else) have to wrap their minds around what the mock-up team wants of them, leading to "would you use this if" scenario-inventing.

This approach is not helpful to the café customer, nor to the product team. Some organizations have matured beyond this, but quite a few still frame their evaluative or generative studies around the use of the solution rather than the purpose people have.

Instead of this unguided, biased, and solution-based approach, you center the person and their purpose. Don't just recruit "whoever happens to be in that one café near our office from 1:30 – 4:00 PM this Thursday." Rather, specifically and intentionally recruit as broad a range of people *who have the purpose and have done thinking about it* as possible.

This is part of the mental shift that problem-space research in general, and listening sessions specifically, requires. It's a shift away from the solution and toward the person's perspective.

A person who has done a lot of thinking to address a purpose cares about that purpose. If you approach them with the opportunity to participate in a study, they want to know:

- If the experience is worth my time
- If you respect my perspective
- What am I going to get out of this in the long-term? Will you make solutions to better fit my approach to my purpose?

There is more than just money in it for the person. So you need some way to let that person decide if participating will be worth it in these ways. And you need a way to double check that the person has done a lot of interior cognition about the purpose. I facilitate this decision-making process by meeting with the person (via the study's chosen communication method) for an information session, before I officially invite them to participate in the study.

The Information Session

An **information session** is an initial conversation with the person in which you both decide whether to engage in the listening session for the study. (I used to call this the "spoken screener." I've moved away from "spoken screener" recently because the word "spoken" implies an audio format, and because the word "screener" implies that the judgement occurs on your side, not on theirs. In reality, it's a two-way decision-making session, so I've adopted a different name for it.) The information session can be done via any communication format.

An **information session** is a back-and-forth communication with each candidate for the study before doing a listening session—usually a few *days* before the listening session. It takes 15-20 minutes. At the end of the information session, if both you and the other person feel comfortable that you are a good match, then you will schedule a time for the actual deep-dive listening session.

Respecting Consent

Before scheduling an information session, you will also want to double check that the candidate is able to give full consent to participate, by confirming with them in the information session that they are participating of their own free will. Research is ethical only if the person participating can actually give their consent. A person may feel required to participate due to some external pressure. Or they may worry about harm that might happen to them because they participated, such as arrest or deportation, discrimination, stress, or any number of other possible harms. In both cases, you need to be doubly sure you understand how participating in the study will affect the external factors in the person's world. Then you can decide whether it is ethical to invite this person to participate, or not.

If the candidate, the person who has done a lot of thinking about the purpose, is not independent (e.g. a child, an incarcerated person, communicating through a translator) or has a condition that you are not expert in supporting (e.g. neurodivergence, major depression), you may need to include a support person with them in the listening session. Depending on the situation, you may need to coordinate having the support person there for the information session as well.

Another factor to consider is that there are laws in some countries which state that you must have support available to a study participant if something triggering or traumatic happens during the study, and/or that you must report the trauma to a central authority. If this is the case in your country (or the participant's), then it's a good idea to prepare ahead of time to have that support ready, and to have a process in place for doing the reporting. This may require some research on your part to determine what resources you need to have available.

A Warm Connection

When you have the information session, be personable and kind, courteous and respectful, like you are communicating with a colleague of a colleague or a friend of a friend. You can begin to get to know the person, and to show them how much you want to understand their interior cognition correctly. This connection-building is important. It's as important a part of the information session as is making sure the person has done a lot of thinking about their purpose.

If you've built a connection in the information session already, then when the listening session begins a few days later, you can both start where you left off. It's a "warm connection." You will both feel more comfortable at the beginning of the listening session, trusting each other to a degree that allows for diving into the person's purpose more readily. This is the other, unstated purpose of the information session.

Researchers praise the information sessions after they have tried them out. They say that having this warm connection makes the listening sessions feel less tiring. They can set aside participants who haven't thought about the purpose, or ones who cannot get beyond generalities. This helps the speaker get to depth more easily in the listening session, which is fruitful for the development of cognitive empathy, and helps with seeing patterns later. True, it requires more of your time to conduct a series of information sessions, but researchers tell me it doesn't feel significantly harder. The increased richness of the listening session is so worth the investment.

Do Not Delegate

Even if you hire a recruiter, *you or members of your team* should conduct information sessions with each candidate.

This proves tricky, because it's not the way recruiters do business. Many recruiting firms have been fine with selling me two or three times the number of candidate names so that I can do the information sessions then select a subset of people to include in the study. But many of these recruiting firms are uncomfortable with the idea that some of the candidates do not end up engaging in the study itself. It may be the way they have written contracts with the people in their database, or it may be something else.

Why should you conduct the information session instead of delegating it to a recruiter? One big reason is that most recruiters are not prepared to spend an extra 10-20 minutes on each candidate. It's not how they run their business. But the more important reason is that an information session is where you start your relationship with the candidate. If the candidate starts that relationship with the recruiter, then when you start the listening session later, you will not have the same connection with them that you would if you did the information session yourself. You may have notes about the candidate from the recruiter, but you won't have the relationship. This means the listening session will probably unfold more slowly.

Even if the information session is handled by someone else on the research team rather than the listener themselves, the connection will still be a warmer one than if a recruiter handled it. Your team members will be able to convey information about the study and answer questions more effectively than a recruiter would.

Each information session rests upon an open-ended question that you ask the candidate, and this question can vary, as long as it gives the candidate a chance to demonstrate that they can communicate their inner cognition. Typically, the question will either be the same as the germinal question I discussed in the previous chapter, or it will be a variation on it that makes sense for the context.

Giving the Candidate Information

The information session is where both of you make a decision. The candidate is deciding whether participating in a listening session will be a good use of their time, and you are deciding whether the candidate meets some minimum criteria and other attributes. (I'll explain how to come up with criteria and attributes later in this chapter.) There are a couple of components you might want to include in an information session.

The first component of the information session is giving the candidate information that they want to know. They may ask for some of this, and you may fill in the rest.

- What the study is about
- Who is sponsoring the study
- Who you are and what relationship you have with the study sponsor
- How you will protect the participant's privacy
- Who will have access to the transcript/record of the session
- When their questionnaire responses will be deleted
- When the transcript/record will be deleted, if they do the listening session
- The purpose you'd like them to speak about
- What to expect that is different than a typical interview

You'll want to touch on the purpose to be discussed in the listening session, and make sure the person understands what to expect in the listening session. Explain how a listening session is different than an interview, and explain how the candidate will be deciding what topics to bring up. You can reference some of the wording they used in the questionnaire to describe their approach to the purpose, to demonstrate that you actually read their answers.

Since the information session is a friendly back-and-forth, encourage the candidate to ask any other questions they may have.

Verifying Information from the Candidate

The second component of the information session is to discuss the topic being studied: the person's purpose. The candidate has said, in the questionnaire, that they have that purpose, and you will want to verify that they have done enough thinking about the purpose to fill a listening session with interior cognition concepts. To do this, you'll ask an open-ended question or two, which will give you an idea whether the person:

+ Can communicate in depth
+ Can recall past thinking
+ Can communicate that past thinking with clarity

I call these "essay" questions, and they can vary from candidate to candidate. Sometimes you'll use a pre-defined "essay" question, and sometimes you'll forge one based on what the candidate says.

A couple of example questions from our meal-kit team might be:

> *"You say you've tried two ways to get dinner on the table faster. Can you describe your decision process to switch from the first way to the second way?"*

> *"What is a challenge that you faced last week when you made dinner happen?"*

> *"How did you handle a recent situation when there was no time to make dinner?"*

Pick a question that gives the candidate a chance to demonstrate that they can communicate their interior cognition with clarity.

If the candidate answers the essay questions with one sentence, try for more depth. If repeated urging for more detail still results in few words, then this candidate doesn't trust you yet, or isn't going to be able to get to depth in a listening session. You'll want to put this candidate on a "maybe" list and tell them you'll reach out if they are needed.

If the candidate is able to provide a glimpse into their interior cognition, you are likely to have a fruitful listening session with them. Accept them into the study and begin the process of scheduling their listening session.

Scheduling the Listening Session

Together you will find a date and time that works for the listening session and decide upon a communication format that is most comfortable.

On the date chosen, ask if the person will have a comfortable amount of time, or if they something important to attend to at a particular time near when the listening session might end.

If the session will be remote, make sure the person can be in a safe place where others won't disturb them, where they have privacy, and where they aren't in danger of accidents. (Because they can get really caught up in the memory mode of the listening session, the person may not be paying acute attention to their surroundings. You want to make sure they are safe, and everyone proximate to them are safe. Not driving a car, not walking along or crossing a busy street, etc.)

If the pair of you have chosen an audio or video format for the scheduled listening session, you will want to ask permission here to record it. If you have chosen a written format, the text of the chat will become the transcript. If you have chosen a sign language format, or an in-person format, a video of the session will be needed to create a transcript.

If the session is in person, and if you are going to the participant's location, you will be going with another member of your team, never alone. So mention the other team member to the participant. You'll set up ways to reschedule if something comes up.

But before you can conduct an information session with a potential participant, you need to collect a bunch of potential participants. That process is called recruiting.

The Value of Your Own Recruiting

Since your team is going to run the information sessions, consider running your own recruiting as well. Even if you don't have a large team, it's not as hard as you might think. Finding participants who really care about their purpose results in significantly better listening sessions. Moreover, I mentioned some of the issues with using recruiters previously in this chapter, and those are major factors in why I do my own recruiting. There are a few other reasons as well.

When you run the recruiting, you gain a lot more control over:

- The tone and method of the initial invitation (more about this in a moment)
- Respondent expectations for the information session and listening session
- The potential respondent pool: you can decide who to invite based on the voices you need for the study and who your organization has **not** listened to in the past
- How information about the study is presented to respondents
- How respondents' privacy and compensation are handled
- Scheduling, and communications with respondents

The Qualifying Process

You will want to think of potential candidates as moving through a process, from responding to an invitation to pre-qualifying as a potential candidate to becoming a participant in the study.

Respondent --> Candidate --> Participant

At each step there are guidelines to follow which I will lightly outline in the next sections.

The Invitation to Potential Respondents

To begin the process, there is yet another mental adjustment to make. You are not "recruiting" but instead "inviting respondents" by placing invitations in physical and digital locations where people who have that purpose may run across them. The invitation has special properties.

- The invitation is easy to ignore, so that you don't interrupt people who are in the middle of something.

- The invitation has a few interest-catching words, images, or sounds about how the study will help them in the long-term. It briefly answers the question, "What's in it for me?" beyond just "you get a gift card at the end." Explain how your organization might produce solutions that support their purpose.

- It's an invitation with no immediate strings attached—it's basically a short message that conveys the idea of "put your name in the hat, and you can decide later whether to spend time in the study, if we reach out to you."

This invitation is not a "one size fits all" invitation. Instead, it is *several different* invitations, crafted in different tones of voice to match the different people you want to attract. The medium or mediums you choose for the invitations will also be based on who you are inviting. Some invitations will be in writing, others in audio, others with visual explanations, or combinations of these. Some invitations will be ones you make to people in person.

Just like the butterfly garden, you'll also want to provide solid value in return for a participant's presence. You don't put out fake flowers in a garden and you don't stand there with a net to capture the butterflies who visit.

For the meal-kit study example, you might ask several take-out restaurants in various cities and towns if you can post the invitation there for a few days. You might ask grocery stores if you (and remote colleagues) can hand out flyers in the frozen pizza aisle for a couple of evenings. You can buy ads in apps that help people order food. It depends up on who you are determined to understand in this study. (I will continue this example below.)

As I briefly mentioned in Chapter Two, you don't want to choose candidates who know you, or who know of you. You want to avoid a "colleague of a colleague" or "friend of a friend," looking at least three or more degrees out from yourself, the farther the better. This is one reason to avoid using social networks to recruit, especially if you are trying to listen to people your company has ignored so far. Inviting through your social network makes it easier to accidentally reach people who know you, who know of you, or who may just be too much like you. There are exceptions, however.

Some research requires understanding people who are experts in their field, and too busy for studies. In this case, networking is important—especially when you search for that first expert who sees a benefit in spending time with you in a listening session. Then you may ask that expert if they can connect you to other experts with the same purpose. If the listening session has indeed benefitted the first expert, generally they are happy to connect you. If the listening session has not benefitted them, don't ask.

Carefully thinking through the invitation and its placement will yield much stronger connections with the people who come forward to spend their time sharing their interior cognition about the purpose. They will see the care you take and be a little more certain that participating in the study could benefit their approach.

Who are these people? Now it's time to define the criteria and attributes of the participants you'd like to respond to the invitation.

Criteria for Qualifying Candidates

Criteria are minimum requirements for the people you choose to participate in the study. With problem space research, there are some built-in criteria you will need to find in respondents, and there are some criteria that come from the person's purpose.

First, you must make sure the person has done enough thinking about their purpose to fill a listening session with interior cognition concepts:

- Make sure the respondent has a deep history addressing this purpose

Second, in every study you also want to hear from people who do not already have a relationship with your solution or organization ("customers," "users," "employees," etc.). This is because you want to look outside the lens of your solution and understand the wider purpose. Here's the guideline:

- Avoid your "customer" list if possible
- If you invite "customers," let them fill less than half of the slots in the study

There are exceptions, of course, but this is a guideline to aim for. In the meal kit example, it will be easy to find study respondents who are not using a meal kit to fulfill their purpose—they will fill half of your available places.

In other situations, like understanding the organization's employees better to support them more effectively, it makes sense to invite people from within the organization. (Although even in cases like this, there may be a lot of value in seeking out different perspectives: inviting former employees, or even prospective ones, for instance.)

Last, you will determine the rest of the criteria based on the person's purpose. Consider what criteria make sense to look for, and the priority of each.

In the meal kit example, the second half of the study's purpose statement is, "given the increased demands on my time." So you will need to set the following criterion for participants:

- People who have recently increased demands on their time

You might also want to add other requirements, to further define who you want to try to invite. For instance, you might consider:

- Do we want to understand people who have steady demands on their time, even if they are overwhelmed?
- Do we want people who are not overwhelmed?

Here's where other knowledge your organization holds, its goals, and the knowledge in the public sphere, might help you decide. You might simply choose to rewrite the earlier criterion:

- People who have become overwhelmed because of increased demands on their time

Attributes for Qualifying Candidates

Attributes are the way that you make sure you get a representative range of participants in your study. For example, many studies include only people who fit the "average user" description for an organization. You'll discuss with your team which other attributes matter to your particular study.

Here is where you want to push your team beyond typical demographic representations of groups, and instead focus on the thinking that actually affects the way people approach their purpose. It may be difficult at first to move away from demographic assumptions, but it is a really worthwhile step for recruiting.

In the meal-kit study example, you could also consider the concept of getting dinner on the table and develop it more specifically. You team might bring up questions like:

- Are these people doing this every night?
- Do they have dependents, or is dinner just for themselves?
- Do they trade-off or have dinners they aren't responsible for?
- Have they tried other ways to get meals on the table faster?
- How much effort have they put into searching for these other ways?

Depending on how the team decides, the questions above could turn into these attributes:

- Get dinner on the table most nights a week, without many breaks
- Feed dinner to dependents, not just self
- Have tried 2+ different ways to get dinner on the table faster
- Have been trying different ways for 4+ months (Here, effort is described in terms of length of time, but it could be described differently.)

Any attributes you choose can be valid. However, you will want to discuss attributes carefully, based on what your organization already understands about the people it supports. The goal is to invite people who have done deep thinking about the purpose, and who are likely to have different approaches from the "average user."This is especially important when you're intentionally looking outside the middle of the bell curve that your organization has historically served.

An Opportunity for Ethical Treatment

There are more attributes you can define. You have an opportunity to do good, and insert some ethics into your organizational strategy, right here in the framing of your knowledge-creation research. The choices you make in recruiting for your study have consequences that need to be considered.

There are two kinds of possible outcomes of your study I want to draw your attention to:

1. Unintended consequences to people your organization already supports
2. Consequences that happen to people your organization has ignored (These kinds of consequences are also known as "externalities.")

An ethical researcher considers both areas when they are recruiting for a study, but it can be more challenging to notice when your organization has been ignoring people. It will require you to think deeply about who has been ignored or harmed by your solutions.

You can guess at who these people are, but it's better if you have an idea from the organization's history. For example, you can discuss this with customer service or sales colleagues, if that is how your organization is set up. But that method is limited. It will only give you information about ignored people who have the wherewithal to make their voices heard to customer service or sales.

I encourage you to **include people in the study who have not been supported by existing solutions** and who have developed some inner thinking, emotional reactions, and/or guiding principles because of that lack of support. These people have experienced harm from not being able to comfortably address their purpose. The harm can be mild, but it can also be systematic and long-reaching, such as the harm that is experienced as discrimination or lack of accessibility or support for neurodiverse thinking.

You may need to think laterally to find out who your organization has been ignoring. Or the knowledge may be the elephant in the room that everyone knows about, but nobody mentions. Either way, intentionally inviting these unsupported people to join the study and speak their truth is the path to the greatest opportunities, both for your organization and for the people who have been ignored.

With respect to the meal-kit example, how could the team find out who has experienced harm related to "getting dinner on the table, given increased demands on their time"? It will probably take some research and discussion.

They could begin by exploring the harms caused by increasing food costs, loss of food-support programs, credit card debt, etc.

Or they could explore the harm of deteriorating nutrition or onset of health issues, caused by less-supportive solutions to the purpose.

Or the harm of stress and being overwhelmed. There are lots of avenues of harm to discuss.

Choose one that is especially connected to where you, your team, and your organization want to go, and start there. That will get you going in the right direction.

Start somewhere, bring the thinking of these people into your understanding, and start creating in support of that thinking.

Asking a Minumum of Questions

Once you've settled on who to invite and invitation methods, you'll need to actually create the invitation. This is where you give respondents a little information about the study and get some information from them to help you decide if you want to add them to your list of candidates.

So, you have a few questions for them. But don't barf all your criteria and attributes on them at once. That will show them that you don't respect their time or their point of view.

Respondents are interested in:

- If the experience is worth my time
- If you respect my perspective
- What am I going to get out of this in the long-term? Will you make solutions to better fit my approach to my purpose?

Their first decision is to start engaging with your invitation in some way. Afterwards, the respondent will make a second decision whether to answer your questions. Part of respecting them is asking a minimum of questions. Three or four questions should suffice to describe all the criteria and attributes you are looking for. Each question can cover several points in your list of criteria and attributes.

These questions then take the form of a little questionnaire that you present to respondents, either in person or via an online survey app. For each question, allow respondents to select several answers and also fill in their own answer. Avoid single-choice radio buttons; they don't belong in this questionnaire.

At the beginning of the questionnaire, you may briefly (one sentence) explain who you are, what knowledge you are building, and how that knowledge will be used. (e.g. How might the information from this study help improve support for their dinnertime time-crunch?) This is especially important for people whom your organization has ignored.

You will also want to mention the study timeline:

- When you will close the questionnaire
- The date range and time zones for the listening sessions
- The date you will delete their questionnaire responses, to protect their privacy

The final question to ask a respondent is how they would like to be contacted. Let them specify how they'd like to be contacted in a big text field.

Turning a Candidate into a Participant

After a respondent has answered your questions, you will have a chance to decide if their answers fall within your criteria and attributes. If they do, then you convert the respondent into a candidate. You move to the next step—setting up the **information session** with this candidate. (The information session is so important that I put it at the beginning of this chapter, even though it comes here, at the end of the qualifying process.)

If you are reaching out to a candidate remotely, not in person, you first want to establish whether they are still interested in going further. Something may have happened in the interim that has changed the candidate's availability. Next you'll want to set up a date and time for the information session and find out their preferred method of communication for the information session.

After the **information session**, if they still want to participate and you think they are a good fit, then you're ready to schedule a **listening session**.

We're almost ready to move on to what goes on inside the listening session itself, but there are a few other things in this chapter that I want to cover.

Calculating How Many Participants

When choosing participants for a study, you can only approximate in advance how many you will need. The actual answer will be determined by how well patterns develop from the concepts people have expressed. If patterns of topics are not developing, that means you need to add more participants, and possibly narrow the person's purpose you are exploring

Approximate Minimum Study Size

Person's Purpose	Begin with This Many Participants
Narrow	2
Medium	8
Broad	14
Exploratory	15-20

Other Attributes	Add This Many Participants
Specific	+3
Range	+10
Not Defined	+15-20

Thinking Styles	Add This Many Participants
Two	+3
Three	+5
Not Yet Defined	+0-7

The first of the three variables that affect approximate minimum study size is **how broad** the person's purpose is: narrow, medium, broad, or exploratory. You will need to hear from more people if the person's purpose is broad, and even more if you have set an exploratory purpose to help you discover what purposes are out there.

Person's Purpose: "size" definitions:

- Narrow: conceptual or chronological subset of the purpose
- Medium: allows for several parts of the purpose
- Broad: the whole purpose, from start to end
- Exploratory: if you can't name the purpose clearly

The second variable is the **other attribute**s your team has chosen. Pick a value from Person's Purpose and from Other Attributes and **add them together** to determine the approximate minimum study size.

If you have specific attributes defined, for example, people who have been harmed with respect to loss of food-support programs, then you will see patterns develop after fewer participants. If you let your attributes range a lot, like including people who are on food-support programs and also people who have never been on food-support, then you will need more people in your study. If you had not defined any attributes, you are saying that you want to include anyone with the purpose. In this case you will need to add quite a few more participants to see patterns emerge. Therefore, it's in your interest to define attributes, so that you have a study that you can complete within team and organization limitations.

The third variable is **thinking styles.** If you have thinking styles defined, then you will add 3-5 more to the total. If you are trying to define thinking styles for this purpose, then you might add up to 7 more to the total.

Logistics

You don't have to schedule each listening session in exactly the same way for each participant. Instead, together you both choose the logistics that work best. Here are some things to consider.

Listening Isn't Audio-Specific

I have mentioned this already, but allowing a choice of how to communicate is so important that it deserves its own section in this chapter. In selecting people to bring broader understanding to your organization, you will be adding people to studies who will want to communicate in their own way. Not only that, your own team may include people who have preferences in how to communicate. So, for the information session and the listening session, it's important to avoid assuming that the communication will always happen by audio.

It's totally fine to conduct a listening session by written messages, even over the course of days. I've experienced amazing depth with chat messaging—where the extra time between messages, hours or days even, allows for more introspection and ability to unfold just why a participant was thinking in a certain way. This also gives the listener more space to breathe and be thoughtful about where they see opportunity to dive deeper on a topic the participant brought up. Chatting also allows for emojis, which can supply a stronger awareness of emotion, especially when used during the memory mode of the listening session.

It's also fine to conduct a listening session in person or via video. These are perfect for communicating by sign language and lip reading. These also can allow for communicating by drawing, sketching, and diagramming. Audio or chat are good choices, if they are available, since they offer you as a researcher (and the participant) a little more protection.

However, as long as the method of communication has room for back-and-forth between listener and participant, and as long as it allows for privacy and space to express truth, any method is welcome. There are so many ways for two people to connect and build understanding.

You want to ask the respondent and participant what works best for them. Someone may find the visual aspect of communicating overwhelming, headache-inducing. If you have a team to help you conduct information sessions and listening sessions, pair up listeners and participants who have compatible communication preferences.

You can add body language as a means of communication, but I want to mention that "body language" gets most of its attention in a certain contrasting circumstance. Body language gets mentioned when researchers are doing *observational* evaluative studies. These are studies where the participant's behavior is observed and interpreted. A lot of the examples I've seen of this observational method come down to guessing what the participant is thinking or feeling. I think it's wrong to guess; you're not omniscient. Ask instead. But I'll admit that I'm not a practitioner of observational methods, so maybe guesses are more accurate when studying your solution.

One Person at a Time

When you schedule information sessions or listening sessions, schedule one participant at a time. Deep listening is only going to work one-on-one. If a participant knows that other people besides the listener will be able to respond to their words, that person will think twice before talking deeply about their inner thinking. To share something that is personal requires a safe space, and it's far more reliable to create a safe space for the participant if there is only one listener and one participant.

Sometimes there are reasons to include multiple *listeners,* for instance if an additional listener is learning and wants practice, someone needs to be present as a liaison with the participant, or someone like an interpreter or a parent needs to be present with a non-independent participant. But keep all extra listeners silent. Designate only one real listener. If the other listeners have questions, they can message the primary listener to ask on their behalf.

Never include multiple participants. Even if they are good friends and know each other deeply, they will subconsciously seek to influence or impress each other. You will get better depth from listening to each person separately.

One Listening Session a Day, per Listener

Because listening sessions take intense concentration, even the most rested, relaxed, and alert person can't conduct more than one a day. I've done two listening sessions in one day a few times, and halfway through the second one my brains starts to mix up the concepts from the first speaker with the second speaker. My ability to focus suffers. So give yourself healthy space in your schedule to take in what each speaker is telling you. Give yourself space to think about it in the background for a few hours afterward.

You cannot cram six or seven listening sessions in one day. Your mind will melt, and you will fail at the sessions after the first two. If someone tries to force a more intense schedule on you, let them know it will destroy chances that the study will build solid knowledge. Show that person this section of the book.

You can interleave other activities into each day that you do a listening session, such as finding participants, running spoken screeners, and doing the synthesis. These other activities will still move the project along, yet give your mind room to restore itself after the intensity of going deep in a listening session.

A Habitual or Subconscious Purpose

Here's something else to consider: when the person's purpose is something they have done so frequently that it has become habit, or that their thinking has become subconscious, schedule two listening sessions. The first listening session will be a typical listening session, where the speaker will be spending time in memory mode, recounting their interior cognition from a past event. The second listening session will be in the field with the speaker as they are addressing that purpose.

The first listening session allows you to understand a lot of the inner thinking, emotional reactions, and guiding principles, as well as develop a connection with the person. When the second in-the-field listening session begins, you both have that first session as a foundation, making it easier to jump into a currently unfolding instance of the person addressing their purpose. Cooking dinner is a great example here. For people who have cooked dinner a lot, high-resolution interior cognition may be difficult to recall from memory. So being in the field with that person as they cook dinner will give you both a chance to dive into topics that flow past in real time.

Thank-You Gifts

The best thank-you gift to the participant is two-fold:

1. Making solutions to better fit different participants' approaches to the purpose, and

2. Giving the participant something of value, like money or a gift card, in the interim, for their time in the listening session—and often also for their time in the information session. An alternative is a donation in their name, in case they can't receive money.

The first is one that I've only personally only seen a couple of organizations do, unfortunately. And it has the greater value to the participant. As a community of product creators, we can make this history change, instead of just "extracting data" from participants.

Your organization probably has its traditions for giving the participant something of value, so I'm not going to go into detail here. Except this: always offer some options, especially options with no strings attached, that are easy for the participant to apply to their life. Sending them a store gift card when that store is an hour away is a negative outcome. Apply ethics and consider consequences here.

Summing Up

Framing your study is a complex topic. While I don't have the space to cover all the details and possible circumstances in this book, I have given you a good overview, and hopefully some understanding of how to approach framing the study, in this chapter.

These are critical components of framing a problem space research study:

- Think about what knowledge is needed.
- Think about what criteria and attributes are important for the purpose you're trying to understand.
- Determine where to look for the people that have the purpose, as well as what criteria and attributes they should fit.
- Consider the ethics involved in who you are recruiting.
- Ask yourself how you can bring in people that the organization has ignored or harmed.
- Conduct the information sessions yourself, if at all possible, to build the connection with the participant right from the start.

Taking the time to frame your study carefully will pay off. The effort will show through in the patterns that form out of the many topics and concepts that the participants bring up. Those patterns, in turn, will provide you and your organization with insight into new opportunities for supporting people more effectively with your solutions.

Now it's time to dive deep into the listening session itself, in the next chapter.

Additional Resources

Mixed Methods: A short guide to applied mixed methods research, by Sam Ladner PhD.

Qualitative Research Practice: A Guide for Social Science Students & Researchers, by Jane Ritchie, Jane Lewis, Carol McNaughton Nicholls, and Rachel Ormston.

INSIDE THE LISTENING SESSION 147

CHAPTER 6

CHAPTER 6

Inside the Listening Session

Y>ou have carefully framed your study and set the conditions for your participant to easily talk about their interior cognition. You've chosen a person's purpose to study that represents what they were addressing, doing, pursuing, making progress on, deciding, planning, or even putting off. By re-centering on a purpose, rather than your solutions, you have set the stage for business leaders to embrace an approach that provides an opportunity map for growth based on people's perspectives rather than the narrow aperture of the product lens.

In the information session, you (or a member of your team) asked the participant if they wanted to take part in a listening session in a way that showed them you are not just trying to "extract data" from them. The two of you have agreed on a method of communication that feels appropriate. The participant feels comfortable because they know what to expect, and they are ready to lead you on a tour of their past thinking.

For your part, you've practiced becoming aware of what is being said at what level. You've become wary about your own assumptions, and the assumptions of your organization.

Both you and the participant are ready to begin.

Now you are ready to do a listening session. This chapter answers a number of questions. How do you get started? How do you know what to ask without a list of interview questions? How do you help them return to topics that you would like to understand more deeply?

I'll start at the beginning.

Starting a Listening Session

If you were able to do the information session with this participant yourself, then starting the listening session will likely feel enjoyable for both you and them because you have already developed some level of connection. If that's the case, and it seems appropriate for this person's context, you can use the connection you've already developed to start the listening session with a "warm reconnect."

The Warm Reconnect

Both of you have had some time to anticipate this listening session. Start out by **mentioning something you communicated about before**. Try to be genuine and bring your own personality to the session. Remember, you are not "the expert," or "the researcher," rather you are a person listening to another person to try to understand their approach to a purpose.

If this listening session is for a research study, you have likely already communicated with the participant in the information session. If another person on your team did the information session with this person, briefly mention why you are doing the listening session instead, and what that team member told you about this participant. Try to be open about how you and your team are working together.

In a non-research context, you might have a listening session with someone you already know, like a colleague or family member, to better understand their perspective. If this is the case, and if your past with this person is fraught with negativity, tell the person that you intend this session to be about them and their thinking so you can learn and understand. Reassure them it will not be about you or your thinking.

As you reconnect with this person, let a little time elapse. Wait for them to reply. Let them lead the conversation, to bring up a question or something on their mind.

A warm reconnect might look like this example:

Listener: Hi <name>, it's good to have this time with you. How are you?

Person: Good, good actually!

Listener: Last time we connected, your son was about to graduate. How was that?

Person: Oh! You remember that? Yes, he graduated, and it was <description>. So, for this session, you said we're going to record it, right?

Listener: Yes, with your permission. And we will delete the recordings after the study, by <date>.

Person: I wonder if I could ... if I say something about someone in particular, if you could delete ... well, not keep that person's name in the recording?

Listener: Yes, we can do that. I can replace all the names you mention with other labels, like person1 and person2.

Person: (with relief) Oh, that's good. I was a little worried ... so yes, thank you. I was worrying that talking about them is a violation of their privacy, so I was wondering how to handle it ...

Even if you're doing a listening session with the goal of building relationships instead of research, it is nice to spend a little time touching base with the other person in a human way.

A Culturally Sensitive Introduction

After reading this chapter, Pei Ling Chin, a colleague from Malaysia, observed that this approach to beginning a listening session is not always culturally appropriate.

In her experience in listening sessions with Malaysians, she says the session starts right after they join the remote call, without the warm reconnect. "It's understood that the participant and the listener are not 'really friends' and both agree to get to the point of the call quickly. This doesn't mean there isn't any rapport or warmth, but the rapport is within the scope of the topic of study, rather than sharing unrelated information about a person's current circumstances," she says.

Pei Ling Chin has done listening sessions with Americans and Europeans as well, and in general they tend to be more chatty and friendly. In Malaysia, "a sense of getting down to business is normal."

Although this may not apply to all Malaysians, or it may apply to other cultural contexts as well, these kinds of cultural differences are why listening sessions are best done by listeners who are part of the same way of life, whenever possible.

Clarifying Details

After the warm reconnect, there are two or three things to clarify with the person before you use the germinal question to begin the session.

Here are all the components of starting a listening session. The boldface items can occur in any order:

- Warm reconnect (if appropriate) from the information session, or from your relationship
- **Check in if the participant needs to stop the session by a specific time (a hard stop)**
- **Mention the reason for the listening session**
- **Mention the person's purpose**
- **Remind them they have free rein to bring up the topics (not a typical interview style)**
- **Ask if they have any questions before you start**
- **Ask permission to make a record of the listening session (audio, video, written, etc.)**
- Germinal question

Since a listening session does not traditionally take a set amount of time, the only place you might mention the clock is if the person does have something important they need to do at a particular hour. You'll have already asked this question in the information session, but something may have changed for the person since then.

It's a good idea to **double-check their schedule** again at the beginning of the listening session. On the other hand, if your organization or culture prefers to stick to a pre-set time block, now is the time to mention that span of time.

Next, re-iterate **the reason behind the listening session**—that you want to understand this person's inner thinking as they addressed **their purpose** at specific points in the past. Cite the purpose clearly. To pull from the meal-kit example from the previous chapter, this might be something like, "I'd love to understand everything you've thought about to get dinner on the table, given the recent increased demands on your time."

Mention why you want to understand, and how you hope to help support people better with this knowledge.

Then, give the participant a chance to **ask any further questions** before you begin.

In my career, I've mostly heard questions about privacy, for example who will see the transcript or their name. I tell them who on my team will work with the transcript, when it will be deleted, and that their name will never be associated with it. When I synthesize the concepts across all the transcripts, the data is summarized anonymously, and the original wording is re-summarized. Doing things in this way means you can honestly tell participants that their personal details will not be as-sociated with the data or revealed to the organization. Regardless of whether this is the case for your study, be open and clear about the level of privacy you are providing for the participant. (See Chapter Nine.)

Other questions besides privacy could come up. Answer as openly as you can. Sense if the person is feeling uncomfortable. If they are not ready to trust you, offer them the option of not participating in the lis-tening session after all.

If all goes smoothly, now is the time to **ask the person for permission to record** the listening session. You will have already brought this up in the information session, so the participant will have answered or had time to think about it further. If they say, "Yes you have my permission," then you will turn on the audio or video recording device. If you are communicating via written text, the text itself is the transcript. In many countries, laws require you to ensure the person's permission is evident there at the beginning of the record. It's important to examine the laws for your country (and the participant's country of residence, if different) to find out what procedures are required regarding research transcripts and recordings.

And now, you can begin the listening session by using the germinal question.

Using the Germinal Question

In a previous chapter, you saw how to *form* the germinal question. Here, whether it's the germinal question for research or for relationship-building, you take a moment to formally roll it out.

The way in which you ask the germinal question indicates to the person that you are handing them the lead of the conversation. It can be something like, "Can you tell me about a time when you were trying to get dinner on the table, even though there were other demands on your time? What was going through your mind then?"

Sometimes the person is not quite ready to gain control and replies, "Where do you want me to start?" That's an understandable reaction. People are not used to being in control of a study session.

I'll often answer this reaction with, "What just came up for you when I asked that?" Usually there's a topic, and I can encourage them to go into it. Let the participant start off in any direction. The surprise of the initial direction is part of the fun of a listening session. It's also the way that this kind of research stretches the way your organization looks at the problem space and the thinking styles within it.

If the person freezes up, sometimes I'll mention a topic that the person brought up in the information session. I don't worry about "starting at the beginning" nor any sort of chronology, because the whole listening session is going to wander here and there in memory, often diving deeper and further back, and sometimes looping around to cover earlier ground. Eventually you'll cover everything the person wants to cover, so it does not matter where they begin.

In this example, the person's purpose is "decide whether to eat at a restaurant during the first six months of the COVID pandemic." But the first topic the person brings up is about choosing a restaurant in general, and not specific to the pandemic. That's okay.

Listener: So, you have made a decision about going to a restaurant during this pandemic. I'd love to know, **as you were making that decision, what was running through your mind**? [germinal question]

Person06: Okay. So, I guess usually whenever I decide to want to eat at a restaurant, for me, first things first.

I think the most important thing for me is, is this something that I could make at home? [explanation or inner thinking] Because to me, I've noticed something with a lot of different restaurants where they have good food, but again, a lot of it is stuff that like I can make at home, or that I usually make anyways. [statement of fact]

So, there's not much of an incentive for me to go out and try something. [emotional reaction or inner thinking] So, like if a food is from a specific geographical area that I don't normally cook with, or maybe a place is known for their cocktails or just something that's different from my everyday diet, then I'm more likely to go to a place. [preference or inner thinking]

Listener: Yeah [support], speaking of everyday diet [micro-reflection], now that we're all cooped up ... [session mode]

Which Concept Type?

You probably noticed that in the above example, some of the in-line notes show two concept types, like [preference **or** inner thinking]. In a world obsessed with categorizing things, here is where you can let go. Embrace the ambiguity. Any statement could be taken to be one concept type or the other. You won't know for sure until you do synthesis, and even then, it may not matter. For now, in the listening session, you don't care. All you care about is if the person has conveyed their interior cognition, or not. Don't worry about identifying which concept type it is, because you are listening with your whole self.

Example of Starting a Session

Here is a complete example of all the parts of starting a session. It's a different participant in the same study about deciding whether to eat at a restaurant during the early part of the COVID pandemic. The **warm reconnect** happened before the record started, so that part of starting the listening session is missing. That's normal and usual, because having the reconnect "off the record" makes it more comfortable and natural for both of you. At the end of the reconnect is when you ask for permission to record the session.

You'll notice that a different team member than the listener did the information session with this participant, so there is a little reference to the fact that the listener and their teammate shared information.

Before the record began, the listener also asked if there were **questions before we start**.

Listener:	For purposes of the recording, may we have your consent to record this? [permission to record, in this case audio]
Person62:	Yes.
Listener:	Thank you very much. <person name> probably talked to you about this during the information session. What we're really interested in is your inner reasoning, your reactions, about eating out during COVID. [person's purpose] So, in preparation for this session, <person name> asked you to think about the last time that you were making a decision about going out to eat, and not takeout or delivery. [session mode] I'd like you to remember where you were, what you were doing, maybe who you were with, time of day or night. Just really place yourself there. [set-up for what went through your mind]
Person62:	Do you want feedback from the last time I tried to eat out? Or do you want feedback from the last time I *successfully* ate out? They're like two different things. [where do you want me to start]
Listener:	Those are both great and so I'd like you to choose whichever one you'd like first, and then I'd like to talk to you about the other one. [session mode]

And you'll probably talk about them interchangeably, which is fine too. [how the session works] So, the last time that you were making a decision about this. Get that in your mind. What was going through your mind when you were making that determination? [germinal question]

Person62: So, it was a group decision. It wasn't just mine. [statement of fact] My in-laws and my husband and I, and my daughter were together after quarantining and taking a COVID test and we wanted to go out. Actually, they own a boat and so we were going to take the boat to a local restaurant. [scene setting] Obviously, via boat, there aren't a lot of choices. So, it was more of a "do you want to do this, or not?"

It wasn't a decision about which restaurant. It was more about "are you guys up for this, or is it too nerve-wracking?" [explanation] I think we were open to it. We called; we made a reservation. We knew that they had outdoor seating. We confirmed that. [explanation] When we arrived it was very clear that while people, in fact, had masks, there a lot of people inside.

And it turned out that our "reservation" was for inside, not for outside seating. [scene setting] So, we made the decision, as a group, that we didn't feel comfortable eating our meal inside. [explanation] So, instead, we switched to a takeout order and ended up eating lunch on the boat, which was fine. [explanation]

So, that was kind of the most recent that I can recall. [session mode] The decision making process really is, "Are you comfortable and do you feel like this is a safe situation? Or, do you feel like it's too risky?" And in that case, it felt too risky for us. [explanation]

Listener: Ah, okay. [support] So, you said that when you were first talking amongst yourselves, the conversation was, "This can be too nerve-wracking." [simple reflection]

Person62: Yeah. Sort of like, "Is this an excursion that you're up for, or do you feel like we should just stay home?" kind of thing. [explanation or inner thinking]

Listener: A little bit of that – was this like a – do you – is being with your in-laws, as a family group . . . Was this like a special event? [verification of scene]

Person62: Yeah it was. So, in the beginning of the pandemic, we probably didn't see them at all from March until, I think, July because we were trying to be very careful, just because, you know, they're a little bit older . . . [explanation]

It's normal to have some back-and-forth at the beginning of the recorded part of the session where the participant is trying to get a grasp on the situation. They want to know what they should talk about, how they should talk about it, and what role you, the listener, will play in the conversation. These opening minutes of the session are about modeling the general guidelines for the session in a respectful way. This is the right time to convey a few key things:

- You are interested in *their* perspective, specifically
- You want to know about what went through their mind during experiential moments from their past that have to do with the purpose (in a specific time and place)
- You are really listening to them, not taking notes and analyzing as they talk
- You are not judging them
- *They* are leading the conversation, and you are following along

Help them feel out the session space and feel comfortable in it.

How a Session Unfolds

Participants who are new to listening sessions are usually not used to talking while someone listens closely. It's okay if they stop and start in a choppy fashion. You may go back and forth with them to help them feel comfortable leading the conversation. Accepting the topic they start with is your first signal to them that you truly want to hear what they have to say. Stick with whatever topics the person brings up, to demonstrate the way you are interested in what is said. Follow them from topic to topic as they hop around.

In this next example you can see the listener sticking to each topic that's brought up until there is one where the person goes into their interior cognition. You'll see that the listener repeats their interest in *what went through the person's mind*, and after a while, the person dives in. The first topic is about prescreening a restaurant, then the topics of signage and grocery store shopping come up, then the topic of having a cough.

Listener: What's gone through your mind about eating out at restaurants since April? [what went through your mind]

[Topic: prescreening a restaurant and waiting until next year]

Person15:   I've thought about it several times, and either the weather was bad, or I made a different plan. [statement of fact] I just didn't feel comfortable. [emotional reaction]

I didn't know if the place had a good setup. So, I sort of wanted to go scope it out first, [inner thinking] and I didn't have time to sort of prescreen the restaurant. [statement of fact] So, every time I think about doing it, I kind of tell myself it's not worth it. I can do that next year. [inner thinking]

Listener: When you think about prescreening, what went into that? [what went through your mind]

Person15:   I would do a drive-by to see how they're seating people on a day that I wasn't planning to go, and I would just look at how they have the tables set up and how close they have people together. Just kind of see how they're doing it. [explanation]

Listener: Are there any other things besides layout and distance that you were thinking about for at a particular restaurant? [more about that]

[Topic: prescreening, then signage is introduced]

Person15:   If I was able to drive close enough, I would check to see what signage they had up and whether masks are required, and people were using them. [explanation and pull-tab]

Listener: And then for signage, what went through your mind? [what went through your mind]

[Topic: signage in grocery stores]

Person15:   I see it mostly in grocery stores and things like that where I have to go get things. You know they have signs when you come in the door that say you need to wear a mask. And some of them have arrows that tell you which way to go and things like that. [statement of fact]

Listener: Cool. Interesting. [support] What was your thinking when you first saw the arrows? [what went through your mind] [still asking, to help the participant understand about telling their interior cognition]

[Topic: grocery shopping is introduced, then grocery delivery]

Person15: I think it's to kind of avoid bottlenecks in the grocery stores. [opinion or assumption]

However, every time I've gone shopping there, there are so few people shopping that the arrows don't really matter. [statement of fact]

If there were more people there, I think people would mind them a little better, [opinion or assumption] but usually I pick a time when it's pretty light, either by accident, or it's always light. I don't know. [statement of fact]

Listener: Um-hmm. This was when the pandemic was first starting? [verification of scene]

Person15: Well when it first started, I did delivery only. I actually didn't go. [statement of fact] And that was not unusual for me because I've been doing delivery in the past when I worked, before, when I was too busy. [explanation] And I thought well, I know how to do that, I can just do that. [inner thinking] [finally!!]

Listener: What was going through your mind when you decided at that time to do delivery only? [what went through your mind]

[Topic: my cough]

Person15: I had a cough early on in March that turned out to probably be more related to allergies, [explanation] but it made me feel cognizant of my health [inner thinking] and just thought, well, I had been out somewhere where there could have been people before we knew what this was, [inner thinking] and I wanted to give it at least two weeks to find out what was going on. [inner thinking]

So, I just got my computer out ... <continues>

After the participant has an initial taste of communicating their inner thinking, they will probably be more likely to return to the interior cognition core in further topics they bring up. And once they seem more comfortable with communicating their interior cognition, you can return to topics they mentioned earlier—if they don't revisit those topics naturally. (I call this idea, a topic that seems to have some inner thinking behind it that you want to return to, a "pull-tab." I will cover pull-tabs in detail in a bit.)

A Permeable Perimeter

As the participant unfolds topic after topic, following their own line of thinking throughout the listening session, they will probably wander outside of the scope for your research. Go ahead and follow them out there, because certainly the new topic is related to the last topic within this person's mind. And it usually comes with a strong connection to the person's purpose—even though it is a new idea for you and your organization. This new topic may or may not be something other participants talk about, and it may or may not build into a pattern. If it does become a pattern across participants, your organization may or may not deem it central to your strategy. But if you do, this is how your organization gains truly new insights about where to head, and how to support people in more ways.

So, when the participant crosses the permeable perimeter of your research scope, that's an exciting moment.

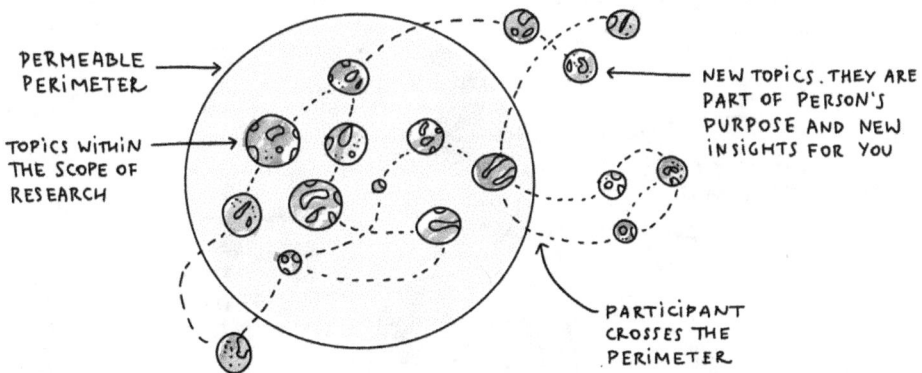

Yes, there are cases when the person does introduce a topic that is not related to their purpose. It's rare, but it happens. For example, when a person telling you about restaurants and grocery shopping during the early part of the COVID pandemic starts talking about meeting a friend for wine tasting, that's probably related to the purpose for them. But when they switch to talking about their niece's new baby, and going for a visit during COVID, that's maybe less related. Keep following to see where it goes. If the topic turns to what they were thinking of buying for a baby gift, then that's probably too far from the purpose.

At this latter point, you can think about pulling them back inside the perimeter, using another topic they brought up earlier. But wait until they have finished their story, out of respect. (See later in this chapter about how to switch to another topic.)

Monitor the Concept Types

In Chapter Three you saw the different types of concepts as layers in a jawbreaker candy, where each candy is a separate topic. In the example above, seven or so topics (candies) come up. One of the topics, deciding to do grocery delivery, is where the participant goes into their interior cognition. Many of those seven topics stay in the description layer and the expression-presentation layer. Any of those seven topics are candidates for the participant to return to later, to describe more of their interior cognition. But for now, ignore them. Focus on the topic where the person *did* go to the core.

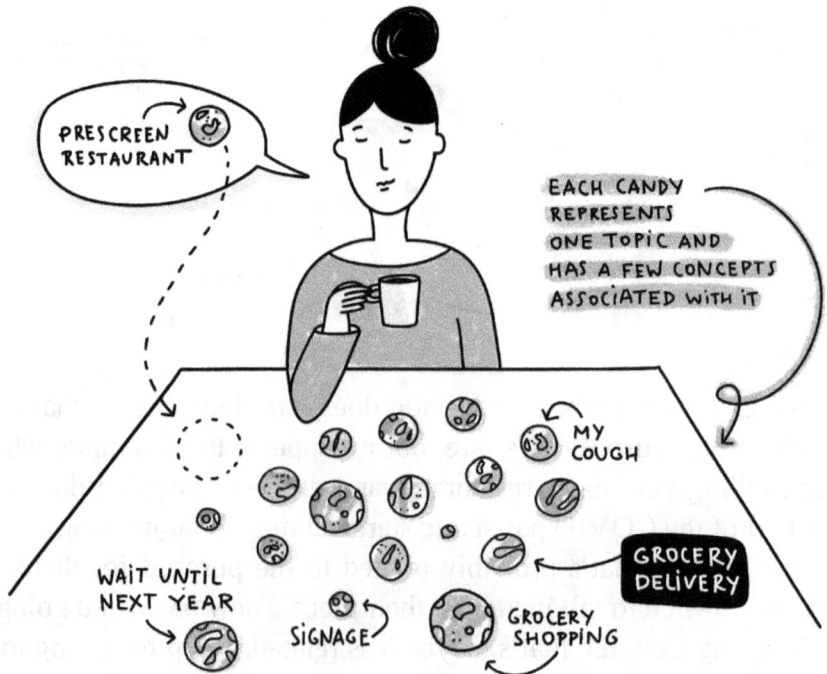

Here's something to realize:

After a listening session, you will crack open all these topics (jawbreaker candies) and save only the concepts mentioned at the interior cognition cores.

The **core** is what's most important; the rest of the layers will only be used as supporting detail to the interior cognition concepts. So, during the listening session, it's vital that you help the person convey their core interior cognition for most of their topics. To do this, you narrow your own cognition to the listener's three cognitive activities I mentioned in Chapter Three.

This time I want to expand on the second point.

A listener's three cognitive activities:

1. Pay rapt attention
2. **Monitor whether the concept type is exterior or interior**
   - ◆ Monitor for signs that there might be interior cognition behind an idea the person brings up (**pull-tabs**)
   - ◆ If the person does not dive into a topic, help them to do so at some point in the listening session
3. Be aware if the person has popped back into the session mode of the listening session

---

Pull-tabs

How do you notice a place where there might be interior cognition that the person hasn't unfolded yet? Potential interior cognition often shows up as *phrases or hints* that seem to have a deeper meaning behind them, or as *emotional shading*. You may even experience them as an *intuition* that the person has something more to say about a topic.

These indications are like the green tops of carrots, growing out of the ground. All you notice are the green leaves, but if you pull them, up comes the root—the orange carrot itself. As an analogy, that carrot root is the interior cognition layer. I call these indications "pull-tabs."

You could visualize them as the tab on a soda can instead of green carrot tops. They are little handles that you can use as questions to encourage the person to unfold their interior cognition.

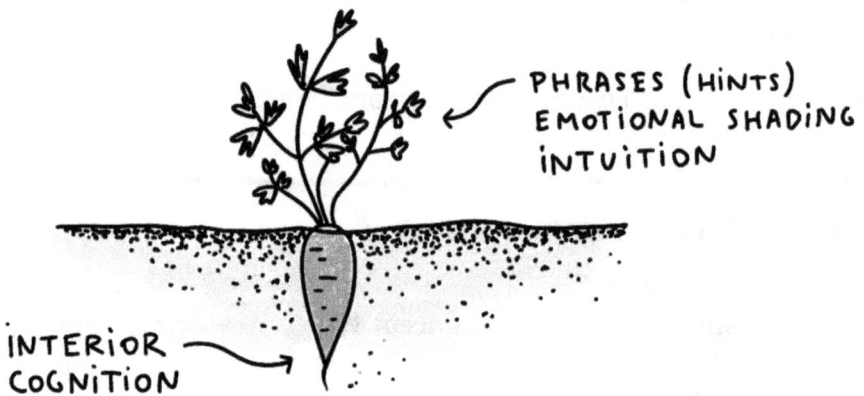

PHRASES (HINTS)
EMOTIONAL SHADING
INTUITION

INTERIOR COGNITION

Any concept type at any layer can be a pull-tab: description, expression, almost cognition, and interior cognition concepts. Pull-tabs indicate there is possibly some more depth there; you monitor for pull-tabs throughout the listening session.

To continue the example above, the listener helps the participant unfold a bit more of their inner thinking about the grocery delivery. The participant tells of her emotional reaction at the time of her decision to return to grocery delivery and goes further back in time to before she retired to tell of her inner thinking about her decision to quit delivery back then. The listener notices a couple of phrases that indicate there could be more interior cognition, "I taught myself" and "recently I have gone back to some shopping in between." These are two potential pull-tabs.

Person15: ... So, I just got my computer out. I hadn't ordered with the delivery service for a while and just went ahead and did it. [explanation]

Listener: What went through your mind?

Person15: Oh, it's great. I love it. [preference] I feel a little bit decadent doing it because they bring it right to your kitchen. [emotional reaction] I've always loved doing it, [preference] but once I retired, **I taught myself** how to shop again because I thought, "I have time." I don't need someone to deliver my food. [inner thinking and pull-tab]

So, COVID gave me the excuse to let someone deliver my food again. [inner thinking]

Person15: **Recently I have gone back to some shopping in between my large orders,** [explanation and pull-tab] and that's when I saw the signage. [explanation]

Here's an example of some emotional shading that could contain deeper thinking, if the participant would unfold it: "made me feel compassion," and "trying to deal with all this."

Person15: It just felt uncomfortable. [emotional reaction] You were inside, you knew the air was recirculating, [statement of fact] so that just **made me feel compassion** for parents with kids going through this, and for whatever reason having to go out to eat.

Also, for waiters and waitresses **trying to deal with all this**. [emotional reaction and pull-tab] I want to go out and eat, but my brain says I don't need to, I can cook at home. [inner thinking] So, I keep staying home. [statement of fact]

Both the phrases and the emotional shading in these two examples indicate that there might be more interior cognition to be unfolded beneath the outer layer. Sometimes if you let the person continue their story, they will naturally get to the core and tell you their interior cognition from that point in the past. But if they don't, after a while you may want to circle back and encourage them.

Deciding Which Pull-Tab to Encourage

With practice, you will be able to notice pull-tabs more easily, and you will be able to sense what still needs to be resolved. During a listening session, you will have some pull-tabs lurking in your memory, and maybe you will jot a few of them down. (There's more about when to jot down a topic later in this section.) You will know the paths the person is unfolding and what they've already told you.

There might be several pull-tabs that the person mentioned. If you are going to circle back, which one do you pick? There is no hard rule here. Sometimes you'll pick the **most recent** pull-tab mentioned. Sometimes you will jump to a pull-tab that was **emotionally shaded** or emphasized. You can even just pick a pull-tab that was **interesting** to you.

This next example is a continuation from the first example above, about grocery delivery. There were two pull-tabs, "I taught myself" and "recently I have gone back to some shopping in between." The listener decides on the latter pull-tab, because deciding to go back to the grocery store in-person seems more relevant to the purpose of deciding to eat in a restaurant during COVID. Going into a grocery store is similar enough to pursue. The first pull-tab isn't relevant to the purpose because it is about when the person had retired, years before, and quit grocery delivery.

Listener: At what point – do you remember when you decided to switch back from getting delivery only, to going sometimes to the store? [most recent pull-tab]

Person15: I think it happened when there was like something I just couldn't find online, [scene setting] and I wanted to see if it was in the store. [inner thinking] It was like less than five things. Probably June, maybe, [statement of fact] and I just thought well let me just go see what they're doing, and I'll make it quick. [inner thinking]

I'd sent my husband once, and he told me about the arrows and things, [scene setting or explanation] so I said okay let me give it a try. [inner thinking] And I went early in the morning, [statement of fact] and I was fine with just going for a short trip. [implied emotional reaction]

And then I sort of went for a little bit more and a little bit more. [explanation] Now I probably do twice a month in person, maybe once a month delivery. [statement of fact]

Assuming, Of Course

You will also want to monitor for another, more subtle kind of indicator. This subtle indicator reveals itself when people within organizations assume you understand an action and the thinking behind the action— because they assume you work in a similarly functioning organization. "**Manage the team workload**." "**Hold check-in meetings**." These are both examples. These pull-tabs don't reveal the interior cognition behind them in the same way that the others mentioned above do. So, for these, the key is to notice when there is an assumption being made about your knowledge of a behavior or process.

There's yet another indicator, in English at least, which is a big green pull-tab, and that's the phrase, "**of course**." It means that the person assumes what they thought or felt is obvious or common. But as a listener, you want to clarify any assumptions you both might be making.

> **Person15:** I can't even think of what I'd order as take-out that wouldn't be cooked. [statement of fact]
>
> We do order the groceries which, **of course**, there was all the stuff going on with "do you wash them down?" and all that kind of stuff. [inner thinking and pull-tab]

In this example, the participant continues, on her own, to explain her interior cognition behind the "of course" phrase. The listener did not have to intervene. This is a good example of letting the person finish their point before you jump in. They may fill in what you need on their own. Like this, which is a bit generalized but still usable as interior cognition:

> **Person15:** I was never that worried about it. [generalized emotional reaction] I would just set the things aside that were dry goods and then put the things away that were refrigerated [explanation] and just kind of wait a day and then eat them the next day – or starting the next day.
>
> I'd just give them 24 hours, [generalized inner thinking] but I never washed everything, like I heard some of my friends doing. [explanation]
>
> I just felt like just giving them some time, in case there was any contact with the virus. [generalized inner thinking]

TIME TO LISTEN

Pull-Tabs: In Your Memory or Jotted Down

For the most part, you'll probably remember the indicators people mention. But if not, it's fine to jot down a promising pull-tab that you think will be good for a later topic.

How do you know if you can remember topics? Think back to a time where you were in conversation with someone for a while, like when you were seated next to a stranger at a lunch, a wedding, or a community gathering. Were you comfortable remembering topics they mentioned? Assess your capacity based on that experience. Use that as a metric for whether and how many pull-tabs you'll jot down. Also pay attention to how tired you feel; if you're very tired, let yourself jot a few more pull-tabs than you usually do.

I've noted pull-tabs in the examples throughout this chapter and the rest of the book, so you will be able to recognize pull-tabs when you come across them in your work. Not everything is a pull-tab. Some concepts *could* be pull-tabs, but seem less related to the purpose being discussed, so I did not leave a notation in the example.

When jotting pull-tabs, you are not "taking notes." You're just jotting down a *one or two-word reminder for yourself.* If you jot down a pull-tab too frequently, then more of your cognition will by focused on jotting than on paying rapt attention. So, explore what the balance is for you as you engage in more listening sessions.

And it's important to realize that **you won't get to circle back on *all* the pull-tabs you notice**. You'll just keep following the participant until they indicate they are finished. Let it work naturally—this is not a robotic process of listing pull-tabs and then checking all of them off. You will only use perhaps two-thirds of the pull-tabs you have remembered or jotted down. I'll revisit this subject a little later in this chapter, as a part of the Transitions section.

Moving Between Modes

Now I want to look at the third point in the listener's three cognitive activities during a listening session.

166

A listener's three cognitive activities:

1. Pay rapt attention
2. Monitor whether the concept type is exterior or interior
   - Monitor for indications there might be interior cognition (pull-tabs)
   - If the person does not dive into a topic, help them to do so at some point in the listening session
3. **Be aware if the person has popped back into the session mode of the listening session**
   - Help the person feel comfortable in the session

It is the point about being aware which mode, session mode or memory mode, the person is currently in. This is not something you must manipulate; just be aware of it. Throughout the listening session, the person will go from one mode to another naturally. It's like a dolphin or a whale, breathing at the surface of the water and diving beneath to keep swimming.

So, don't be worried when the person pops back into the session mode. It's normal, and it will happen many times during each listening session.

When the person returns to session mode, like a dolphin coming to the water's surface for air, it's likely that they will be wondering about one of a few different things (discussed below). When this happens, respond in a way that helps them feel comfortable. Here are three responses for when the session is going relatively well. I'll cover other responses in the next chapter.

How the Session Is Supposed to Work

Sometimes, a person might "resurface" into session mode because the listening session feels so different from an interview or a typical "research session." You'll explain how the session works in the information session, and also mention it at the start of the listening session.

But it still might feel so different to the participant that they may want to check in with you a few times when they worry they went off course. Reassure them that the session can wander off topic, and that they can take as much time as they want. The person might interject, "I don't know what you want to hear." Explain that you'd like to understand their thinking at that past time, not just a description of what happened. Ask, "Can you take me through a particularly memorable instance?"

Clarification of What Was Meant

Another thing that may pull the participant back into session mode is when they are not sure you understand something they mentioned. It can also happen when you need to ask them to clarify something.

You can satisfy their need to make sure you understand, and model asking for clarification at the same time. You can say something like, "I think you mean <concept>, so let me know if I got it wrong," or "Do you mean that <concept> applies in that situation?"

Encourage the participant to ask clarifying questions as much as they want, too. Make sure they know it's okay to ask for clarification. It's also okay for them to check to see if you understood something, or to ask you to repeat something you said.

Verification of Scene or Identification of Players

Some details of the memories can be complex and overlapping with other memories; there will be times where you both pop back to the session mode to make sure you understand what happened and who was doing it.

In the next section of this chapter, I'll show you techniques to encourage the participant to dive in to their stories, and in the section after that I'll explain how to help the participant transition to an earlier topic that you hope they'll dive into.

Techniques for Interior Cognition

The heart of this book is this section—techniques you can practice to help the person you are following unfold their interior cognition. I'm loading this section with examples so you can see what I mean. I've also divided this section into techniques that will **guide** and **help** versus techniques to **avoid.**

Techniques to Guide the Participant

This first set of techniques allows a listener to gently guide a person toward the core, the interior cognition, of the topic they are communicating about.

There are five techniques:

1. What went through your mind
2. More about that
3. Fill in the blank
4. Reflection
5. Why? versus Because…

1. What Went Through Your Mind

Like the germinal question, you can ask "what went through your mind" in a variety of ways. You'll get a better and better understanding of the person's life experience as the session unfolds, so you can use that understanding to use more appropriate phrasing for this person. You can add your own variations to the examples below.

Questions for "What Went Through Your Mind?"	To Get To
What went through your mind there?	Inner thinking
What was the thinking that went into that <concept>?	Inner thinking
What was the thinking around that?	Inner thinking

With respect to <concept>, what was running through your mind there?	Inner thinking
Was there anything that was running through your mind then?	Inner thinking
Do you recall any of what was going through your mind then?	Inner thinking
What was your reaction?	Emotional Reaction
How is it that you decided that?	Guiding Principle
How were you going back and forth about <concept>?	Guiding Principle
What led to that decision?	Guiding Principle

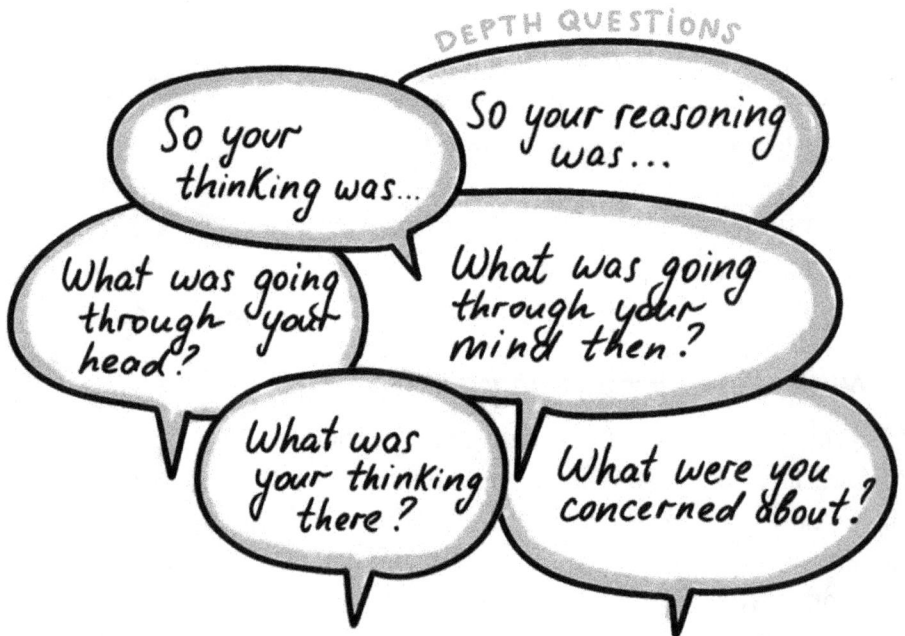

DEPTH QUESTIONS

So your thinking was...

So your reasoning was...

What was going through your head?

What was going through your mind then?

What was your thinking there?

What were you concerned about?

2. More About That

You can also ask other kinds of questions to get at the same interior cognition. Asking someone to tell you "more about that" is common in a traditional interview setting. But for listening sessions you'll want to include a hint that you are interested in the person's interior cognition. There are three ways to do this. One is to use wording like "more about your thinking," and a second way is to use words that encourage the person to continue the story. Here are some examples of these two ways:

Question Variations to Get at Interior Cognition	Two Ways
Tell me a little bit more about your thinking at <time and place>	More about your thinking
Can you talk a little more about your thinking about <concept>	More about your thinking
What else did you think?	Encourage more
It sounds like there is more to that story.	Encourage more
In what way?	Encourage more
When you were thinking about <topic>, it sounds like you <pull-tab>...	Encourage more

3. Fill in the Blank

The third way to encourage more of the story is to simply say, "and …" After a beat, the person will fill in the rest. The word "because …" also works. This type of query where you don't supply any detail turns out to be really valuable for encouraging the person to supply their own perspective. Often, when people participate in "a study," they expect that the "researcher" will have certain expectations about their answers. So, stating "and …" or "because …," with just one word and a trail of silence after it gives the participant agency to fill in the blank any way they choose. In this instance, the participant from the earlier "starting a listening session" example is discussing grocery shopping.

Person62: So, in the beginning of the pandemic, we probably didn't see them at all from March until, I think July, [statement of fact] because we were trying to be very careful. Just because they're a little bit older and we just tried to minimize spread. [inner thinking and pull-tab]

And then it became very clear to us that this was going to be going on for a really long time, [inner thinking and pull-tab] and so we needed to make it a priority to have a visit. [inner thinking and pull-tab]

So, we kind of all got on the same page about what to do and we – I mean we literally grocery shopped more than two weeks out and didn't go out in public for the two weeks before. [explanation and pull-tab]

We've seen them about once a month since, so we're not seeing them all the time. They spend half their time where they're going to retire, and then they spend the rest of their time – they have a place that's like 6 or 7 blocks away from us.

So, they're actually nearby fairly frequently, during the week. [statement of fact] For those visits, we do them outside, [statement of fact] and we social distance because we're just trying to keep it to a minimum. [inner thinking and pull-tab, part of the first one above]

Listener: **And . . .** [fill in the blank]

Person62:   I'm pregnant. [statement of fact] So that's definitely a factor. I don't think there's a lot of evidence yet how that impacts mother and child, [explanation or generalized inner thinking] but I'd prefer not to find out personally. [preference or emotional reaction]

So, we're being careful because of that now. [generalized inner thinking and pull-tab]

Sometimes there are topics where the person seems to be circling the core, stuck in the outer layers. They could be stuck because it's just something that takes some thought to explain. They could be stuck because they can't remember what went through their mind.

When you find out they are circling because they can't remember, leave that topic alone and let them continue in whatever direction they were going.

If they are stuck circling because they are not sure how to explain or what you're looking for, try to find another way to ask for depth. (But stop trying other ways if the person becomes annoyed at your persistence.) In this example, the listener asks a question, but the participant doesn't dive into it. So, the listener asks again, more clearly, to encourage an answer about inner thinking at the time.

Person62:   It's just like a low level of anxiety all the time, it feels like. [generalized emotional reaction] It's just a constant consideration. [generalized inner thinking] For us, I think – luckily my husband and I, kind of without even talking about it, are pretty aligned with our being safe, especially with the pregnancy. [generalized emotional reaction] But it's just, it's just – like logistics and anxiety and a small level of like low-level frustration all the time that we have to deal with this kind of thing.

You know, it's a cautious feeling. [generalized emotional reaction] For us it feels like a **calculated** risk that we even considered going to the restaurant. [generalized inner thinking and pull-tab]

Listener: **Calculated.** [micro-reflection on the pull-tab]

Person62:   Yeah. We both agree that being safe with the pregnancy is important, even though it's frustrating. [generalized inner thinking]

Listener: What are those **calculations** for you?   [encouraging more]

Person62:   Am I going to go crazy if I have to stay in the house for another day? [generalized emotional reaction and pull-tab] Versus, is it a place that is going to feel safe to us? Meaning there is social distancing. Are they observing COVID? Do they have outdoor seating? [generalized inner thinking] We haven't eaten inside of a restaurant since the beginning of the pandemic. [statement of fact] It's kind of those factors, if that makes sense. [session mode]

4. Reflection

In the "calculated" example above, what I show includes a technique called **micro-reflection**. Micro-reflection is when the listener repeats just one or two words the participant has said. These repeated words are the "pull-tab" that the listener noticed. The first "calculated" that the listener responds with in the above example is a micro-reflection.

It's more helpful to the participant if you **use a micro-reflection instead of a question**. Put yourself in their shoes. If the listener is bombarding you with questions formed of the very words you just said, it can get annoying. When a listener instead communicates a reflection as a statement, it sounds more supportive. It could be taken as an **affirmation** of what was just said. "Calculated." *Yes, there are calculations. The listener understands me.* Or it could be taken as an **encouragement** to reveal more. "Calculated." *Yes, we had to discuss the risk of going to the restaurant during my pregnancy, during COVID, and there were a few thoughts and emotions that we discussed while making the decision.* Both meanings are supportive.

In the example, the listener could have micro-reflected two words, "Calculated risk." If this was said, then the extra question, "What are those calculations for you," may not have been necessary. I don't think of this as a mistake, however. Listening sessions are intense, and the way the listener handled it was completely acceptable.

There are two other kinds of reflection in use in the therapy, sociology, and research fields. These two are called **simple reflection** and **complex reflection**. You may have encountered simple reflection in your own work; it's used in product research as a technique to clarify that you understood what the person said correctly and to encourage them to explain more. For these techniques, you use your own words to state someone's concept back to them.

Complex reflection, an approach that William Miller and Stephen Rollnick teach, encourages the person to think about their interior cognition, as a part of a therapy session. There are many ways to do complex reflection in therapy, such as "coming alongside," "agreeing with a twist," or "siding with the negative."[1] In the research field, you can use complex reflection to "continue the paragraph."[2] The listener attempts to say what the participant might say next, if the participant isn't unfolding things on their own.

In listening sessions in general you'll want to use micro-reflection or simple reflection instead of complex reflection. This is because, as a listener, you want your cognition to be limited, and complex reflection requires more brainpower from both you and the participant. However, any kind of reflection is fine to deploy.

In the example below, the listener inserts a simple reflection to encourage the participant to dive further into their interior cognition. In this case, the listener's intuition about where the participant was headed with the topic was incorrect. That is a risk of simple reflections. But in this example the simple reflection still elicits rich guiding principles and a strong emotional reaction.

> **Person62:** So, I feel like it's this new thing that everyone has to deal with. They choose to deal with it in their own way, [explanation or implied guiding principle] but if you're dealing with it differently than someone else, unfortunately, that may mean that they're putting you at a higher risk, right?

Like if they're less conservative than I am, [opinion] aka they're willing to come within six feet of me, without a mask on, indoors, and I'm not comfortable with that, then that feels awkward to me. Because then you have to be like, "can you please back up." I need you to respect my decisions. [generalized inner thinking]

Listener: So, **it is about making clear your position.** [simple reflection]

Person62: It doesn't have to be. [session mode] I don't have to impose my conservativeness on everyone, [guiding principle] but I'm like hey, I'm pregnant and I don't need you to come any closer right now, period.

Like, just stop right there. [inner thinking] You hate to, at least for me, like normally I'm very friendly, very open. I don't have problems talking with random people, [preference] and so for me, it's a little bit hard because all of a sudden, I need to have this like protective bubble around me because of COVID. And I don't like it. It sucks. [generalized emotional reaction]

It's not necessary to micro-reflect anything other than the pull-tabs. Do not consciously micro-reflect explanation, scene-setting, or technical details unless you need clarification. Don't micro-reflect expression concept types like preferences or opinions. Why not? Because the person will respond with detail at one of these outer layers. Clarification is fine if you don't understand something; otherwise, encourage the participant back to the interior cognition core whenever possible.

In the listening session, noticing pull-tabs is meant to be low-level monitoring, not a primary focus. This means you might micro-reflect things that go nowhere. Don't worry about it if you do—the participant may clarify what they meant with more words, they may respond by going sharply in another direction, or they may ignore the micro-reflection completely.

In the example below, the listener keeps sensing that there is more depth to a certain phrase, "this is awkward." The listener brings it up four times, to try to get a full understanding of the depth beneath it.

Person62: We're not going to go inside, are we? [inner thinking] Uhh, this is awkward. [emotional reaction] Because it's unfortunate.

We went with the intention of having a meal outside on the patio and instead it was like, "Oh God, we're definitely not doing this." [emotional reaction] And we knew, pretty much from the instant that we got there. [inner thinking] It was like a 15-mile boat ride, so it wasn't like a quick jaunt. [implied emotional reaction]

You know, I just try to roll with the punches, [implied guiding principle] but at the same time it was very clear, and I think to our whole group, that there's no possible way that we're staying here to eat. [inner thinking]

Honestly, I don't even know that we would have eaten on the patio. Probably [conjecture], but at the information that we didn't have a table outside, that we would have to eat inside, if we wanted to dine in, then we are all on the same page immediately that that was not going to happen. [inner thinking]

Listener: And it was **awkward**. [micro-reflection]

Person62: I mean it sucks. It's unfortunate. There's this dichotomy between what we used to be able to do without a second thought and now everything feels riddled with risk assessment and thinking about germs. [generalized emotional reaction] I am the opposite of a germaphobe, [implied guiding principle] so for me, this is like, "Oh God, I really don't even feel like thinking about this."

There's just a fatigue that goes along with it. [generalized emotional reaction] Like, okay, well we came all this way, but there's no possible chance that we're going to eat – we're not going to have the experience that we thought we were going to have. [emotional reaction]

Listener: When did the awkwardness come in? [encourage more]

Person62: Like – well, more like – well, I hate to say this, but I'll say it. I was little bit judgmental that a business would run in a way that felt so risky. [opinion or emotional reaction] Kind of like a discord between what we would expect and what we were experiencing, maybe, if that makes sense. [generalized emotional reaction]

Listener: Yeah. Tell me a little bit more about that. [more about that]

Person62: I would say most of the businesses that we've frequented have been doing a really good job. [opinion] Pretty much anywhere that could do, like a walk-up window, has been doing it. [explanation] It just seems like, for the most part, people are reacting in a way that protects the public and this just felt like they weren't. [inner thinking or opinion] I think most people did have masks, [statement of fact] but I feel like yeah, but you sit down and eat your food and take your mask off.

You know we're all in the same room and it's the same ventilation system. I don't know. [implied emotional reaction]

Listener: And so that was judgmental about the restaurant itself. [complex reflection]

Person62: Yeah. Sure, because I think it's ultimately their decision how they're going to run their business, right. [inner thinking or guiding principle] It's not – if they took out 60% of their tables and they put a bunch of picnic tables in the field, we would have been like, "This makes sense to us." [conjecture]

But to have basically the same capacity that you would have pre-COVID, inside, just – yeah, I guess I was judging them. [emotional reaction or opinion]

[pause] I get it. Like they need to make money, [guiding principle] but are you going to read on the news about an outbreak at that restaurant and are they going to be closed for two weeks? [conjecture]

Listener: I'm curious about if it felt awkward in any of the other – was anything else about those moments when you got there awkward to you? [encourage more]

Person62: It feels awkward when – I feel like people are used to social norms and there have been occasions where it's like it's clear to me that somebody here doesn't agree with my level of conservativeness, and for that, that's awkward. It's like, "oh we don't agree". [generalized emotional reaction]

For example, we walked up to like a window for ice cream. We intentionally chose this business because you could walk up outside. You didn't have to go inside. [scene setting] And the girl, who was like 16, was like, "Oh you guys are outside, you don't have to wear a mask. You can just step up to the window."

And then we couldn't decide, and she was like, "Well, if you want to come inside and look at the ice cream, you can." [explanation]

It's like, what is going on here? It's like the difference between your opinions on this pandemic and mine are very evident, and that's awkward if that makes sense? [emotional reaction]

Listener: Yeah, yeah. [support] So, social norms, and how those play in that feeling of awkwardness that you have. [simple reflection]

Person62: Well, I feel like day-to-day you don't usually come across an interaction, pre-COVID, like where there's so much possibility of a discrepancy that big, that's *that* evident. Like you don't know if a dude sitting next to you is racist, but if he's not wearing a mask, he's probably – like he probably thinks COVID isn't real. It's kind of an outward social norm, and those normally aren't visible. [generalized emotional reaction]

Listener: Oh, okay. [support]

Person62:   So, I feel like it's this new thing that everyone has to deal with. They choose to deal with it in their own way, [explanation or implied guiding principle] but if you're dealing with it differently than someone else, unfortunately, that may mean that they're putting you at a higher risk, right? Like if they're less conservative than I am, [opinion] aka they're willing to come within 6 feet of me, without a mask on, indoors, and I'm not comfortable with that, then that feels awkward to me. Because then you have to be like, "can you please back up." I need you to respect my decisions. [generalized inner thinking]

This example ends where the previous example begins. You can see how they hook together. The whole example shows a nice variety of "what went through your mind" and reflection techniques.

5. "Why?" vs. "Because..."

At this point in the techniques review, I want to warn you about "the five why's." Researchers and product owners have heard that if they make sure to ask "why?" about a topic five times, then they will get to interior cognition. It's not as simple as that.

First, asking "why?" by itself does not help the person communicate their interior cognition to the listener. It does not guide them in that direction.

Moreover, as a participant, being asked the same "why?" question becomes tedious quickly. It surges into annoyance easily. So, if you value your participant, don't use "the five why's."

You can use the word "why" every once in a while—it's not a forbidden word. But notice that in all the examples I've shown so far, it has not appeared. In all the transcripts I have permission to use as examples, it only appears once.

"Why?" is *not* the strongest technique.

At least in English, one way around this is to use the word "because" instead. When you come to a place where your urge is to ask "why?" try substituting the word "because…" as a statement.

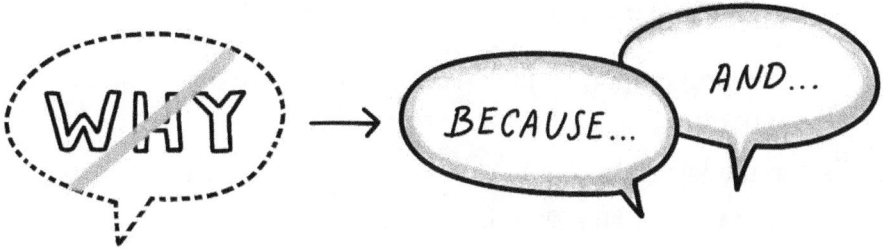

With "because…" you state just one word and leave space after it. Just like "and…" in the section about "what went through your mind," this method gives the participant agency to fill in the blank any way they choose. And it sounds a little more curious, and less like you are challenging their reasoning.

Techniques to Encourage Clarity

When a person is being asked about their inner thinking, emotional reactions, and guiding principles regarding a topic, it is natural for them to respond with concepts at the outer layers: description and expression. This is totally human. Not everyone is clear about or even cognizant of their interior cognition.

So, to help the person articulate their interior cognition clearly, there are three techniques:

- Pin to a past place & time
- Find the roots of an opinion or preference
- Turn passive into active

Pin to a Past Place and Time

As I mentioned in Chapter Two, "memory mode" in a listening session is when the participant is talking about a specific time and place in the past. They go into a past experience and narrate that experience from

179

the inside, in their own words. It's kind of like a flashback in a story. This is where a person's interior cognition really becomes evident.

It is much easier to talk about interior cognition when it is connected to a memory from a particular event.

To help the participant, you may need to remind the participant to focus on a particular memory by using phrases like:

- "so the last time was …"
- "run me through a specific time …"
- "is there a time you remember vividly enough to tell me your inner thinking …"
- "so that Tuesday what went through your mind …"

Here's an example that starts out with generalizations, and when the listener "pins" the discussion to a place and time, the person finds a particular memory to relate.

Person06: So, for the times that I have gone to restaurants, I was involved with picking almost every single one, except for one. [statement of fact]

Listener: You're known in your circles as the one to pick the restaurant. [simple reflection]

Person06: Yes. Begrudgingly, yes. [statement of fact]

Listener: [ironically] Awesome. [support] How did you get that responsibility? [encourage more]

Person06: Um, I feel like – well, I think this just goes back to years ago when we would have like larger group hangouts and stuff. You know everyone would have ideas for something, [explanation] but I would be the one to make logistics and figure out timing with people and choose ideal and appropriate plans for everyone. [explanation]

Listener: Right. Something that would work for everybody. [simple reflection used as support: heard]

Person06: Yeah, and I've seemingly just inherited that responsibility ever since. [explanation or statement of fact] I mean it would be nice if someone else… So, like, I have this problem too where it's like, I would want someone else to do it, but then their level of planning things isn't as great as my level of planning things. [opinion]

Like I could punt off the responsibility, but then they're not going to do as well in it as I would. So, what call do I want to make there? [inner thinking]

Listener: Yeah, may as well do it. [support] So, with respect to the other restaurants that you made the decisions about, **can you tell me about one in particular?** [pin to a place & time] How you were going back and forth about it with respect to pandemic planning, or with respect to supporting small businesses, like you said? [what went through your mind]

Person06: So, I think with one of the more recent restaurants I was supposed to meet up with a friend at a restaurant. [scene setting] I didn't know which one though. I knew I had wanted to do <city name> just because it was more convenient for my friend because she lives in <city name>, and I also just wanted to get away from my immediate area, which is in <different city name>. [inner thinking]

I literally went through maybe, I would say, five pages of like both Yelp and Open Table search results. [explanation] And my friend likes to drink whereas I'm kind of indifferent. [preference or implied inner thinking]

Then the other place is like a little further out, but it does have drink specials, but then the food is pricier, but then it's in a nicer location. [statement of fact] So, for these last two, I actually had my friend pick one because I was kind of like these are like two that I really like, help me pick out which one. [explanation and pull-tab]

At the end of the day, we decided to go with Restaurant A because of the more vast amount of food options. [explanation and pull-tab]

Listener: You said that that friend likes the drink specials. [simple reflection, hoping for more on the decision pull-tabs]

Person06: She likes the drink specials, but I think what had happened – well, on the day that I was asking her, she was also helping a friend move.

So, maybe she was just more focused on like eating something. [explanation or assumption]

In the transcript, the person continues with this story and a bit more about their interior cognition.

Here is another example with the same person where pinning to a place and time did not work:

Listener: Can you think back to **a memory of a restaurant that you picked that you wanted to go to** [pin to a place & time], and how you made that choice? [what went through your mind] Like a particular restaurant on a particular night? Any time of day really, but a particular meal? [pin to a place & time, albeit fumbled]

Person06: I think pre-pandemic it was more or less like what are the surrounding activities we would do beforehand? [generalized inner thinking] For example, if I were to go out and see a show at the <event venue name> or something, with a significant other, [scene setting] you try to like look at restaurants that are around there and then eat, and then do the activity, or like vice versa. [generalized inner thinking or explanation]

Listener: Can you tell me about **one of those events in particular** [pin to a place & time] so that we can maybe touch on the thinking that was unique to that? [what went through your mind]

Person06: Sure. Actually, the moment that I was thinking about, we were going to go see a show at the – I forget what it was called – at some theater in <city name>. [scene setting]

And we were just looking at restaurants in the nearby area to eat at first, before going to the show. [explanation]

Listener: Uh-huh. [support]

Person06: So, I mean that's what we did. And in terms of picking out the restaurant, it was like in <neighborhood name>, so it's not as much of a variety in terms of the food type as it is other areas of <city name>. [statement of fact or opinion]

I mean I would say <neighborhood name> is more like a fancy type of area. It's like more high-end restaurants and high-end new American, European style restaurants. [statement of fact or opinion]

Honestly, to me it almost all tastes the same, so there's not much variety [opinion], but we picked one place that wasn't as pricey as the others, and ate there, and then went to our show. [explanation as pull-tab]

You can see that even though the listener attempted to pin the topic to a specific place and time twice, the participant kept returning to scene-setting, then moving into statements of fact and opinions rather than diving into a memory.

The last paragraph only contains explanation and opinion—all from the outer layers. The pull-tab in that last paragraph is "wasn't as pricey." The listener tries that pull-tab next. And still gets nowhere.

> **Listener:** So you were looking at prices before you even chose the restaurant? [simple reflection]
>
> **Person06:** Yes.

So, the listener tries another technique, called "find the roots."

Find the Roots of an Opinion or Preference

"Find the roots" involves asking about a person's expression layer concepts to understand the interior cognition behind them. If they tell you about an opinion or an attitude, don't just leave it at that. Go back toward the time when the person first formed that opinion or attitude. Why did the person form it? What was going on in their mind? If they have a memory of when it formed, that is where you will discover their interior cognition. The inner thinking, emotional reactions, and guiding principles that played a part in creating their opinion will be exposed as "the roots" of the opinion or attitude.

The interior cognition in these roots is what you want to know, in order to understand this person.

Finding the roots does go "back in history," so it sounds similar to "pin to a place and time." But here, it's not about a time when they were pursuing their purpose; it's about the roots of an opinion, preference, perception, behavior, or attitude. You ask about it differently. Here is a continuation from the "pin to a place and time" example above.

> **Listener:** How did you come to this conclusion that *they all kind of taste the same?* [that opinion of theirs] **Where did that come from? Did you have an experience, or something?** [find the root]
>
> **Person06:** I've been to about two or three different restaurants in that same area and I can't think of anything that differentiates the two or three experiences that I've had in terms of like taste. [pull-tab about differentiation in tastes]

Listener: Right. [support] As opposed to some other experience where something did differentiate. [complex reflection] Can you tell me an example from those in the pre-pandemic days? [pin to a place and time]

Person06: Well, this would be in another area of <city name> which is probably maybe half a mile, or a mile, away.

Usually, more towards, I would say, like the <neighborhood name> area of <city name>, like that <subway name> line part, near where <street name> is, is where you start to see more ethnic food. So, food from different ethnic groups. [scene setting]

I guess you said one experience [session mode], so one experience that I had with food that was different was Puerto Rican food in <city name> actually. I'm Puerto Rican, so I'm really picky about this stuff. [statement of fact or explanation]

Listener: Awesome. [support]

Person06: Well, okay. Sorry, I might talk about two different experiences if that's okay with you. [session mode]

Listener: That's totally fine. [session mode]

Person06: I remember in <city name>, pre-pandemic days, of course, there was this really hyped restaurant. [scene setting] I think it's overhyped, [opinion] but it was this really hyped restaurant called <restaurant name>, which is somewhere in between <neighborhood name> and <street name>. It was this restaurant where it was only open for dinner. [statement of fact] People would wait two hours. [scene setting]

Listener: We have one of those kind. [support]

Person06: Like limited seating space and stuff. You know, since we showed up like two hours beforehand. [scene setting] Yes, we literally waited two hours because I wanted to see what the hype was. [inner thinking]

Listener: Right. [support]

Person06: We were one of the very first groups in line, so we were able to get a table by the time it opened. [explanation]

Person06: We went there, we ate the food and I remember feeling like angry? I know that's kind of like an out there reaction, [emotional reaction] but to me, like I grew up on food where for like $7 or $8 a plate is like a really huge plate of rice and meat and vegetables and all this other stuff. [explanation]

But here I am paying $16 for like four dumplings [statement of fact] and a plate of this fried pork dish where the pork wasn't even cooked correctly, [opinion] and like some other stuff to it.

The worst thing of it all is they try to advertise this whole experience as like family-style, and I'm kind of like – like a family of four can't eat like four dumplings. Who are you trying to sell this to? [emotional reaction] Like really, really, really poor families in Puerto Rico? Like no. [emotional reaction]

Listener: Wow, $16 for four dumplings! [support]

Person06:   Yeah, exactly. And you know I have a friend who is like a really picky eater, but even she said she was like hungry after having a meal there. [explanation] I mean I think I was just kind of irritated because the food wasn't – I mean the food was good, but it was just like very small and it was like at very extraordinary prices. [emotional reaction]

I felt like I was paying more for the vibe, and for the brand, rather than the actual food.

I get nowadays that's how restaurants stand out, but like your first point of business as a restaurant is the food. [inner thinking or guiding principle]

Listener: Is the food. Hello! [support]

Person06:   Like please focus on that first before all this other stuff. I don't mind eating in a hut if the food is good. [preference or guiding principle]

Listener: Right. [support]

Person06:   That was like my first disappointing Puerto Rican food experience in <city name>. [emotional reaction] And then my second one was at another place, also in the same area, but a little different and less pretentious, I think. It was a place called <restaurant name>. [scene setting]

While the food there was still expensive, at least it was enough to fill me up. [opinion] Like I had an appetizer and a meal and then like some dessert. Honestly, it was like about the same price as whatever food I paid at the other restaurant, but I got more food. [statement of fact]

Listener: And it was better? [encourage more]

Person06:   I think taste-wise it's still the same. [opinion] It was just more. [statement of fact]

So, in this example, the opinion that *the food at all the restaurants tastes the same* has some connection to emotional roots. The person had two experiences of eating familiar ethnic food that they are picky about, at extraordinary prices, which irritated, disappointed, and angered them. People in the home country of the ethnic food wouldn't be able to feed themselves enough at those prices. This emotional reaction is a pull-tab to find out why the person was thinking about people in the home country. There wasn't even enough food at one restaurant to feel full. But, at the end of this topic the person is again unwilling to get into their interior cognition. They return to opinion and statement of fact. Both places tasted the same, and we don't know *why* that is a metric this person mentions for how they make decisions about restaurants.

You can use this technique outside of the research context as well. Finding the root is *especially* powerful as you **develop relationships** with people. It helps you see where people are coming from, and why they have the opinions and behaviors that they have. In cases where you are not getting along with the other person, it helps you see past any labels you have put on them. You can see what they experienced and thought, and how it informs the way they respond to situations now. (In Chapter Seven I describe how envisioning a dragon helps you stay out of judgement.)

In cases where a person has a habit that they can't explain, finding the root can help them find their way back to when their habit formed. Exploring their interior cognition, if they can remember it, can fill in deeper understanding for both of you. The examples about people deciding about restaurants during the early COVID pandemic involve recent habits and related approaches, which people could explain. An example of another habit that would benefit from finding the root is someone's approach to a medical condition they live with.

Turn Passive into Active

Active statements are something that someone *does*. Passive statements are something that *happens to* someone. For example, "I got stung by a bee at the park." The action is "sting," and the person reporting the bee sting is not doing that action, the bee is.

Interior cognition won't come up (or at least will not be stated clearly) when a person is communicating in passive statements. This is because their focus is outward on the environment around them, rather than inward on their own thoughts, emotions, and actions.

You will want to help the person focus on their action, like:

Person:	I got stung by a bee at the park.
Listener:	**How did you react?** [turn passive to active]
Person:	Well, I'm not allergic, [statement of fact] which is a relief because I know people who have to rush off to the hospital. [generalized emotion] I just **put ice on it** and [laughs] **whined to my friends**. [explanation and pull-tabs]

What the person talks about after the listener turns passive into active will probably include concepts all up and down the layers, from scene-setting to opinion and generalization. If you combine "passive into active" with your other techniques, you will then get inner thinking, emotional reactions, and guiding principles.

Listener:	[laughing along] Whined! [micro-reflection]
Person:	Yeah. I'm gonna mine it for all the attention I can get! [laughs] [implied guiding principle] Actually, it hurt a LOT, [statement of fact] and to cope the pain, I got loud about it. [inner thinking or emotional reaction] My friends were sympathetic, luckily, and their support helped the pain a lot. [implied emotional reaction]
	They started distracting me with stupid jokes, and at one point I totally forgot the pain. I was grateful. [emotional reaction]
	But I didn't tell them that—I just joked back. [guiding principle] It all turned out okay about 20 minutes later, [explanation] and I didn't have to look like a wimp who is too sensitive about a little bee sting. [guiding principle]

Here's a second, even simpler example:

Person:	I got an invitation to speak at the conference. [statement of fact]
Listener:	**How did you react?** [turn passive to active]

| **Person:** | It literally made my heart skip a beat and my stomach drop. [emotional reaction] I've never been comfortable on stage. [preference or emotional reaction] So I was thinking how could I respectfully decline. [inner thinking] |

There's another, more subtle kind of "passive" you will want to monitor for. This subtle version happens when people focus on the thing that triggered a cascade of interior cognition, and they get stuck on the trigger. You can help them past it using the same "how did you react" phrase.

Person:	I read that email that he sent to everyone. [the trigger]
Listener:	And ... [fill-in-the-blank]
Person:	And it was horrifying. [opinion or emotional reaction] The manager, who is new to our group, berated my colleague about missing a deadline—and sent the email to the whole group! [scene setting]
	My colleague's dad needed people to harvest, because the crew he'd hired ended up double-booked, and the fruit was really ready. [explanation] This new manager had even approved it! [implied emotional reaction] I was horrified to see it all get turned around. In an email! [emotional reaction]
Listener:	Well, what did you do? **How did you react next?** [turn passive to active]
Person:	I remember thinking how I could calm everyone down. How can I calm everyone down and avoid anyone getting fired? [inner thinking] So, I got up and went to tell my manager that something got lost in communication, and we needed to do some mediation. [pull-tabs]
Listener:	Wow. [support]
Person:	It helped too. My manager.... (conversation continues)

Often, participants will use passive focus with the assumption that you know what they're talking about. They reference ideas in passing, or they imply messages, assuming you'll fill in the rest. However, if you fill in the rest it will be from your perspective, not from theirs. Instead, when you notice passive statements like the ones in the above examples, ask about them. Find out the details from the person.

Techniques to Avoid

There are some techniques that have been propagated among product creators and researchers based on misinformed instruction. What I mean is that a lot of practitioners learn on-the-job—which isn't the problem. It is happening for totally valid reasons. The problem is that the instruction practitioners are picking up on-the-job is often just based on what other practitioners are doing. It's lacking in formal, proven roots. And you can't tell which instruction has this formal background and which doesn't. So, practitioners pick up some techniques that are considered bad form in professional and in academic research practice.

The following techniques will lead the listening session in a direction that is either unhelpful for getting to interior cognition, or that wrests control of the session back from the participant, so that the listener is no longer truly following.

Here are the techniques that will **not** work for listening deeply:

- Leading questions (avoid universally)
- Questions about future cognition (avoid in all but market research, co-creation)
- Description-layer questions (avoid for deep listening, except for clarification)
- Expression-layer questions (avoid for deep listening, except as support)
- Introducing new terminology (avoid universally)
- Introducing new topics (avoid for deep listening)

Avoid Leading Questions

Here is a familiar rule. In most interviews, and in legal court proceedings, you avoid leading questions. Leading questions are worded in a way that betrays to the other person how you think they will answer. These kinds of questions start with the words "did" or "does," or with "was" or "is." The questions finish by describing an event or context you expect might have happened. "Did you hang out near the cozy fire for a while?"

"Is being with your in-laws something you enjoy?" "Was that something you couldn't control?"

Leading questions suggest what you think the answer is, and they guide the person in the direction you indicate. You're not following them anymore when you use leading questions, you're manipulating them to follow you. Also, the participant may have an emotional reaction to the question itself. It will pull them back into session mode and make them wonder what you want of them.

Worse, leading questions usually elicit yes or no answers. You will not get much interior cognition as the result of a leading question.

> **Person62:** Honestly, no, because we'll do takeout. [statement of fact] We're pretty comfortable with the idea that you can go pick something up, or something can be dropped off. [generalized emotional reaction] So, that's kind of our release from cooking and dishes. [generalized emotional reaction and pull-tab]
>
> But of course, it still comes with parameters. [generalized inner thinking and pull-tab] It's not the same as going out to a fancy dinner, but it will have to do for now. [generalized emotional reaction and pull-tab]
>
> **Listener:** Did this feel like going out to a fancy dinner? [leading question, not getting to any of the pull-tabs]
>
> **Person62:** Yeah, it felt like a treat, yeah. [yes or no answer]

It's okay to ask leading questions when you need clarification of what the person meant, or if you need verification of some detail to that you have a clear understanding of the scene and the people involved. But you want to avoid leading questions during the rest of the session.

If you ask a leading question by accident, and you realize it in the moment, just let it continue. Don't try to correct it, or you risk popping the participant out of memory mode. Let the participant answer yes or no, then try again with another technique.

Avoid Questions About Future Cognition

Asking about cognition that might happen in the future is another mistake for a listening session. It is asking for Conjecture. You are asking someone to imagine what their future inner thinking, emotional reaction, or decision will be. It's a mistake because it is a query in the almost-cognition layer of the jawbreaker candy topic (rather than getting to the core). And because it's asking the person to guess.

In a listening session, you are exploring what *went* through a person's mind at a point in the past, not what *will go* through a person's mind at some point in the future.

Conjecture questions are often used in market research, when a participant is asked to imagine using, buying, or interacting with a product, service, or brand. With this imagined scenario in mind, the participant will answer questions about potential preferences, opinions, behavior, and attitudes. Market research uses conjecture for a certain purpose. There may also be other scenarios, such as co-creation exercises, where conjecture is useful, but listening sessions are not one of them.

Often, a conjecture question looks innocent because it follows the topic at hand. Here's an example:

Person62:	I don't worry too much about actually getting it. I worry about spreading it. [generalized emotional reaction] And as a citizen, you don't want to be like the one that made a mistake and then spread it. We're trying to keep this to a minimum. I'd like to do my part, if that makes sense. [generalized guiding principle]
Listener:	Un-huh. [support]
Person62:	So, I don't spend a lot of time with anxiety about me personally being diagnosed with COVID. Now I say that. [generalized emotional reaction] There have been a couple of times where my Mom had a false positive COVID test. [scene setting] That brings your anxiety level up.
	I wasn't too bad until I spoke with my brother and he was like, "Yeah, if she gets sick and goes in the hospital we might never see her again," and then I was like pure panic. You know, like that incident in particular, in my mind, was anxiety inducing. [emotional reaction and pull-tab]
	But day to day I don't worry [generalized explanation] like, "Oh, I could get COVID and these are the things that could happen to me and this is what my symptoms would be," or anything like that. [not my inner thinking]

Listener:	Okay. Okay. [support] You said you worry most about spreading it to somebody more vulnerable [simple reflection] and that, let's say family, and you're fairly confident that **even if they have the same risk level as you, you'd still be anxious?** [conjecture]
Person62:	Yeah, just generally. **It would be lower anxiety.** [guess at future emotional reaction]

Don't ask them to guess at their future thinking. A person might guess with some level of accurate prediction about their own future thinking and reactions, but no matter the accuracy, it's still guessing. There's a chance they would have different thinking or reactions when they actually experience that imaginary future scenario. It's not reliable, and you can't use it to build solid knowledge for your organization.

Avoid Description-Layer Questions

The techniques discussed earlier in this chapter all have one goal: to guide or help the participant to unfold their inner thinking, emotional reactions and guiding principles about a topic. The description layer of the topic "jawbreaker candy" includes explanation, scene setting, and statement of fact. If you ask questions about the description layer, you will usually get answers in the description layer.

Here's an example:

Person15:	Tomorrow I might actually go out for my first trip to a winery. Somebody called me yesterday. She wants to go tomorrow. It's beautiful weather. We know we can sit outside, [explanation or scene setting] so I think we're going to do it. [inner thinking and pull-tab]
Listener:	What went through your mind when your friend asked you to go? [what went through your mind]
Person15:	I just looked up the winery. A) to be sure they were open. B) to see what their procedures are with COVID. [explanation] As I suspected, they don't let people sit up next to the bar. You get a takeaway box that you can take to a picnic table in a field. [statement of fact]
	It's not the same as it used to be, [implied emotional reaction] but that's one reason we want to go on a weekday. She only works part-time so we're going to go tomorrow afternoon, so that hopefully it's less busy than the weekend. [inner thinking]
Listener:	Um-hmm, um-hmm. [support]

Person15:	We both agreed if it looks too busy, or it looks unsafe, we can walk away. So, we're going to go and see what it's like. [inner thinking and explanation]
Listener:	Um-hmm. When you looked online to see the information they had, **what kind of info did you find?** [description-layer question]
Person15:	So, they immediately had like a little square at the top saying, "Due to COVID we're not using the bar area. This is how it goes." That was the first thing you would see and then it gave a little more detail farther in about what their hours were and which days they're open. The old stuff was still there, but clearly the COVID part came first. [statement of fact]

And it was very gentle and friendly. [opinion] It just said you'll need to wear your mask unless you're drinking and get your things and then go to the tables that are separated. [statement of fact] |

The person's answer above mostly stays in the description layer. The listener's question did not elicit any interior cognition. You're allowed to ask for clarification about scene-setting and explanation that confuses you, and you are allowed to ask out of pure curiosity or for relationship-building. But it does not usually lead you to a person's interior cognition.

Avoid Expression-Layer Questions

Like description-layer questions, questions in the expression layer tend to get answers that are also in the expression layer. Asking about a person's opinion, preference, perception, behavior, or attitude about something will usually not bring up interior cognition. It's fine to ask these kinds of questions to establish support for the other person, or if you need clarification. There's also a chance they will bring up some implied inner thinking or emotional reaction. However, they are not helpful for getting to interior cognition. Here's an example:

Listener:	And then how has it been, being retired?
Person15:	Fantastic. I highly recommend it. [opinion]
Listener:	Oh, nice. **What's fantastic about it?** [expression-layer question or support]
Person15:	Well, it depends how retirement is for each person, but there are many things I love doing that I just didn't have enough time for. [statement of fact]

So I can choose now what I want to do with my time. [generalized explanation and pull-tab] I did prepare for it and save for it, so I have enough money to do what I want. [statement of fact] So, that makes it fantastic. [opinion and pull-tab]

Avoid Introducing New Terminology

In listening sessions, I try to stick to the vocabulary the participant has used in the session. Introducing new terminology, like professional lingo or technical jargon, often has the effect of changing how the person is communicating. This is not always a big deal, but it can throw the participant out of their own perspective. Introducing new terminology can pull the participant back into the session mode of the listening session, with heightened awareness of what you expect from them.

This can be especially damaging in a scenario where you introduce a new word that sounds like a correction to something they said. As an example, if they say "jail," don't say "correctional facility" in your responses. This is worse than pulling them briefly out of their own perspective, because it seems judgmental regardless of your motive. It threatens the safe space the two of you established at the beginning of the session, and it may cause the participant to close off their interior cognition completely.

Limit yourself to the vocabulary the participant uses, whenever possible. This will keep you focused on their perspective, and it helps keep them focused on their own thinking by not bumping them out of it with a different word.

Avoid Introducing a New Topic

As with new terminology, bringing up a new topic as a listener usually disrupts a listening session. Introducing your own topic is not listening. This might seem obvious, but it can be easy to accidentally introduce a new topic by asking questions that aren't about what the participant is saying.

If the participant is talking about how they decided to handle a bad experience they had while riding on a train, and during a long pause you respond, "And probably with your planes, too," then you have derailed the conversation. Even though you're still talking about the bad experience, you have taken over control of the direction of the conversation.

Stick to the topics the participant brings up and avoid introducing your own.

These techniques in the three sections above:

- **Starting a Listening Session**
- **How a Session Works**
- **Techniques for Getting to Interior Cognition**

are the heart of this book. They are the tools you will practice using, so that they become second nature—so that your attention is wholly on what the person is communicating, and what layers and modes they are in.

Transitions

Topics come and topics go. Some topics come around again. Some topics are nested or tangled together. The person who is describing the topics will often return to those they brought up before, to fill in more detail for the listener. Or sometimes they won't. Your first job is to follow the person.

Your second job as the listener is to decide whether a prior topic is worth returning to for the pull-tabs that haven't been covered. If you have the urge to go back to an old topic, wait for the end of the current one to introduce any change.

The End of a Topic

You can sense when a person has finished a topic by the finality of their tone and rhetorical expressions, or by a shift back to the session mode. You can sense these in written communication as well as audio and video.

If you don't notice the tone or expression or shift in mode, sometimes you can notice a topic end by the space the person leaves. It's the tiny pause at the end of a topic.

Let some time tick by, a heartbeat or two. And then wait a heartbeat longer. That's what this kind of space feels like.

This example starts with the topic of going to a cozy restaurant, and then when that ends, there is a space.

Person15:	A friend had had a funeral meeting at a restaurant that I ended up liking a lot, and I enjoyed the big group atmosphere, but it also had a nice, cozy area. [implied emotional reaction and pull-tab] So, I told my husband we've got to go back there and actually have a nice, cozy dining experience. [explanation] It was great. They had fireplaces, and nice tables, and good food. We had a good time. [implied emotional reaction and pull-tab]
Listener:	Nice. [support] So, you went the first time, and it was a funeral, and that was the first time you had been to that restaurant? [simple reflection or verification]
Person15:	Yeah. I'd never realized it was there, and I was like, oh I've passed this by, I don't know how I never walked in there. [inner thinking] The group was using a room in the back, so we didn't really eat out in the main area. [statement of fact] So, I thought I want to try the actual restaurant someday. [inner thinking]
Listener:	Umm. Nice Yeah, that sounds great [support] with the fireplaces, and cozy. [micro-reflection]
Person15:	I think we went right after work and did like drinks and then had a full meal and just kind of relaxed and then went home. [explanation]
	[pause]
Listener:	Um-hmm. Um-hmm. You mentioned earlier that you somewhat recently retired. [earlier you said]

Allow the space to exist for a moment when the person comes to the end of a topic. Sometimes the person will pick up another topic on their own after the space, so you don't have to do anything. Sometimes they'll decide to add more detail to the current topic after a space.

Especially later in the listening session, if they have grasped the idea of communicating from memory what went through their mind about a topic, they are likely to add some interior cognition detail after a space. You don't have to do anything but notice and pause along with them.

Listening sessions are full of spaces. These sessions are not hurried. You are not trying to keep the person talking. If this feels new to you, you'll want to practice letting space exist in your casual conversations. It might be hard, at first, but practicing with space is valuable. Learning to allow the space to exist can make the listening session a special place, for both the listener and the participant.

These spaces also give you an opportunity to consider the next topic.

Deciding Whether to Shift Topics

If there is a space or a topic-end, and if the person has not picked up and continued on their own, your job as the listener is to decide whether an old topic is worth returning to for the pull-tabs that haven't been covered.

You can do a little cognition at this point. Here are three things to think about:

- Of all the pull-tabs that are still lurking, does it feel like there is more interior cognition that could be unfolded from them?
- Does the person have an interest in this topic, or from what they've talked about so far, is it far from their main focus?
- Is your urge to return to a topic that the person has covered a couple of times already? Here, you run the risk of belaboring the topic and annoying the person.

So, based on this thinking, how do you know which of the topic pull-tabs to shift to?

Deciding on a Topic

This is the easy part. Just like with deciding which pull-tab to encourage, the only rule with deciding on a next topic is that it must be something the participant has already mentioned.

Sometimes you'll pick the most recent topic. Sometimes you'll choose a topic that the person was emotional about or emphasized, or one that has been repeated several times. You can also pick a topic that interested you or which seemed significant in some way.

Go with what feels right in the moment.

Earlier You Mentioned

When you shift the topic, you want to keep the person in flow. You want them to easily return to leading the conversation. So, this means that you can't say, "I want to change the topic." That would interrupt them.

Instead, there are some other phrases that you can use, which don't call attention to the change. These are all statements except the last one, which mimics a statement because it leaves all the details of how to proceed up to the other person:

- "Earlier you said <topic>"
- "You mentioned <topic>"
- "So, that <topic> you referred to"
- "<Topic> ..." and a trail of silence after it
- "What about <topic>?"

At the end of each of these phrases, let there be enough silence that the lead returns back to the participant. The person can use the phrase as a place to start their response.

Sometimes they will need time to think about the answer because this is something that they haven't reflected on. Notice when that is happening and don't pressure them into giving you an answer right away. Give them time to articulate.

Here's an example that includes the end of a topic about a sister coming to visit. You can see some indications that it's the end of that topic; the person just didn't have much to say about it. The listener then decides to shift to an earlier related topic about a friend visiting, to try to get to interior cognition there.

Person06: Yeah. I mean my sister and I, we tried to like – we tried to come to an agreement on how much, or how less social interaction – I guess like the amount of appropriate social interactions we could have before we met up. [explanation and pull-tab]

Listener: Got it. [support] How far was she traveling to see you? [verification]

Person06: I mean she was traveling from Las Vegas to see me. [statement of fact and hint at end of topic]

Listener: So it's a bit of an investment. [complex reflection, which fails]

Person06: Yeah. [indication of end of topic] (pause)

Listener: That makes sense, totally. [support] So, you skipped that one invite to eat out with friends because it was too much risk and because your sister was coming. [simple reflection]

What about this one where your friend came and stayed 5 days with you? You did go out, you said, a couple of times. [shift to earlier topic]

Person06: Um, oh, so my risk calculations behind that? [session mode]

Listener: Yeah. [session mode]

Person06: So, for myself I avoided anything – I mean my friend did go to large gatherings, [statement of fact] but she says they were all outside, and I saw pictures. So, I'm like, "Okay, I trust you on that." And everyone looked like they were wearing their mask. So, it's like, "Fine, I trust you on that." [emotional reaction]

For me personally though, like, I could have gone out and met these other people too, but I was only comfortable socializing with her and our other mutual friends. [emotional reaction and pull-tab] So, those are the only interactions that I actually participated in. [statement of fact]

Another Instance of This Purpose

You started the listening session by asking the person to relate a story from a particular past time and place. If topics for the first story seem complete, yet you don't feel like you have a good understanding of this person's interior cognition, you can ask for another story where they addressed this purpose.

I used to have a deep listening exercise in my in-person audio workshops. The purpose was "decide whether to attend a performance." I paired people up, asked them to choose who is the first listener, and set 10 minutes for a practice listening session. I roved around the room listening in and helping people. Frequently I would find a pair who were each looking at their devices, instead of interacting with each other. "What's going on?" I'd ask. "Oh, we finished the topic. There was nothing more to say about it." This is how I realized that I need to emphasize that the listening session is to understand someone's interior cognition regarding the purpose, not to ask questions about one topic. I told these pairs, "Go ahead and try again, with another performance you were considering."

In the example listening sessions about deciding whether to go to a restaurant in the pandemic, at one point the participant couldn't think of any particular time they had made a decision about going to a restaurant. This was a bit disconcerting to this person and to the listener. The person might have had a memory block because of feeling nervous at the start of the listening session.

The listener takes it in stride and asks about another instance of a similar purpose the participant had mentioned: grocery delivery instead of going to the grocery store.

> **Listener:** Yeah. [session mode]
>
> **Person06:** No, I'm sorry, I don't remember. [session mode]
>
> (silence for a moment)
>
> **Listener:** No problem. [support] Perhaps we can talk about other similar decisions. Is there a time you remember making a similar decision? [another instance of this purpose]

Person06: Well, what's similar? [session mode]

Listener: I heard you talk about this delivery of groceries. [earlier you said] Have you done any thinking about how you make decisions around grocery delivery? [what went through your mind]

Person06: Yes! That I remember. [session mode] Last Tuesday I ... [goes into scene setting]

In this case, the person regained their confidence and was able to relax and remember some of the restaurant trips that they had been thinking about for the listening session.

Here's another example, where the purpose is "cooking dinner as a creative home chef." The participant had already described their guiding principle about sustainably raised salmon, and this is the wind-up of the topic. Here you can see both a phrase that indicates the end of a topic, "that was that" in this case, and the end-of-topic pause. Then the listener asks about another instance of cooking dinner that had come up earlier. This listening session was done via text chat, with the emojis inserted.

Person: So after I got the manager, and it was pretty clear that no store in the county had the sustainably raised salmon I wanted, 🐟 the fishmonger and I settled on the black cod. [explanation] The meal turned out well, I think. 🍽 I had to tone down the mandarin orange a bit by adding more garlic, [explanation] but my mother had seconds. [implied emotional reaction] So that was that dinner. [signals end of topic]

Listener: All right! 🙌 [support] (pause) So on to the other meal that you were going to tell me about. [another instance of this purpose]

Note that the listener transitioned to another instance, and did so in a way that kept the focus on the person's purpose. The exact wording of the transition varies based on what's natural to the listener. When there's a lull, if the previous thread has been explored in enough depth, move forward by exploring other instances of the same purpose.

When you have covered the promising pull-tabs, when the person seems to have gotten to depth on the topics they were focused on, that's when the session is ready to wind down.

Ending the Listening Session

Ending the listening session is a process. There are a few conditions to look for, and a response in each case.

You will have recognized that the person is winding down. Take a moment to run through the topics in your memory or where you jotted them down. See if you feel comfortable that most were covered, and that you heard interior cognition regarding many of them.

If you feel like you have gotten a good understanding of the participant's interior cognition about their purpose, and the participant also seems finished discussing this purpose, then begin the process of ending the session:

- The closing question
- How did that go?
- The thank-you gift
- The recording

But there is one thing to mention first, before I explain each of these parts of the process. It is a reminder that you're not watching the clock.

No Time Limit, Except Hard Stops

In a listening session, you are paying rapt attention to the person. You're confident and relaxed, unlike some other contexts where you are, for example, trying to "get through" six participants a day. So you're not watching the clock, anxious about timing.

Like I mentioned in Chapter Two, a listening session usually ends when it's over, not because it has reached a certain clock time. So let the session continue until you sense the person winding down. The session might end earlier than you expect, but still be rich with interior cognition. Don't draw the session out longer just because it falls short of the time you expected it to take. End it when everything feels wrapped up.

If the person did mention that they have a "hard stop" at a certain time, or if it's culturally normal to have a set time in your specific context, when that clock time arrives, mention it. "I notice that it's 11 o'clock." (Making sure you use a number from their time zone.) Let the person respond, rather than assuming you must stop the session now. There is a greater than 50 percent chance that the person will say, "I can go a little bit longer to finish explaining this." Usually what follows is important to the person, and frequently contains quite a few concepts at the interior cognition layer.

The Closing Question

When you sense that all the topics have been explained well enough, you will indicate to the person that you are ready to wrap up. Begin with a statement about how much you have covered in your time together. The statement should be one that feels natural to you, and that indicates that you're satisfied with the conversation. You can use something like one of these examples:

| Listener: | We've covered a lot, and this has been fabulous. |
| Listener: | It feels like we've explored so many topics together. |

Next comes the closing question that you pose at the end of every listening session. Sometimes the answer loops back into the listening session again. The closing question is this:

| Listener: | Is there anything else you expected to cover when you agreed to this session? |

The wording is special. You can vary it a little, but make sure you guide the person back to the information session, and the days when they were anticipating the listening session. If you word the closing question this way, then you avoid putting the person in a position where they need to take a step back and think fast.

Notice how the wording of the question above differs from "Is there anything we haven't covered?" It's hard for a person to think of new topics at a moment's notice, so the answer to that question is usually, "No. I think we covered everything." The person is ready to end the session.

If you insert the "when you agreed to this session" or "as you anticipated this session," you are pinning the topic to a past time and place. That is one of the techniques in this chapter, and it's so helpful to give the person a past memory to go back to. They can more easily see if they were indeed thinking they'd bring up something that they didn't.

Asking the question by *pinning it to that past* often results in a "yes" answer. And then the person will open a new topic and you can both dive in together, again.

It's possible to vary the wording of the closing question I suggest. You can reference that they signed up for the study or agreed to a relationship-developing chat in different ways. You'll see a variation in the example below.

Listener:	You've shared so much great thinking and information about what your experience has been. Are there any other – I know we went a little bit off of thinking about restaurants, but the whole picture is important. [session mode]
	Were there any other things that you expected to share when <person's name> asked you to participate in this study? [closing question]
Person15:	The other thing I remember was in the beginning, what I did when I felt like I couldn't go to the restaurant, is I bought gift cards from the restaurant. And I haven't used them yet. [explanation] I just bought them so they could have some business. That to me was the fastest way to support somebody. [inner thinking or guiding principle]
	If I decide I can't go in again I'll probably do that, or I'll just see if I can pick up some food and give them a big tip, or something like that. [conjecture] I just felt like I had to do something, so gift cards were the first thing that I did before we even ordered out. [inner thinking or guiding principle]
Listener:	Yeah, yeah. [support] I'm glad you remembered that. [session mode] That's a great point [support] and it seems like giving a big tip is also important to you. That came up, both with the delivery . . . [earlier you said]

Person15:	The same thing did happen in the restaurants. When we did that, we did always give a big tip [explanation] since they were taking the chance too, to have to come to work. [inner thinking]
Listener:	They were taking a chance. [simple reflection]
Person15:	I just think it's something we instinctively felt. [implied emotional reaction] We've always been generous tippers to begin with, [explanation] but it just felt like this is a weird world we're living in. [emotional reaction]
	And there weren't many people in the restaurant, so we were getting good service. So, there's no reason not to give a big tip. [inner thinking]

How Did That Go?

This part is optional, but if it feels right, you can chat with the person a bit, in session mode, about how the session itself felt for them. Back in the Recruiting for Research chapter, I listed what a potential candidate is wondering, before they agree to participate. This even applies to stakeholders and colleagues that you want to do listening sessions with. Here are the three things they're wondering:

- If the experience is worth my time
- If you respect my perspective
- What am I going to get out of this in the long-term? Will you make solutions to better fit my approach to my purpose?

So, at the end of the listening session, you can ask, *"How did that go?"* and find out if they mention anything in these categories.

The Thank-You Gift

If this is a research study, and if there is time, you will want to revisit the thank-you gift option that the participant chose in the information session, to make sure it's still their preferred choice. Or if the participant did not specify a choice at that time, you can go over the choices and note their preference. You can also do this with the participant later, via another communication method.

Remember from the previous chapter, the best thank-you gift to the participant is two-fold, and that the first bullet point is the one that many organizations fail at:

+ Make solutions to better fit different participants' approaches to the purpose, and
+ Giving the participant something of value, like money or a gift card, in the interim, for their time in the listening session—and often also for their time in the information session. An alternative is a donation in their name, in case they can't receive money.

Communicating with the participants after the listening sessions is part of providing participants with greater value. At the end of the listening session, you can chat with them about what to expect in this regard. Here is an example:

Listener:	Okay. It has been excellent to get to know you. Is there anything else that you thought we would be chatting about that you want to bring up? [the closing question]
Person06:	I had something, but I'm trying to figure out the words for that something. [session mode]
	So, this whole recording and everything, this is just going to be used for teaching how to do research, right? [how the research might improve the purpose of deciding to go to a restaurant during the pandemic]
Listener:	Yes, without any identifying information. [session mode, reassuring]
Person06:	And it might be used for potential like – I think when I talked to \<person's name\>, he was telling me about how he wants to know how restaurants are affected by the pandemic and he also wanted to know how patrons are affected by the pandemic too, right? [reference to information session]
Listener:	Right. I think one of the things that he's interested in doing is understanding how patrons are affected and what the thinking is **so that restaurants can communicate more clearly**.
	Like that shock that you had with the tip being added in already. It's like if it was communicated then you wouldn't have to feel that shock. That kind of thing.

> Generally what we do is we have a transcript made and delete the recordings within a certain period of time. Ordinarily the restaurants, they will not see the transcript. It's too much for them to take in.
>
> What they will see is some concepts that various people said, not associated with your name, but maybe a little quote summarized as a concept, like "feel shocked when I saw the amount, the bill total, which made me double check."

Even in listening sessions meant for relationship-development, this part of the ending process is important. If you are listening to a colleague that you want to collaborate with more smoothly, you can mention insights you have now. You can show your understanding of where their actions or preferences come from. (If you need time to process what you learned, you can save this communication for later.)

If you are listening to a project stakeholder, you can take this time to explain how the patterns across all the project stakeholders will help you guide that project. Or you can explain that if there is a lack of patterns it means there is probably some miscommunication or misalignment among the group members.

In cases where your team can work on ideas and solutions with people, a great way to wrap up the listening session is to mention opportunities for collaborating, idea-generation, co-creation, or seeing if any of them want to evaluate the solution ideas you land on. You might chat about how to include this person and/or others in their community and outline a schedule for this.

The Recording

If you are doing audio or video, don't turn off the recording until the person has left the conversation. It's a common phenomenon for people to feel a bit freer to delve into personal stories when you tell them that you turned off the recording—and in that case you will lose the story. (Don't "trick" them into doing this by saying you're turning off the recording, but not actually doing it. That's not legal.)

If you are doing the listening session via text chat, then you might need to remember to save the chat.

Right After the Listening Session

Now the listening session is over. Yes, you can reach out to the person later to clarify something that they mentioned. But for today, you have two more things to do.

Whether you are doing research or relationship-building, reserve the twenty minutes immediately after the listening session to accomplish these two things. I like to set a timer and make myself do it within that timeframe, while my mind is still filled with the person's thinking.

1. Crack open the topics that you remember and scribble down just the interior cognition concepts (as summaries) from those topics.
2. Create a nickname for this person in a research study, so you don't use their real name in your team work.

The majority of your twenty minutes will be devoted to the first step. Scribbling a set of interior cognition concepts that you remember replaces written notes about the session. (The record of the session, as a transcript, also replaces written notes.) Listening deeply is about understanding another person's way of thinking as they address their purpose, and so you want to avoid introducing your own point of view in notes *about* the person. Instead, write a list of interior cognition concepts from *their* point of view, using some of their language.

Only write down interior cognition concepts: inner thinking, emotional reactions, or guiding principles. You can use some of the explanation, scene setting, or opinion as supporting details of these summaries. But the summary itself starts with the verb representing the inner thinking, or the emotional reaction, or the guiding principle. The verb is followed by the key point—the thing the person was "verb"-ing.

You've seen some of these summaries already in Chapter Three. Here is that list again, but just showing the interior cognition concepts:

Concept	Concept Type
Re-start grocery delivery at the start of the pandemic, after having stopped when I retired because it felt too decadent for a person who had time to get to the store	Inner thinking
Recognize that my cough could be more than just allergies, because I had been out where there were people who could have had COVID	Inner thinking
Quarantine myself for two weeks to see what's going on with my cough	Inner thinking
Feel confident setting up a grocery order with Giant Delivery because I have done it before	Emotional reaction
Feel pleasure that COVID gave me the excuse to let someone deliver my groceries right to my kitchen again	Emotional reaction

It takes a little practice to format these summaries, but it's worth it in the end. These summaries are a direct way for you to remember this person's thinking quickly. During synthesis, I go through the record of the session and write a summary of *every* interior cognition concept, so I can compare them with other participants' summaries and see the patterns more easily. For now, just write the ones that you remember, for a quick reference before you do synthesis.

The second step is to choose a unique nickname using some of the memorable wording the person used. You want a short name unique to this person that helps you remember this person months or years later. The only rule is that this name must be something this person would be happy to associate with.

Here are some examples that are phrases people from different studies used about themselves:

- Stronger, Tougher, Kinder
- Neat & Pressed
- Just be Prepared
- Integrate My Life

- I'm a Tinkerer
- Black Octopus

Don't use generic phrases that depict your idea of this person's personality. "Always Trying," or "Tentative But Determined." Personality nicknames will *not* help you distinguish this person later. Worse, personality nicknames include some judgment on your part about the person. So, avoid personality-based nicknames.

Often, I'm near the end of my twenty minutes when I have to make the nickname, which forces me to pick something quickly.

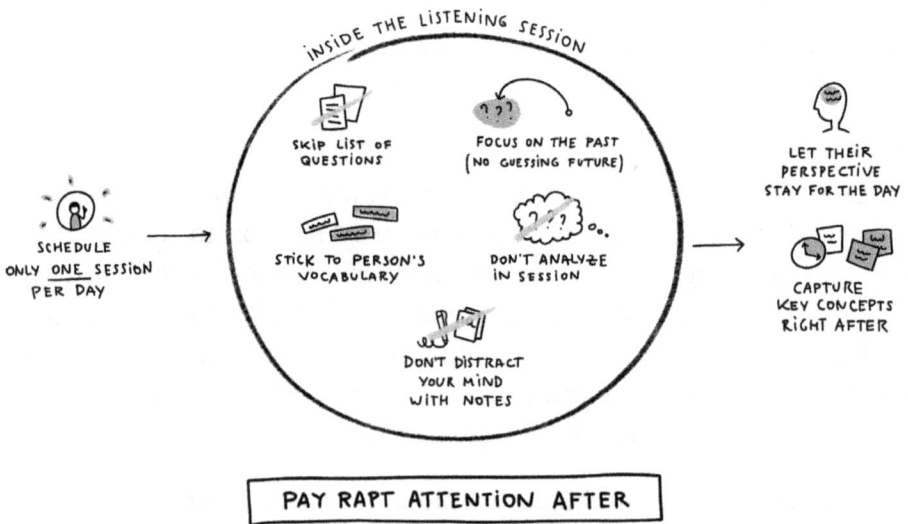

INSIDE THE LISTENING SESSION

SCHEDULE ONLY ONE SESSION PER DAY

SKIP LIST OF QUESTIONS

FOCUS ON THE PAST (NO GUESSING FUTURE)

STICK TO PERSON'S VOCABULARY

DON'T ANALYZE IN SESSION

DON'T DISTRACT YOUR MIND WITH NOTES

LET THEIR PERSPECTIVE STAY FOR THE DAY

CAPTURE KEY CONCEPTS RIGHT AFTER

PAY RAPT ATTENTION AFTER

Practice Listening Deeply

Introduce techniques one-by-one to your listening practice, rather than all at once. You may wish to arrange practice listening sessions, perhaps with colleagues or stakeholders that you want to build relationships with through deeper understanding.

Here are the first three techniques that I suggest focusing on:

- Asking what went through your mind
- Pinning to a past time & place
- Allowing space in conversation

After a few formal listening sessions, you will start to feel comfortable with the techniques above. At that point, here are two more to introduce to your practice:

- Noticing pull-tabs
- Micro-reflections (as well as simple-reflections, if you want)

Stick with these techniques for a few weeks or months, then go back to sections of this chapter that you're aware are missing in your listening practice, and pick a few. Maybe focus on transitions, or ending the listening session. Review the sections that you connect with. And have fun! Listening deeply can be very rewarding for both people involved.

Summing Up

Getting to a person's interior cognition is the heart of listening deeply. Listen, therefore, with a mindset of respect and support for the person. Use the techniques described here to hand the lead over to the participant. Ask how their thinking came about. Pay rapt attention. That, in turn, allows you a chance to understand their perspective without your own cognition shading what you learn.

At the end of the session, if everything goes well, the person will have had a chance to delve into concepts no one else has asked them about. They will hopefully come away with a sense of feeling understood. They may even thank you for the experience.

Feeling understood is so rare and precious.

That's what you want to make happen. For the space of the listening session, the goals of your organization fall away. Your own goals fall away. You are free to focus only on that person. It's often an experience where you feel so engrossed in the person's approach to the purpose that you don't notice time passing. You will likely end the session with the feeling that you have been elsewhere for a while, and that you are changed when you return.

Vocabulary List

Closing question: to make it easy for the person, guide them back to what they were thinking as they anticipated the listening session, and what they expected to bring up: "Is there anything else you expected to cover today?"

Conjecture: a question about a person's future actions, expression, or interior cognition, which causes them to guess (avoid in all but market research, co-creation).

Description-layer question: asking for more detail about an explanation, scene, or fact that the person mentioned, which usually results in more of the same (avoid for deep listening, except for clarification).

Expression-layer question: asking about a person's opinion, preference, perception, behavior, or attitude, which will usually not bring up interior cognition (avoid for deep listening, except as support).

Fill in the blank: encouraging the person to go into detail by saying "and …" followed by a pause; similar words like "because …" will also work.

Find the roots: help the person return to the time when an opinion, preference, perception, behavior, or attitude initially formed, to understand their interior cognition back then.

Leading question: a question worded in a way that suggests you know what the answer is, guiding the person in the direction you indicate (avoid universally).

Micro-reflection: mentioning a pull-tab the person brought up, but not as a complete sentence, to encourage the person to unfold more details about a topic.

More about that: broadly asking a person to give more details, in hopes of understanding their interior cognition.

Pin to a past place & time: help the participant more easily talk about their interior cognition by connecting it to a particular event in the past.

Pull-tab: words that indicate there might be interior cognition that the person hasn't unfolded yet; phrases, hints, emotional shading, assumed understanding, "of course".

Turn passive into active: passive action happens to a person, and you can help them more easily speak of their interior cognition by asking about their intentional actions and reactions.

What went through your mind: specifically asking about a person's interior cognition.

Endnotes

1   Angel R Bethea, "Types of Reflections," Georgia Department of Behavioral Health and Developmental Disabilities, accessed December 31, 2021, https://dbhdd.georgia.gov/sites/dbhdd.georgia.gov/files/related_files/site_page/Types of Reflections.pdf.
2   William R. Miller, in Listening Well: The Art of Empathic Understanding (Eugene, OR: Wipf & Stock, 2018), 27-28.

CHAPTER 7

ENSURING A SAFE SPACE   216

CHAPTER 7

Ensuring a Safe Space

When listening deeply, ethics are involved. You are dealing with people's interior cognition, and it is your responsibility to build a safe environment for your participant, to avoid negative consequences to them.

You never want to force, coerce, or entreat a person to relate their interior cognition. You are there not to extract stories nor to forge insights. You are there to hold a safe space for the other person, and to notice when that space does not feel safe. If something makes them feel vulnerable to your judgment, to privacy invasion, to lack of control over what you'll do with their "data," then you will take steps to repair, support, or let them exit the listening session.

You are not an expert in how they think; you are a witness. You can notice their signals, be sensitive to their emotions and experience, and show yourself worthy of trust. You can ensure the session is ethical. This chapter will show you how.

What Is a Safe Space?

Culturally, a safe space is somewhere for people to meet and communicate without being harassed, discriminated against, or harmed for being who they are. Many universities have a designated safe space. Places of worship, your home, a bar or pub—safe spaces take many forms, including virtual safe spaces, now that we have them. In some countries, there is legal protection associated with safe spaces. The concept of a safe space is part of therapy, as well, meaning a place for two people to communicate deeply without fear that the topics will be repeated outside of that session.

A safe space in a listening session is necessary for the person to feel comfortable discussing their interior cognition. It is the foundation on which the listener and participant will build their connection and mutual trust. There are lots of things that can affect a safe space, like if you are listening to a stakeholder who has authority over your position and could potentially fire you. Likewise, if the participant sees you as a person who can bring attention and support to a need of their community, but you don't act that way, it affects the safe space. I'll explain how to recognize when this is happening, and what to do.

Security, Trust, and Connection

During the listening session you are monitoring the natural rhythm of the person moving in between session mode and memory mode. In the beginning of Chapter Six, I used the analogy of a dolphin or whale coming to the surface of the water to breathe and then going back down. Monitoring this surfacing and diving is a mental program running in the background of your mind.

A listener's three cognitive activities:
1. Pay rapt attention
2. Monitor whether the concept type is exterior or interior
   - Monitor for indications there might be interior cognition (pull-tabs)
   - If the person does not dive into a topic, help them to do so at some point in the listening session
3. Be aware if the person has popped back into the session mode of the listening session
   - Help the person feel comfortable in the session
   - **Help the person feel safe in the session, or let them exit**

Most participants need to feel secure that you will respect their point of view and not extract information they consider private or that makes them feel vulnerable. It is your job to begin building the safe space in the information session, and to continue it throughout the listening session. Applied ethics[1] includes paying attention to consequences, and the consequences of not supporting a person in a safe space include mental and emotional harms, such as these examples:

- feeling triggered
- feeling accused or criticized
- being made to think my interior cognition is not "right" somehow
- being treated as someone who does not have human rights

I'll cover some specific techniques to avoid these harms and to recover from mistakes, or to let the person exit the listening session. Later in this chapter are techniques for exiting the session.

Over and over during a session you will show your support. When a person feels safe, it is possible to trust. You saw some of this notation in the last chapter: [support]. The frequency of this notation in the examples is an indication of typical ongoing reassurances that the listening session is a safe space. There are a few other flavors of that notation that I will explain below.

Trust

Trust is an emotion that informs you whether it's okay to rely on someone or something. *Can I rely on the vendor to set up the software on time? Can I be sure my manager will keep their promise not to yell at me in front of the whole team? Is my new co-worker going to give me a hard time because of the way I like to dress? Will I need to suppress my political views to avoid people telling me I'm wrong?* People trust others when there is evidence that they and their ideas will be treated with respect and care. Some people are quick to trust; others are more wary. When trust fades, people engage the guiding principles they have built up over time for situations like this: for example, "Change the subject when someone asks me, 'But where are you really from?'"

Trust isn't usually total; you tend to trust others on a spectrum between "total trust" and "no trust" at all, and where you are on that spectrum moves. A person tends to build trust and withdraw trust, like a snail pulling its head into its shell, then poking it out later, unfurling antennae to sense the world again. This means a listener can often repair a mistake they make.

How Trust Works In a Listening Session

The decisions that a participant makes at each step of entering a partnership with you—putting their name in the hat for your research study, agreeing to the information session, being present for the listening session, telling you their truth, going to depth—each of these are decisions whether to trust you.

Throughout the listening session, the person will continue making decisions about whether you are safe and interested in what they are saying. They decide based on your responses. They'll poke out of their shell briefly at first, with less-vulnerable topics. Then as you show your constant support for them, they may open up more deeply and touch upon topics closer to their heart.

It generally takes 7 to 15 minutes for a participant to begin to trust you, and to have confidence as to what level of depth you are interested in. Once you hit that state of connection and depth, you'll be able to feel it. The person's responses will pick up more personality and self-direction.

Here's an example. In one study, I did a number of listening sessions about how different people had figured out how to save for retirement. Here is the moment when the person felt safe and understood, and began sharing their interior cognition.

Person: My parents didn't make enough money for retirement. They're almost penniless. [statement of fact] I'm having to give them money for food. [explanation]

I would do anything not to see them hurt like this. 😖 [implied inner thinking and pull-tab]

Listener: Oh ... oh 😰 [support] ... basics like food. [simple reflection] Oh, that's like ... the hurt is so real. ... [support]

They paused. I waited. And then they decided to trust me.

Person: I'm terrified. I mean, really terrified. What if that's me? 😟 [emotional reaction] If I skip happy hour, but then I'm not starving later. [inner thinking] That's a good thing, right? [emotional reaction] I don't have any kids. There's nobody to bail me out. [emotional reaction]

Listener: So you skip happy hour. [simple reflection]

Person: Yeah. I don't have a choice, do I? [emotional reaction or inner thinking and pull-tab] But how do I save for my retirement when I'm already giving them money? 😟 [inner thinking and pull-tab]

This person's depth of feelings and pain are what are currently forming some guiding principles for them. The pull-tabs can lead there, to see what has emerged so far. That's where we went next in the session.

This level of vulnerability isn't unusual in a listening session. In this session, the person felt safe being vulnerable because I was able to demonstrate that they were in a safe space. The participant thanked me after the session for allowing them to explore their relationship with retirement and their parents in a new way.

Techniques for Hosting a Safe Space

Safety in a listening session means that the person believes you won't trample on their sense of self. They know they won't be doubted or manipulated or dismissed. They can speak about themselves without posturing or judgement. They can explain their experiences, their inner thinking, guiding principles, and emotional reactions. They can feel understood. Fortunately, this kind of safety can be cultivated with intention.

There are four techniques that I use to promote this kind of emotional safety:

1. Recognize and acknowledge the other person's mood
2. Demonstrate that you are listening closely

3. Show that you are not judging them, that their thinking and emotions are valid

4. Bring the warmth of your own personality to the conversation

Each technique can take you a long way toward creating a safe space, but they become especially powerful when you use all four. Used together, they create a "feedback loop" of attention, validation, and respect that the person can feel.

Let's explore each of them in turn.

1. Recognize and Acknowledge the Person's Mood

An important part of creating emotional safety is showing the other person that you sense and respect their mood. If you can say something that **shows them you notice their mood**, the participant may unconsciously feel reassured that you understand them. This is easiest in person, and it gets more difficult when you are communicating remotely or in a written form.

The mood-reflecting technique can help you navigate all sorts of interactions in addition to listening sessions. For example, for several years I have helped direct traffic arriving at the beach finish line of a large footrace. Inevitably, the non-racing beachgoers arrive around the same time and are irritated to find the beach parking lots already teeming with spectators. Drivers have often been stuck in unexpected traffic for 30-40 minutes. When each driver pulls up to my traffic control position, they're on edge. I start with eye contact, smile, and an open-ended question or observation to reflect their current mood.

If I sense frustration and despair from the other person:

Me: Oh my gosh, this traffic is crazy.

If I see a haggard driver with a car full of sullen passengers and beach things:

Me: Not the beach day you were anticipating.

If I sense anxiety, and the person seems worried about trying to get somewhere in time, with no beach things in their car:

Me: You're here to find your runner?

Acknowledging the driver's mood aloud takes the person from ready to yell at me to ready to engage. When they finish complaining about the traffic, they are ready to focus on what they need to do next.

The technique has three simple steps:

1. Sense the person's mood. Do you know why they're feeling what they're feeling?
2. Pick an informal, open-ended comment that references the circumstance.
3. Say the comment with an emotional tone and language that matches theirs.

The emotional tone and language are key. At the race, if I address the driver with neutral tone and body language, as if I didn't notice or didn't care what they were going through, the mismatch between my tone and the person's mood would tend to make them more upset. Acknowledging their mood shows them that you are paying attention to them, that their feelings are valid, and that you are not judging them.

Noticing someone's mood in a remote session is slightly more difficult because, in session mode, you must sense their implied emotion about the session itself. This can be accomplished while you are starting the session, paying attention to whether the person's greetings and responses are terse or more friendly. As the session unfolds, you'll have a better sense of how the person expresses themselves, and you can then notice when the length of their responses changes. Longer responses might indicate feelings of comfort with the session, whereas short responses might indicate a shift in mood. This is not always true for every person, though.

You'll also pay attention to what implied emotion about the session is being conveyed in those responses. The person might indicate distrust with words that dismiss your question or that signal unwillingness to talk about a topic anymore. "My schedule has gotten busier than I anticipated today." "I am not sure why you are asking." "I'm running out of time." "That's everything." "Enough about that." In audio communication, you might notice indications the person makes with their breath—sighs or huffs that might mean impatience. In non-audio communication, you will rely solely on those words, though.

2. Demonstrate That You Are Listening

Use signals to affirm the participant. Connect with their story by using small exclamations and agreements. Phrases like, "yeah" or "mm-hmm" work in the U.S. culture, and other cultures have more phrases. You can use these phrases in written communication, too. In person, you can also use laughter, chuckling, out-breaths, snorts, and small sounds that indicate surprise or amazement. Emojis take the place of these in text. In emotionally charged moments, respond with a little more intensity than usual, to match. You can use wording like, "Oh no!" or "crazy!" or "That's wonderful!" The goal is to show you're paying attention.

For example, a person might say:

Person:	Oh, I was under a lot of pressure. The clock was ticking, [explanation or implied emotional reaction] and I was wracking my brain for a way to write the conclusion [inner thinking]—and then it came to me! [implied emotional reaction] I could tell my brother's story. But I totally forgot the scientific detail. So, I called him, and I got his voicemail." [explanation]
Listener:	Voicemail! [support]

You could also say something as simple as, "Oh no!" to show you are following them closely. Any one of many responses can show the participant you are paying attention.

Also, try referencing something they said earlier in a way that connects to the present conversation. It will demonstrate that you have been listening, which makes it safe for them to speak at more length.

Person:	So how can I help people act within the constraints of this capitalist, patriarchal society? I'm a big believer in helping people act to help make things better for everybody. 🖐
Listener:	That's why you started the non-profit?

| Person: | 👍The thing I was trying to do then was … |

Connecting to earlier points shows that you are tracking. Occasionally, you will get the reference wrong, but the person will correct you. And, if you accept the correction without defense, you promote trust here as well.

Person:	I want my son to grow up surrounded by aunts and grandparents. [preference] That kind of familial connection is important to me. [implied guiding principle] But since I moved away from my family—I had to get out of that small town [implied inner thinking]—we don't get to see each other much. My son doesn't get to become familiar with his grandparents and aunts. [explanation] So, that's what we're stuck with. [implied emotional reaction]
Listener:	You're a little wistful not having family close by. [complex reflection]
Person:	Well, not exactly. [session mode] I really had to move; I always wanted to get out of that small town. Since I was little. [generalized inner thinking or explanation] So it's more about how to create a version of that family closeness but while living away. [generalized inner thinking]
Listener:	Oh! So … [fill-in-the-blank]
Person:	So, that's why I was thinking about
	(story continues)

Of course, it is possible to say too much, or respond too often, or use the same "oh wow!" response every time. If what you say distracts the person, it can disrupt the conversation and their sense of trust. If the participant goes quiet, they may be wondering what's going on with you.

As always, if you make a mistake, gently bring yourself and the person back to the last thing they said.

3. Show that You are Not Judging Them

Participants want to be sure that the person listening won't belittle their inner thinking, dismiss their emotional reactions, or judge them. The easiest way to demonstrate lack of judgment is to use words to show that you recognize their interior cognition is authentic.

When they have introduced a concept representing their perspective, in-ject a small sentence that shows you believe their perspective is valid. It doesn't have to be anything big.

In this example, the participant is talking about plane travel to visit fam-ily during the COVID pandemic of 2020. Their husband was already exposed to COVID at his work and had to quarantine for two weeks. Nonetheless, they allowed a relative to come for a visit to see the new baby. There is a good chance the person could feel judged for what they decided to do, if the listener responds in reserved manner.

Person:	I knew, from the get-go I was going to pick her up at the airport and just deal with it because she's family, [guiding principle] and when else do you have the first niece born in your lifetime. [inner thinking] She lost her job due to COVID, so I really wanted to make sure she had something good happen during COVID. [inner thinking]
Listener:	And it seems like it was important to you to sort of support her in having something positive happen after that. [support: not judging]
Person:	Yeah. She's had a lot of hard knocks in her life and I just thought she doesn't need this one – missing her niece. [inner thinking] As an aunt, she just wanted to see that baby. [explanation]
Listener:	Um-hmm, um-hmm. [support: not judging]
Person:	She had a very good visit. [opinion]
Listener:	That's so wonderful that she got to do that. [support: not judging]
Person:	My husband supported me on that too because it would affect him, obviously, if she brought something in the house. [explanation or implied emotional reaction] But we talked about that too [explanation] and decided family was worth taking the risk. [guiding principle]

In this example, the listener may not agree with the person's decision around COVID issues. It doesn't matter. To listen effectively, try not to let your opinions on the subject enter into your mind during the conversation. Do your best not to judge the person at all. Instead, keep your mind fully focused on supporting them. (The next chapter will outline what to do when you face statements that make you feel a stronger reaction.)

A Dragon Can Help You Stay Out of Judgment

Judgment is disruptive to a listening session. Even if you say nothing or try to hide it, your attention to what the person is saying has been blocked for a moment. You may not follow this particular topic the way you need to. When judgment enters the session, it also tends to break the feeling of trust that the participant needs to keep going. You may not be able to get to interior cognition with that person on that topic again.

Responding with judgment is a normal, human instinct. Here's a way to help you past it.

Once you recognize your judgment, it may be helpful to remember that you're only seeing a few moments of the person's life. They have had a whole lifetime of inner thinking, a whole lifetime of reactions, defenses and self-defenses. To get past your judgment, picture the person as a dragon, like the traditional Chinese dragons. These dragons have large heads with a mane around their head, and very long, sinuous bodies that extend behind them. The head of the dragon is how the person shows up as they address their purpose, and the long body is the person's past, always there.

PRESENT →
• THOUGHTS
• EMOTIONS
• ACTIONS
• SPEECH

PAST
EXPERIENCE
(influences present)

Each person has a long history that brought them to each moment in their purpose. In each of those moments, their long, sinuous body of experience is influencing their inner thinking, emotional reactions, and guiding principles. In each moment, they are the whole dragon.

When you have a reaction to what they did, their inner thinking, emotional reaction, or guiding principle, remember that it was driven by *their* experience, not yours. They are recounting *their* memory. Even if you were there for that memory, it's *their* dragon body, not yours, driving their interior cognition.

The next time you encounter someone whose reasoning feels very wrong to you, picture the dragon, and respect their history.

Another point related to not judging the person is when you notice contradictions in what they said. This often happens when a person is exploring what went through their mind, peeling back layers of self-understanding. A person might tell you one thing about their inner thinking or emotional reaction, then change it a little bit later when an insight occurs to them about what was really going through their mind at the time. People aren't always clear about what's going on in their mind, so the process of explaining it to a listener often results in these kinds of clarifications. Let this process unfold for the person. Refrain from pointing out contradictions, because that shows you've been judging them all along.

4. Bring the Warmth of Your Personality

In a listening session, it's important to be your authentic self. Specifically, you need to be *you*, not the stereotypical "researcher" or "professional." This means you can relax and show some of your personality. If you are worried you are going to make a mistake, if you are doubtful that a listening session can be empirical, recognize that in yourself, and set it aside so that you can approach the session in a relaxed way and take pleasure in getting to know this other human being.

I see many listeners fumble the trust connection with a participant because they act too formal, and that formality calls attention to the traditional, research-defined relationship between "subject" and "researcher." Formal phrasing like, "thank-you-for-that," tends to interrupt the participant's sense of safety in the session and pulls them out memory mode back to session mode. It keeps the conversation focused on your needs rather than their purpose.

Why do I encourage you to show up as yourself? Most people you are interacting with will be able to unconsciously tell when you are not feeling positive about hearing from them. This kind of disconnect clangs around in the person's awareness, making the listening session more like an obligation than an engaging exploration of their thoughts. They won't be able to give you their full attention if they keep wondering about what feels "off."

So don't worry about seeming "unprofessional" or fumbling a few seconds for what to say next. Strings of words like, "Uh, okay … yeah, this is … you know…" as you find your way to a response are fine. You're not going to confuse them. They will realize it's okay if they also wander as they try to express what went through their mind. Many less-than-perfectly-clear concepts will pass between you, and if there is trust, you can delve into the concepts to make sense of them together.

Example 1: A Warm Conversation

What does "being yourself" look like in practice? Let's look at one example of what happens when a listener shows warmth and personality. The person's purpose is taking care of their clothing.

Listener: So, back to that whole idea of you mentioning "the preservationist in me." [earlier you said] Where did that come from? [find the root]

Person: I like to take good care of things. [preference or implied guiding principle] I just generally in my life get a little bit annoyed when things get marked and kind of ruined because of unconscious treatment of things—just disregard. Like for example, wearing jeans on a sofa that then rubs off slightly blue. [slightly generalized emotional reaction and pull-tab]

I kind of try not to do those things and try to keep on top of those things to make things stay nice for longer because it costs so much to replace stuff. [guiding principle] So, it does apply to a lot of things in my life. [generalization]

Listener: Agh, jeans rubbing off blue. [support] It sounds like maybe there's a story that caused you to develop this habit? [find the root]

Person: Yeah, so, at points in my life where I have money, I spend money on nice clothes. [guiding principle] At points where I don't have any money, I'm like, "Thank goodness I bought those nice things because now I still look smart and I've got lots of things I can wear." [slightly generalized inner thinking]

Yeah, if I can afford it, I will spend as much as I can on something nice. [same guiding principle] Which might be a price that would make someone's jaw drop. They would go, "Why would you spend that on that?" [explanation or scene setting] And I would be like, "Well, because it's beautiful and because I know it will last and I know I will get good wear out of it and it looks sharp and it makes me feel great." [inner thinking and implied emotional reaction]

So, I would buy just that one item that I know will go with a few other things and that I will be able to [generalized inner thinking] – It's not high demand items. It's not something you wear once in a blue moon. [explanation] It's something that will transcend day and night normally and will transcend little bit of going out during the day, early evening, and maybe a little bit of work as well. [generalized inner thinking]

I'm actually thinking of a jacket, a tailored jacket that I have that is a designer jacket and it's made out of – it's a very thin, fine wool with a pinstripe through it, and it's also got a little bit of detail on it that actually looks like seller tape, like sticky tape, [statement of fact] but it's got a design and it's super cool; I love that jacket. [opinion]

Listener: So there is this idea of preserving a beautifully designed item for as long as possible [simple reflection] and this idea that you just mentioned of the way it can work for a lot of different situations. [simple reflection] But the whole idea is that you really want to look smart. [earlier you said]

Person: Yeah. [session mode]

Listener: What does that mean? [non-embarrassed]

Person: Okay, so it's not necessarily immaculate, but it's looking clean and the clothes looking as sharp as they did when I bought them. So that means the shape of the clothing; it hasn't lost its shape. [explanation and reference to earlier guiding principle]

For example, you have tracksuit bottoms that go out in the knee and have derrière marks... So, it loses its line, and it doesn't look as sharp as it used to. It's the same with the T-shirt, the same with a pair of trousers. [explanation] So, I take care of that designer jacket. [same guiding principle] I could never, ever replace that jacket. It's from a collection a long time ago, [statement of fact] and it's also a very timeless shape, [explanation] so I kind of imagine having that one for years. [inner thinking]

And I also imagine that being something that in maybe 10, 20 years that somebody says, you know when things come around again, and someone says, "Hey, where did you get that?" [conjecture]

And I'm like, "Hey, it's vintage, this." You know? [projected strong emotional reaction, joy]

Both: (Laughter)

Person: I think that's gonna fill me with like a big smile, yeah. [a driver of that same guiding principle]

Both: (Laughter)

Example 2: Distant and Formal

Repeating a single phrase like "I understand," or "I hear you," can feel cold and mechanical. Sometimes I hear a researcher say, "thank you for that," which puts too much focus on the transaction of the listening session itself. The participant is giving something, and the listener is thanking them for it. That exchange feels unnatural, especially if it's done repeatedly.

Here's an example of how this dynamic plays out, in this case from a practice listening session.

Person: When I pay to go out and see something, I generally go to see live music. [generalization] I am trying to think. [session mode] It's kind of funny... I was getting my car fixed recently, and people were rehearsing this dance show on the side of the building.

So, they were actually hanging from the building by ropes. They were doing a whole performance, [scene setting] and that was kind of cool to see. [opinion and pull-tab]

I didn't actually go there to see that, but I just happened to be in the neighborhood, and I watched it for a few minutes. [statement of fact] That was really different. [opinion and pull-tab]

Listener: That's really interesting to know. [session mode, distant and formal]

Person: (pauses, wondering if they said something wrong)

Listener: Well, now I want to move to another topic. [session mode, in control instead of following]

Notice how "that's really interesting to know" acts almost like a judgment. It pulls the participant away from their topic, making them pause to figure out what the listener wants.

Instead of "that's really interesting to know," a more experienced listener might have continued with something like:

Listener:	Wow! [support] Dancing on the side of the building! [simple reflection]
Person:	Yep! It stopped me in my tracks. [implied emotional reaction or inner thinking and pull-tab]
Listener:	What went through your mind at that point? [what went through your mind]

If they had continued the conversation in this way, it is likely the person would have explained what they were thinking and feeling at that moment. They might have described being in a hurry and the mindfulness they put into staying to watch. They could have talked about an experience they'd had which made them vow to enjoy random life events like this. Instead, because the listener chose transactional wording, the participant thought that part of the conversation was at an end. The listener only got the shallow and passing statement, "that was really different," from the participant.

When you recognize and match the other person's mood, demonstrate that you are listening, stay out of judgment, and bring warmth and your authentic personality, you create a safe environment for your participant.

Signals That Safety is Fading

It's natural to lose a small degree of trust at various points in every listening session, and then repair your connection with the other person. But it's less common for the safety to truly fade. So, it's helpful to know the signals that indicate the evaporation of safety. When you notice these signals, you probably need to end the session.

These signals can appear at any point in the listening session. Be alert for them, because it's part of a listener's three cognitive activities. Later in this chapter I explain how to end a session that is no longer feeling safe.

Less Willingness to Answer at Length

At any point in the listening session, you might sense that the participant is just tired of your prodding to speak about their interior cognition. They might just be exhausted. Either way, you'll want to return to session mode to see how the person is feeling. You'll encounter phrases showing reluctance to get into detail, like, "That's just how it goes." "That seems like something that would be clear."

Uneasiness About the Nature of the Listening Session

If the participant is trying to figure out what kind of answers you want and doesn't seem comfortable telling you what went through their mind, then possibly they are uncomfortable with unfolding their interior cognition for you. Or possibly it's just a topic they wish they had not brought up. Phrases like, "I don't know how to answer," and, "I feel like I'm not being useful," will appear in their discourse.

Getting Testy About Repeating Their Answer

Sometimes without knowing it, in your pursuit of their interior cognition, you will annoy the person with your persistence after one topic. The participant will feel as if they've explained everything they know about it, but you just keep asking. Their answers will become short and pointed. "I've already explained it." "Like I said before..." "I think you haven't heard me."

Growing Distrust About How You Will Use Their Answers

As the listening session unfolds, the participant may begin to feel like their answers about interior cognition are painting *too* detailed a picture for you. They worry that the depth of their answers may be used against them, or against an organization they're associated with. If this happens, they may withdraw from answering at all. Instead they may use phrases like, "Tell me again what this study is for?" "I feel like you're trying to get our company secrets."

Wanting to Be Finished

If the person is getting antsy, pausing to pay attention to other messages, responding to interruptions away from the session, or (in an audio method of communication) making sighs or other similar vocalizations, it's probably a signal that they want to get on with other things in their day. You might encounter phrasing like, "Sorry, I'll be right back," or, "How much longer are we going to be?"

The above are indications that you need to check with the person in session mode and make a decision together whether to end the session. There are likely to be other, additional signals that you may encounter in your own work.

Situations That May Challenge Safety

There are a few situations where there is a potential for serious erosion of trust, where it's necessary to return to session mode immediately and let the person know they don't have to continue. You can offer to move on to another topic or to end the session. Continue only if the other person affirms that they are willing.

Sensitive Topics

There are topics that a participant may feel hesitant to share, for worry of disapproval or embarrassment. There are always specific topics sensitive to one person that may not be sensitive to others, but some common topics that may come up in your research are:

- Experiences of discrimination or harassment
- Eating habits
- Medication usage
- Spending or saving habits
- Salary and other assets

- Productivity
- In countries with authoritarian regimes, any topics that challenge the regime

(These examples are related to purposes that organizations have been interested in understanding. However, you might find yourself studying something like physical or mental abuse, sports or coach abuse, death, religion and religious practices, etc. You will want to make sure you have advanced training in those kinds of topics or employ a certified psychologist or social worker to conduct the session.)

With sensitive topics it is especially critical to show respect and non-judgment. Go slowly; keep checking in with them to ask if they'd like to proceed. If they want to continue, gauge how comfortable they are with discussing the topic at the description and expression layers before going for interior cognition. The person might be fine at the outer layers, but not any deeper.

Monitor for the signals of fading trust listed above. Even if you can't identify exactly why the person suddenly seems uncomfortable, don't hesitate. If the moment is causing stress, return to the session mode to offer the person other options.

If your awareness of hitting sensitive ground is not your best skill, and you expect a particular listening session to cover these sorts of topics, consider asking someone else with better sensitivity to conduct that session. The emotional safety and comfort of the participant is *important*. If there is no one else to step in, then begin the session with an explanation that you would like the person to let you know when you've reached sensitive ground. If you've already built a little trust with this person in the information session, then they will probably be happy to let you know.

An Insider Connection

When sensitive topics come up, a person will sometimes react to the topic by becoming silent or shortening answers. In other cases, they may actually speak at *more* length. This often happens when they pick up on something about you that they assume you have in common with them, such as a philosophy, culture, or lived experience. If they assume the two of you have this important thing in common, they may share interior cognition on a sensitive topic that you would not have heard otherwise. This is a dynamic that Jazmyn Latimer calls "insider-outsider," as "insiders" may automatically get more depth and truth than "outsiders" are entitled to.

Jazmyn, a researcher who is the daughter of a police officer, tells the story of a situation she experienced. In 2019 she was conducting a study for Code for America's *Clear My Record* initiative, aiming to help District Attorneys across California implement a law about marijuana conviction relief, since marijuana was no longer illegal. To see how DAs currently helped clients clear their arrest records, she sat in on many meetings between DAs and their clients. (Note that she was listening in person, and this is important.) Jazmyn is Black, and in one meeting, so was the DA's client. When the DA walked out of the room briefly, the client turned to her and said, "Hey, we Black people have to advocate for ourselves." And then went on to tell her some details he wouldn't have told someone else. He assumed she'd had experiences that would help her understand him.

Jazmyn tells us, "The trust is just *there* when it's another person who's Black." It's like she has an insider connection with the person, even though she may not have the same background and experiences. "The trust that forms can be insightful, but also awkward. There can be un-wanted information you are privy to. You can begin to doubt whether the person is being truthful or code switching."

This assumed trust was based on physical appearance. That visual layer of the communication can trigger assumptions. In my work, I try to avoid these assumptions by leaning toward audio or written listening sessions, when these formats work for the participant. This removes some of the opportunity for the insider connection to enter the session. While it means you can miss an easy chance at connection, you can still build that connection, and build it more accurately by acknowledging what a person is saying.

Jazmyn Latimer and other practitioners have larger questions about the inside-outsider dynamic in the context of ethics. When a conversation is conveying a truth that would not otherwise come up, when is it ethical to try to represent that truth, especially to stakeholders who are likely to deny it? Should the information be reported, to improve the organization and solution? Or was that information shared privately in the belief that it would remain that way? What are the consequences, for the participant, of me sharing the information?

As you develop your own trust relationships with participants, consider the terms of those relationships in the participant's context. If you can, discuss with the participant the appropriateness of sharing certain sensitive topics that they mentioned. If you decide it's appropriate to share, make sure to do it in a way that respects the agency, perspective, and personhood of the participant. Additionally, never use a study participant's name in your reporting, to protect their privacy.

Triggers in a Listening Session

There are situations where a strong response to a topic occurs, and you must end the session. It can happen to the participant, and it can happen to you. This section of the chapter describes how to notice these triggers, and the next section describes how to end the session.

Accidentally Triggering Someone

As a listener you have a responsibility to avoid triggering someone else. No matter how careful you are, you might cause someone a memory that causes a strong emotion, like anger, alarm, or pain. You might use a phrase that causes another person to focus on the differences between you, or to remember something difficult that happened to them.

How you handle this kind of mistake should depend on the severity of the trigger and the connection you've already built with the person. If you have built a strong connection, you have a chance that they will be willing to continue. Immediately admit your mistake, submit an apology, and see how the person responds.

You are most likely to be able to repair their trust if you notice and apologize immediately, without prompting. If you take too long to notice the infraction or to address it, you are unlikely to recover. Their feeling of safety may already have disappeared, in which case you will need to end the session.

Sometimes, you may notice the connection is broken, and you're not sure what has happened. In these cases, it's likely you've made a micro-aggression or other kind of triggering mistake of intent or of wording, without apologizing. Go ahead and end the session, embracing the fact that something went wrong. Then see if you can identify the issue in the transcript later, in case it's something you can avoid in the future.

How to Notice a Triggered Participant

A person who has been triggered is likely flooded with emotion. Their minds might also jump to the inner thinking and guiding principles that rush in because of this trigger. Because of what the person is experiencing, you may notice a long pause, a change in mood, or a shift to a different subject. People who are triggered may deal with you by ignoring what you said, making a passive comment about it, or directly mentioning the trigger.

Any of these responses will probably cause an emotional reaction in you, like embarrassment or defensiveness. Notice when these kinds of reactions occur and guide them out of your body. When you have guided your reaction away, focus on an apology, and on acknowledging with words the validity of their reaction.

There will be time for you to deal with your own emotions about your mistake after the session. Don't make it worse by talking about yourself in this moment.

Preparation to Avoid Triggering Someone

Earlier in this book I have said that you cannot do up-front preparation to understand a person's interior cognition. It is also unlikely that you can predict what might trigger a person. But you can learn the "loaded" phrases that connotate power imbalances, abuse, and painful cultural histories. You can find documentaries, texts, podcasts, and more which explore these topics in detail.

Pay particular attention if your own background has significant advantages that your participant may not have access to—for example, if you have been to university, grew up without having to be aware of disabilities, live in an area with access to fresh food, or feel welcome in places that your participant feels are off limits to them, and so on. These imbalances mean you are more likely to cause unintentional harm if you do not carefully prepare to be sensitive to their context.

The need for this preparation is an additional reason for hiring listeners from the culture and language of the person, especially for international work.

When You Get Triggered

There may be also times when the participant may trigger *you*. You will need to notice this in yourself and clear your mind just enough to decide whether the person has crossed a important **threshold**. On inside of the threshold, the person is talking about their thinking related to their purpose. On the outside of the threshold, the person is *not* communicating about the purpose they are addressing. They have gone outside the permeable boundary of the scope of the session. You get to make a choice.

On the inside of the threshold, where the person is talking about *their thinking related to their purpose*, you can either gather yourself and continue with the upsetting topic, or you can interrupt and end the session. If you believe there is something to be learned, and if you feel capable of dealing with the emotions from the trigger, you can forge ahead. Or your whirling, triggered mind may prefer to end the session. That's perfectly valid.

On the outside of the threshold, where the person is *not* communicating about the purpose they are addressing, then you have little chance of encountering the knowledge that you want to understand. You can interrupt and pull the person back to an earlier topic to explore, or you can interrupt to end the session. Your choice depends upon how safe you feel with the person, and whether they refuse to leave the topic that triggered you.

Whatever you decide, be very clear and settled within yourself about this decision. If you are doing the listening session remotely, that may feel like enough of a shield for you. But continuing in a circumstance where you might experience trauma or nightmares because of what was expressed is not a good idea.

When you are triggered, you are not obliged to continue the listening session. Your own mental health is at risk. I've heard researchers tell me, "But my boss insists that I must collect the data." There are laws in many countries that prevent employers from willfully putting their employee in harm's way. Being triggered counts as being harmed.

As an example, there is another story that Jazmyn Latimer told me. Jazmyn, as I've mentioned before, is the daughter of a police officer. So, when she found herself doing a study listening to police officers tell their stories about their work, a few of them knew her father. They felt free to speak to her as if she was one of them, using several racist phrases and epithets in course of describing their thinking about their work. (They did this despite clearly seeing that she is Black, in person.) She wasn't sure if they were saying these things because they thought she understood "the way things are" within the "police tribe" or because they thought her father spoke to her that way. She was triggered, overwhelmed with strong layers of emotions and confusion despite her many years of professional experience.

Jazmyn was able to push her feelings to the side in the moment and guide the conversation elsewhere, but the damage was done. She says the session affected her for days.

Here is another choice you can make, before the listening session even begins. If you legitimately suspect that a specific participant may trigger you, try to find another listener for them. Or, if that can't be accomplished, consider recruiting a different participant. Everyone deserves to be in a listening situation that is safe and free of pain, including you.

Deliberate Harassment

Rarely does a participant intentionally aim prejudice at a listener, but it does happen. Someone with harassment tendencies gets past the recruiting information session. During the listening session, they can pick up on certain cues, such as the timbre of your voice or the style of your wording. Unfortunately, these rare trolls use the cues to harass you, personally.

If they leave the subject of their purpose to bait you, that is a clear sign that the session needs to end. When a person tries to make you get emotional, that is harassment, and that is wrong.

Sometimes I've been confused by a sudden change in the participant towards trying to make me emotional; other times I know exactly what is happening. In the first instance, it may take me a few more minutes to figure out that they are manipulating me. It's grueling, and my heart races and my palms get sweaty. When I finally recognize these symptoms and realize what is happening, I end the session.

Some researchers are willing to give an aggressive participant a few warnings before deciding to end the session. You can do that if you feel comfortable and powerful enough in the context. In one case, when I had the shield of doing the session remotely by audio, I did manage to talk a person into behaving appropriately. In other cases, I have felt so uncomfortable I have ended the session. In general, I encourage you to err on the side of ending the session. Your mental health is important.

You should *never* feel obliged to stick with the session only to complete the study or fulfill your manager's expectations. Harassment and triggering are things no one should have to tolerate. The session has gone off course and will produce no more useful data. There are always other participants out there to recruit.

Communicating with Your Manager

Ordinarily the participant is the most important person involved in a listening session, but you, the listener, are next in line. When the participant harasses or triggers you, they give up their priority position, and you become priority. Your manager and your team are third in line, after you. They are not on the front-line facing this; you are.

If you encounter a trigger or harassment, even if you end the session quickly, be aware you may have sustained an injury. Just like any workplace injury, you might want to make your team and managers aware of it. You may also need to take some time to remove the power of the barbs that were thrown at you and to care for your mental state.

Protect yourself, and—if it is safe to do so—go back to your manager and team to report what happened. Tell your manager that the data you were aiming to collect was not present, so it was not worth the time investment. Perhaps your teammates can be spared a similar experience. Perhaps you can be given space and time to address your injury.

Regardless, what has happened is *not* your fault, and *not* okay. Take time to care for yourself and recover.

How To Exit an Unsafe Session

Here are the techniques for ending a session. In any of the situations described in this chapter, if a participant is not feeling safe, or if you do not feel safe, you have permission to end the session. You can exit the session no matter how long you've been at it, two minutes or two hours. You don't have to draw out the torture if one of these situations occurs.

Here are three circumstances that you might encounter, and some suggested phrasing that you can use. Feel free to change the phrasing to suit your circumstance, and even add new phrases for additional scenarios that you anticipate.

Early in the Session

If signals that a participant feels uncomfortable appear early in the session, often it's not something you did, but a circumstance surrounding the person before the listening session began. Things happen. Moods change. Someone may have just learned that their brother-in-law has stage four cancer. The person may not want to do the session after all and might feel obligated to do it anyway.

When you become aware of the signals, give the participant a choice to either postpone or to cancel entirely.

Listener: It sounds like now isn't such a great time for this session. Do you want to postpone? Or cancel? Either is fine.

You can add a statement about the thank-you gift, if it makes sense to you at that point.

Listener: We're happy to send you a partial thank-you gift.

You'll probably sense their relief in the way that they answer.

If there are circumstances before the listening session that would prevent *you* from feeling able to host a safe space—or pay rapt attention to another person—reach out to that person and postpone or cancel the session. Your own life matters, too.

Farther Into the Session

If you have gotten farther in the session, there are several different ways to end the session, depending on the severity of what has happened. These "endings" are polite, to help telegraph to the person that they are not at fault.

You can skip to the closing question and let the participant make the decision whether there is anything more to be said. There won't be, because of the erosion of trust, but you can give them the final decision.

| Listener: | We have covered a lot of topics already, and I truly apologize for making this last one a little difficult for you. Is there anything else that you thought we would be talking about during this session that we haven't touched on yet? |

Or, you can skip to the closing comment, without the closing question.

| Listener: | Well, I think we've covered what I hoped to understand. And I am sorry for making this last topic upsetting. We can end now, and we will send you the thank-you gift that you chose. |

Or another variation:

| Listener: | I think that we should skip this last topic and maybe end now. You've given me such a good understanding of your thinking, so I want to thank you for your time. Let's talk about which form of thank-you gift you'd prefer. |

If you make the sentence about yourself, rather than about the participant, it will give that person a sense that you respect them and are not accusing them of quitting early. Mentioning the thank-you gift is a must, here. You want to show them that you do appreciate what they've tried to communicate so far, even if it didn't work out at the depth you hoped for.

For a Listener Who Feels Unsafe

If you are the person feeling unsafe, and you want to leave the listening session, there are a variety of ways to exit that vary from polite to simply leaving. You can use a variation on any of these phrases or prepare your own.

| Listener: | Well, I think I've learned what I need for this session. I'm going to end it here. We will send you the thank-you gift that you chose during the information session. |

Or you can invent an emergency, if you don't want the participant to realize you are not feeling comfortable.

Listener: Oh! (pause) I've just gotten an emergency notification, and I have to go now. We'll send you the thank-you gift. Sorry, I really have to leave now.

You can be terse, too, especially if you think your words could betray the strong emotion you are feeling—if you don't want the participant to realize you are upset.

Listener: I'm sorry, but I'm going to end this session here. We'll send you the thank-you gift. Goodbye.

Or,

Listener: ... And, I have to end this session here. Goodbye.

Or, you might *want* to let the participant know that you are feeling harassed or triggered, and you can tell them so, and let them feel a bit of your emotion. This is for extreme cases.

Listener: You have said some rude things to me. This session is over.

If it's a remote session, you also have the option to not say or write anything at all, and to just end the connection.

If it's an in-person session, it's much harder to get up and walk out the door, but not impossible. I have heard that it feels more possible to get up and leave if you look at your phone or other device and then use the "emergency notification" excuse. Assuming the session is in a location where your managers are present, ask one of them to escort the participant out.

However, if you are at the participant's location, you need to focus on your own safety. And if you go to the participant's location, ***never go alone***. When you arrive, you want to pay attention to any signals at the location that you may experience harassment or triggering words, and just call off the whole session.

Steve Portigal's book[2] ***Doorbells, Danger, and Dead Batteries*** has a good section on personal safety.

Self-Care

While I'm on the subject of protecting yourself, there are a few other things worth mentioning. Many practitioners are in jobs where little thought is given to the sustainability of the work. Historically, there has been some attention given to physical labor in this respect, but not all that much to mental labor. So here are a few topics that are germane to the current world of product and service creators. Hopefully in ten years these will have changed for the better.

Overworking

Spending so much time in other people's worlds can be draining. While your team can help, you try to to be intentional with your own practice to ensure you don't burn out—especially in this era's milieu of moving fast and self-identification with work. It's easy to believe that working more, doing more, is better. And so, you may repeatedly over-schedule yourself, which leads to mental injury.

Globally, many employers are demanding more and more time in people's days, helped along by always-on internet connections. There is a meme that started in China called "revenge bedtime procrastination." It's about staying up late in an attempt to eke out some leisure time for your mind, but in a way that drives you to worse health because of less sleep. It's easy to fall into a two hour "entertainment" hole every night, looking at variously sized screens to try to recharge. According to psychologists studying bedtime-procrastination, it often isn't successful in overcoming exhaustion. The instinctual steps we take to try to retain our leisure time are often counterproductive. Overwork injury is real, even if it is not visible

Look at your schedule and the demands on your time. How are those demands affecting your mental health? Do you need more downtime in your workday or evening? Can you schedule mentally demanding things farther apart?

One thing I do to protect and sustain my mind is to schedule only one listening session a day. It gives me a chance to take 15 minutes to clear my head before the session and then work my mind back out of that person's world slowly for a few hours after, while I'm doing other less-involving work.

Team Support

One listening session per day also gives you a chance to recognize when you've dealt with a particularly haunting topic. If you are a member of a team, and if your team is not overworked, you can support each other after a difficult listening session. Chatting about it, hearing another person's thoughts about it, helps to make the topic have less power over your mind. I've had long conversations with a teammate about what a participant said, where we helped each other work toward seeing the participant's perspective more clearly. If haunting topics are likely to come up, you can even budget extra time for these kinds of conversations during a study.

When you make your teammate a part of such of conversations, remember that they also run a risk of becoming haunted by a topic. Make sure to check in with that teammate to ensure that they are comfortable with the content before you begin sharing specifics. Make sure as well that you are available to them in return, if they need a safe place to review a session as well.

If You Work in an Unsafe Space

Not everyone has supportive team members. If you find yourself in an unsupportive work environment, especially with respect to overworking, you can try to talk to someone about it. That someone might be in the hiring department, might be a mentor, might be a therapist, might be a friend, or might be your journal or meditation practice. You need time to explore your thinking about the situation in order to do something about it. Hopefully there are local resources to help you make decisions in this situation, especially if leaving a job is not a good option for you.

Taking Care to Avoid Injury

Listening deeply is hard work. It takes concentration. I've said it's like wearing a heavy hat, and you cannot wear that hat for very long, maybe an hour or two, without taking a break. Early in your listening career, don't expect to be able to listen deeply for even a full hour. You want to work up to it, like an athlete training for an event. If your manager has expectations beyond your capabilities, alert them to your present limitations, and make a training plan together. You will become injured otherwise, and that manager will lose your productivity, or they will lose you entirely if you decide to quit the job. Circle this section and show it to them.

Most countries don't yet have labor protection laws for people working with their minds. There's some history as to why, which involves the mind-worker class of employees looking down upon the physical-worker class, and renouncing unions and labor laws. Nevertheless, mind-workers can be injured on the job. There are efforts underway to get protection laws in place—efforts that are up against well-funded opposition and systemic thinking. To the degree that it is safe, be open with your manager and teammates about the hazards of the work so that everyone can work together to create sustainable work practices.

If you are part of a team, you might create a list where each team member identifies where they are best qualified to pitch in, and then assign work together according to each person's areas of strength. This list would include all the parts of deep listening, from setting the person's purpose, recruiting, information sessions, and the listening session itself. Forcing anyone to do something that chills their heart means they won't do a good job of it. On the other hand, supporting team members as they try new things, even things they might be uncomfortable with at first, means the team builds a safe space to make mistakes as you improve. This is where listening deeply within your team can be helpful in finding the right balance for the people involved.

With care, the team can progress together, and the knowledge you build for the organization will improve as well.

Summing Up

I've discussed what a safe space is, techniques for building that space for the participant, and signals that will help you recognize when the integrity of that space is eroding. I've also discussed situations you may encounter where sensitivities or triggers may make someone feel vulnerable—and how to end the session if that occurs.

You are the person responsible for your own boundaries. Your organization does not get to set them. Make sure to define your boundaries in advance, recognize them in a session, and stay true to them. Use your own judgment, not your manager's, to recognize when an experience is unsafe for you.

The next chapter explains common challenges and complexities that arise in listening sessions and gives suggestions on how you might best react.

Additional Resources

HmntyCntrd – an award-winning organization focused on supporting people in their personal and professional growth. https://hmntycntrd.com

Endnotes

1   See a definition of applied ethics at the Markkula Center for Applied Ethics,
    https://www.scu.edu/ethics/ethics-resources/ethical-decision-making/what-is-ethics/
2   Steve Portigal, *Doorbells, Danger, and Dead Batteries User Research War Stories* (New York, NY: Rosenfeld Media, 2016).

CHAPTER 8

CHAPTER 8

Handling Complexity Well

No matter how practiced you are at deep listening, you will encounter awkwardness and clumsy communication. This chapter is full of stories about what might happen, and ways to feel positive about encountering them yourself. I will share tips how to recover from these blunders. I will discuss common communication habits that play a role in listening sessions, and I'll talk about when it is wise to respond to a specific situation by ending the session politely. In most cases, no one is at fault. The best way to proceed is simply to help the person feel understood.

Be gentle with yourself. When you do run across the unexpected, respond the best way that you can at that moment—learning from the experience as you go.

Recovering Quickly from Blunders

Don't be hard on yourself when you stumble over concepts or words, no matter how flustered you may feel at the time. Inevitably there are misplaced comments, badly-timed responses, and even random interruptions from the environment. This will happen to both you and the other person. So, try to address it in good humor.

When you do break the flow, it's usually something you both can recover from. You will lose momentum, but the person is there in the session because they want to add their thinking to your knowledge. They're usually willing to work with you to regain the flow of the session.

When you have interrupted the train of thought, the trick is to avoid spending too much time explaining your blunder. No matter how flustered you feel in the moment, any explanation will derail the session further. Let it go. Momentum will return as they get back in rhythm.

Accidentally Distracting the Participant

Here's an example of derailing a listening session, and how the listener recovered. In this example, the participant is talking about a job they'd started right after going through a divorce.

Person: Part of recovering was getting a job. I started selling life insurance. I ran across people who did not understand what they were buying, and as I explained life insurance, I realized they had issues with money. [inner thinking] And I could relate, having gone through what I went through. I had been learning so much about money. So, I'd kind of coach them through it. [implied emotional reaction and pull-tab] I really loved doing that. [preference]

(pauses)

Insurance companies are selling you crap that you don't need, in confusing ways, [opinion] and people really don't like spending money around death. [opinion] I just really don't like selling life insurance. [implied emotional reaction]

Listener: Or planning for it. [complex reflection to "death"]

Person: (pauses briefly) Yeah. [session mode] The other terrible thing is planning for it, and it was annoying. [thrown off by the complex reflection] I definitely believe in, you know, if people have dangerous job and dependents, let's have it. [guiding principle] But I forget what I was saying. What was I saying? [session mode]

The participant took "or planning for it" as a cue to go in a different direction. Instead of encouraging their momentum, the listener accidentally stuck a stick in the metaphorical bicycle wheel and brought the participant to a screeching halt.

The listener recovers by reminding them of what they had been saying:

Listener: So, you got this job [simple reflection] and then you found out you loved doing the coaching, but it wasn't paid. [simple reflection]

Person:: Right. I decided that I wanted to start teaching people how to deal with money. [inner thinking] I decided to get licensed as a financial planner so I could earn money that way, plus help people out. [inner thinking] ...

And the participant went on for twelve more sentences. The listener did not dwell on their fumble, but instead let it pass and offered a path back to the original topic. Not every issue in a session is so easy to recover from. This next section is an example.

Compounded Misunderstanding

Occasionally, even the most practiced listeners will fail to listen, or will misunderstand what the person is saying. The following example demonstrates the compounding nature of these types of mistakes, and how important it is to let them go.

Here's an example from the study about deciding to go to a restaurant during the early months of the pandemic. Examples from this participant appear in Chapter Six, so this is a bit of a continuation. Here, the listener seeks clarification of what was meant at first.

Person62: As far as, like, the interaction at the table, just like, you know, you've kind of got to acknowledge as a group [implied inner thinking] – I think we said something like, "It's really nice to be able to do this." It feels like a treat all of a sudden [emotional reaction] instead of like oh, well no big deal, because it does feel like a big deal. [emotional reaction]

Listener: What's a big deal? [clarification]

Person62: Going out to eat. [session mode]

Listener: And a big deal in what way? [accidentally reflecting the emotional reaction]

Person62: Um, just that it's not something we're doing all the time, whereas before it was never a second thought. [explanation]

Listener:	Hmm. So, big deal as in production? [accidental introduction of vocabulary] **Or big deal as in?** [still reflecting the emotional reaction, pulling the topic further away from the participant's experience]
Person62:	I would say big deal as in, like, kind of both risk and reward. Like it feels risky, but we're doing it. [explanation and implied inner thinking, which was covered earlier]

But it's a real privilege to be able to get together in this time because that's not a given. [generalized inner thinking, applied to the whole group of diners] |
Listener:	Hmm. (pause) Um, I was just writing something down. [session mode, calling attention to the fumble] **Yeah, I really hear you,** [support] **how small things are now – I don't know, more visible.** [reference to a topic from earlier, a bit flustered that the "big deal" questions derailed the conversation]
Person62:	Yeah. [session mode]
Listener:	I really hear that in your story. [support, figuring out where to recover]
Person62:	You kind of don't realize what you were taking for granted until all of a sudden you have to think about all of this crap just to go eat dinner. [guiding the listener back to the topic that produced the "big deal"]
Listener:	Yes. That's an excellent point. [support] **I'm curious what you had for dessert?** [distracted, possibly trying to show warmth of personality, although the participant did not bring up dessert at all]
Person62:	Hmm. Did we have dessert? I don't think we did. [session mode]
Listener:	A friend of mine also went out to a restaurant a couple of weeks ago and was just so happy about . . .(trails off) [explaining the blunder, possibly trying to show warmth of personality, this time it's on the topic of the original emotional reaction]
Person62:	It *is* really nice. [session mode] **I've cooked so much. I'm so tired of cooking and dishes. (laughing ruefully)** [generalized emotional reaction]
Listener:	Yeah. [support] **Does that figure into how you're thinking about eating out?** [leading question and generalized what went through your mind]

The session continues in a generalized vein and then *finally* gets back on track. This example is from toward the end of the listening session, and it's possible the listener was getting tired. But it's more likely that there was an interruption in the listener's environment. Nevertheless, it's an example that *could* have ended with the person deciding that they were finished with the session.

Yes, if you have a good connection with the person, if you focus on being supportive and expressing warmth throughout the session, the participant will help you recover the flow.

Generalized Concepts

Generalizations are concepts in the "almost interior" layer of the jawbreaker candy, along with conjecture and implied concepts. You'll encounter generalizations a lot in certain cultures, so here are three ways to try to get down to the interior cognition.

Pin the Generalization

As I mentioned in Chapter Six, when a participant speaks in general terms it's best to pin the topic to a specific time and place when they were pursuing their purpose. Interior cognition is tied to experiences, and experiences are tied to a time and place.

> **Person62:** Like, it's super annoying when we can't, you know, split a bill really quickly. [generalized emotional reaction] I hate that. [preference]
>
> **Listener:** Annoying because … [micro-reflection and fill-in-the-blank]
>
> **Person62:** It's not quick. [explanation]
>
> **Listener:** The last time you had to split a bill, what do you remember thinking as you did it? [pin to a place and time]
>
> **Person62:** I don't know. Just that it's always annoying. [generalized emotional reaction]

In the example above, you see a generalized emotional reaction. The listener tries the technique of pinning it to a place and time, but it goes nowhere. Next, the listener refers back to an earlier topic to try again.

Listener:	Earlier you mentioned that birthday dinner for your friend. You say you usually split the bill when your with your group of friends ... [earlier you said]
Person:	Oh, yeah, that time since it was a birthday, we only split it among ourselves, not the birthday boy. [explanation]
Listener:	(pause) And you did the splitting ... [fill in the blank]
Person:	Yes. Oh, that time in particular I had to talk the waiter into letting us do it. [explanation]

I could tell he was not too happy about putting seven different credit cards through the station in back. [implied inner thinking] So up front, when he brought me the bill, I decided to let him know that we planned to give him a 20% tip.

I figured that would make him feel better about the seven credit cards that people were getting out of their wallets. [inner thinking] I saw his eyebrows go up a little, and then he politely accepted all the cards and went to charge them. [explanation]

I remember feeling pleased that this approach worked. [emotional reaction] Someone had just told me about it, like, a day before. [statement of fact]

So, the person does relate their interior cognition when they were guided to a particular past scene. The listener had to try twice, but it worked. This is typical of how you can help a person who is has a habit of generalizing to move into their interior cognition.

Generalized but Specific

Not everything that sounds like a generalization is actually a generalization. There are two ways that a participant might go to depth even though they are using more general language. If someone is describing inner thinking, emotional reactions, and guiding principles in specific terms, using generalizing language, the conversation is helpful and can proceed like any other listening session, no matter what the phrasing.

Below are some examples of general-sounding language that's actually specific interior cognition.

Speaking in Third Person

I've had sessions with people who will hardly use first-person, even when clearly speaking about themselves. They frame their speech in terms of "you" or "they," "he," "she," or "one."

To determine whether the person is giving you the right layer of information, in your head, replace "you" or other pronouns with "I" or "me." What happens? If the result is still too generalized, proceed in pinning the topic to a place and time. If, however, the "I's" and "me's" allow you to understand concepts as interior cognition, then the "you" "they" wording can be ignored. You can proceed without pinning, letting the person use their preferred language.

In the following example, the participant is discussing how they still have a habit of taking a red-eye flight for a work meeting.

> **Passenger:** You work your ass off and then you've got to go to the airport and deal with flying. [implied emotional reaction] I vowed I wasn't going to do it anymore, and I'm still doing it. [possible guiding principle and pull-tab] Taking a lot of long trips in a short amount of time, it's hard on you physically, and I can't bounce back like I did when I was in my 30's.
>
> What you're doing to yourself [explanation or implied inner thinking] by planning like a young man [reference to the guiding principle above] ... you tell yourself you can probably handle that. You'll just deal with it. Once you get off the plane, you'll find a way to catch a quick nap or something like that. [generalized inner thinking]
>
> And if you're changing time zones, especially, that's a really hard thing to do. [reference to the earlier explanation or generalized inner thinking]
>
> **Listener:** Right. [support]
>
> **Passenger:** You're not really going to have the opportunity to catch up that you might think you will. [explanation or conjecture] You get in and you find the hotel doesn't have your room ready. [scene setting]
>
> What are you going to do? You just sit around, you walk ... [explanation or implied emotional reaction]

These "you's" are mixed with "I's" and "me's", so it's easy to convert them to first person.

Once you do, you will be left with inner thinking, emotional reactions, and a guiding principle:

- **Implied emotional reaction:** (Feel overwhelmed that) after I work my ass off, I've got to go to the airport and deal with flying.
- **Implied inner thinking:** Wonder what I'm doing (to my health) by taking a lot of long trips on red-eyes and changing time zones, because I can't bounce back like I did in my 30's.
- **Inner thinking:** Tell myself that I can still handle the jetlag with a quick nap before the meeting, even though I know the hotel room usually isn't ready

As you can see, the specific detail we're getting out of the general language makes the conversation productive.

Explanations

Another general-sounding but actually specific way of communicating is when a participant extends generalizations into detailed explanations of how something works or how they do something. The person may assume you know nothing about the subject. Often this kind of explanation results in specific guiding principles.

Listener:	You made a vow, but you're still flying red-eyes … [simple reflection of the first pull-tab, to understand the possible guiding principle]
Person::	Red-eyes are cheaper, of course they are. [statement of fact] You should still pay double to get there at a reasonable hour so you can sleep. Charge it to the company, or pick it up yourself. [generalized inner thinking] If it's important enough to send you halfway around the world, it's important enough for you to not be half-dead in the middle of the meeting, [guiding principle] and you're going to be half-dead if you don't get there the evening before, trust me. [conjecture or explanation]
	Maybe you think you can handle it with a nap, but you're not in your twenties anymore. [generalized inner thinking from earlier] And anyway you're not really going to have the opportunity to catch up that you might think you will. [explanation or conjecture]

This generalized explanation language results some usable interior cognition:

- **Inner thinking:** Remind myself not to take the cheap red-eye flight and just pay double for the flight that gets there at a reasonable hour—or charge it to the company.
- **Guiding principle:** Make sure I'm not half-dead in the meeting by arriving the day before and getting sleep, because it's an important meeting that I am flying halfway around the world to get to.

Chronic Generalizing

Sometimes a person's habit of communicating in generalizations is so strong that, no matter how helpful you are in guiding them to their interior cognition, they can't (or feel too uncomfortable to) express themselves at that layer.

In this case, no matter what techniques you use, the person will stick with the "almost interior" layer. If you try for a while without success, visiting several of the topics that they brought up, you can politely end the session. There's no interior cognition to be had. You can skip to the closing question.

Here's an example of how this plays out, from a study about the purpose of getting to the airport gate to board a flight. This passenger has been unable to pin any of his thinking down to a particular trip he took. Here the topic is about bringing coffee on board the flight, but still the passenger is unable to relate their interior cognition. After trying several topics, for about twenty minutes, the listener is going to give up.

Listener: For last Tuesday's flight out of Manila, you took a taxi to the airport. When you got there, what went through your mind? [pin to place and time]

Passenger: I always get coffee at this one coffee stand in the airport, the Acacia Tree. I always go there even if I'm flying out of another part of the airport. 😎☕ [generalized explanation and pull-tab]

Listener: The Acacia Tree ... [micro-reflection on the most recent pull-tab]

Passenger: Yeah, coffee on the plane isn't great. 💀[opinion] So I have to bring coffee with me. [generalized explanation]

Listener: Do you remember the time you first decided to go to the Acacia Tree? [find the root, but checking first]

Passenger: I don't really remember, to tell you the truth. It's been years. [session mode]

Listener: Earlier you were saying there was one trip where traffic was bad, and you couldn't get to the airport early like you prefer. [earlier you said]

(pause)

Passenger: That's right. [session mode]

Listener: What was your thinking in terms of coffee for that trip?

Passenger: Hm, I don't remember, did I go get coffee? [session mode] Probably not. 😓[explanation]

Listener: Okay. Well I think that covers all of your recent trips. Is there anything else you expected to tell me about in this session? [closing question]

Passenger: No, I think that covers everything. [session mode]

Listener: Thank you for chatting with me. 😊 I have a note here that you selected the airline credit thank-you gift. Is that still your preference?

Passenger: Yes, absolutely. 🙏

Listener: The airline will be reaching out to you after some service updates have been made based on this study, just to let you know what is happening. [explain what's next] (considers whether to invite this person to generative co-creation research) So, I think that's it for us here.

Passenger: Great! Thank you for the mileage credit. Bye!

Listener: Have a great day! Bye!

After the session, the listener checked the recruiting notes, because this was a case where a different team member had conducted the information session with this passenger. This participant had been recruited by someone new to the team, and there were no notes. So, the listener reached out to that team member to find out how the participant had responded during the information session. It turns out that generalizations had occurred there, too. Then, the listener asked the new teammate if they were up for some coaching about what to look for in the information session, to recognize the signs of generalization.

The Importance of Silence

In Steve Portigal's book *Interviewing Users,* there is a remarkable chapter on silence.[1] Steve talks about the role of silence in different cultures. He points out cases in which silence can defeat awkwardness. Silence has a powerful effect on human interactions and, when used adroitly, it can smooth out some blunders, but not all. If you can be willing to let silences exist, they can create a space for a person to fill with their interior cognition.

In some cultures (the U.S. culture, for example) it's not easy to let silence be. Many people tend to want to fill silences with words, especially when we're just starting out as deep listeners.

Practice noticing silences in your everyday life. Just notice it. You can fill the silence with words immediately if you need to at first. Over time, if you can allow silences to lengthen, you will often be rewarded with the other person beginning to speak again, sometimes in greater detail or with more in-depth interior cognition. (Or the other person might accuse you of not listening.) It's this practice in your everyday life that will motivate you to try extending silence in a listening session.

Most of the time, silence is an excellent ally. Silence encourages a person to add to their last sentences, to flesh out their ideas into more words. Silence can give them a sense of control, a sense of being in the driver's seat. Silence is often an effective tool to build a safe space. Not every silence is helpful in the moment, however. The reason why the silence exists matters.

In the following three circumstances, I explain when each approach is most helpful.

Use Silence Later in the Session

Early in the listening session, the participant will be trying to get a sense of what you want to hear. They may be new to the format of listening sessions, and may require time to feel out how to lead the direction of the conversation. In this circumstance, silences are not always helpful because you are implicitly asking the person to take the lead when they may not be ready for it.

Later in a listening session, silence can demonstrate to the participant that you are giving them space to pick the next topic or to go further with the current topic. It is most useful after you've established a trust connection. Silence here allows them the safety and room to unpack something they don't have all the words for quite yet. When pauses happen, if you allow space, the person doesn't feel rushed to say something. They can try to find the right words, and what they add is more likely to be their interior cognition. A good scenario of helpful silence is in Chapter Seven, in the example about saving for retirement, in the first section.

Silence Can Indicate Discomfort

Silences can also come up when the subject matter is uncomfortable. It could be the participant is uncomfortable with you, with something they heard in your voice or saw about you online, or really any other reason. If they are uncomfortable, they will be reluctant to share what passed through their mind at a particular moment. They may worry you won't understand, you will judge, or you will become defensive or offended. This is an indication that they feel unsafe, and you may need to use some of the techniques from Chapter Seven to help make the space safe for them. Sometimes differences in culture, education, privilege, or experience can lead to additional discomfort when the listener says something. If you think that differences are causing friction, let the participant know that you are interested in bridging that difference. Tell them that you want to understand their experience from their perspective. Your organization may desperately need additional perspectives from people, and you can encourage this person to help bring positive change by speaking if they are comfortable doing so. If they are still uncomfortable after your explanation, then let them exit the session.

Silence With Sensitive Subjects

Silence rooted in loss or a difficult subject, can be handled differently. I discussed Sensitive Topics in Chapter Seven. Here is a little more. Sometimes a participant will grow silent because the subject itself is painful to them, and this silence must be treated differently. Ongoing suffering, the loss of a loved one, frustration with systemic discrimination—these are all topics that will come up in listening sessions, especially when you recruit to include a realistically broad range of people addressing the same purpose.

With this kind of silence, let the participant know that they don't have to talk about the sensitive topic. Affirm that their experience is important, but that it is theirs. There is no requirement to share it. After a short pause, move back to a previous, more neutral topic.

Also, silence *can* be an indication that something is painful, and if the participant *wants* to confide in you, they may need that silence to get past their own mental protections.

The Person Who Lies

It is unfortunate, but some participants purposely tell stories that are not true. There are people who like to earn extra money by participating in research studies.[2] Others lie to make themselves look good, or for some other unknown reason. It's really, really, really difficult to tell when someone is fabricating concepts for you.

As a rule, you will not be able to spot a falsehood during a listening session. Occasionally you might sense an inability to speak about specifics or a tendency to give extravagant details, but lies are normally not obvious. Humans are great storytellers. Fabrications are typically detected in discussions with team members afterward.

One team I worked with caught a participant in falsehoods while in session. I was mentoring a group of researchers who had been given permission by the participant to listen in silently. The team and I had a shared chat window for the group to exchange observations, which I ignored until I saw far more comments appearing than normal. The person was giving detail in certain areas about an unrelated purpose, in a way that felt "off" to the group—though, notably, not to me at the time. The participant had named a conference in a city on a date, one of the group members looked the conference up and found that it did not exist.

I saw their flurry of comments to each other. I did not confront the person with the information, because that would have resulted in conflict, judgment, and ruining the safe space. I also would not get any interior cognition from the person by confronting them. At that point I decided to end the listening session politely. The team then pointed out several other parts of the story that did not stand up to fact checking. We sent that participant the thank-you gift, but we did not keep the recording, nor pay for a transcript.

Normally, listening sessions are conducted one-on-one, so fact checking in the moment is impossible. That's fine. You will have the transcript after the call, and plenty of time at the synthesis stage to consider items that don't add up.

Complaints & Objections

Sometimes a participant may arrive with concerns or anger about a product, a solution, or something your organization has done. Even if they arrive calm, they may have their anger, frustration, or other feelings towards your organization triggered during the session. The participant may complain about a policy, certain stakeholders, or even object to pricing or perks. This can still be part of a listening session, especially if you can connect it to the person's purpose.

Make sure they feel understood. If the participant is griping about a solution that an organization offers, let them air it. This is the moment for you to demonstrate that you truly are interested in what they are saying. In one session, I helped a participant unfold their emotional reactions about a solution for 40 minutes. We connected the emotion to the purpose, and the person got to air some inner thinking and guiding principles that really clarified what their experience was. I provided non-judging support for the person and followed their topics, guiding them to their interior cognition for those which sounded important and urgent for them. After those 40 minutes, that person said, "I really appreciate you paying attention to me. I'm thrilled that you have understood my thinking! In return, I'm more than happy to give you my time right now to answer what you need for your study."

So we continued the listening session, where I jumped back to a few of the topics they mentioned and could lead to other topics related to their purpose, but unrelated to the solution. After the session, in addition to adding that person's concepts to the opportunity map, I was able to send specific solution-related interior cognition to the product team.

If someone complaining doesn't feel understood, they will continue speak, often louder, and more forcefully, until they do. *Help them feel understood.* This is the simple equation to help someone move past complaints into describing their purpose.

When They Can't Feel Understood

Some participants are so used to not being heard that your listening won't register to them. Even when you've done everything you know to show them you're listening, it may be such a new phenomenon for them that they don't know how to handle it. If you try everything and sense that you are not going to get to interior cognition concepts, end the listening session, thank them as you would any other participant. In this case, you may actually want to make a transcript so you can pass their issues on to the team who deals with evaluative research, or to the customer service or sales teams. This transcript probably won't hold enough interior cognition to add meaningfully to your own synthesis, and if that's the case it's easier to leave it out of the patterns completely.

Stay Grounded

Even if you personally believe that the participant's complaints stem from a misapplication of your solution, or if their complaints seem absurd, you want to ground yourself. Let the words flow through you and out. You're listening to the participant's perspective, and *their pain is real*. Just focus on that. They don't need you to explain how to use the solution correctly.

Afterward, if you want to get their absurd "mis-application" of the solution out of your system, journal it, write your teammates or stakeholders, gripe to your partner or friends about it—just leave the person's name and details out of whatever you say. One thing I do in this situation is play that participant's role myself, using their thinking, emotions, and guiding principles. Within a couple of minutes their "mis-application" suddenly becomes reasonable, an obvious direction for them to take toward their purpose.

If you can understand their perspective in this way, often it leads to surprising understanding and opportunity. In this way, even seemingly absurd usage contexts can lead to actionable knowledge. The listener's perspective is a gift, if you can allow yourself to recognize that their perspective is valid and help your organization learn from it.

Furthermore, if they indicate that they think you are personally to blame, just embrace it. You *are* the organization to them. Reassure them your job is to understand their approach so you can make better solutions. Help them *feel understood* so that you earn their trust and can move on to exploring their purpose at depth with them. If this doesn't happen, you don't have a listening session.

Note that someone being hostile towards your organization is differ-ent from someone being hostile towards *you* because of who you are.

Chapter Seven contains discussion about the threshold a person might cross, and the options you have on both sides of that threshold whether to continue or end the session.

Technological & Scheduling Issues

Rarely, a listening session may become truncated due to technological issues. An audio connection may be bad, or be repeatedly cut off. Possibly the medium of communication the participant has chosen is not working for you—for example you may not be able to write fast enough to keep a text-based session going. Or maybe something isn't working for the participant. If you can, pause to discuss how to handle the situation. If you are cut off, immediately reach out via the communication method you used to schedule the information session. You can agree to try again at a later time.

In other situations, a participant may repeatedly reschedule. In such cases, it's helpful if you try to connect at most two or three times before moving on. If the participant is likely to share a particularly needed perspective, you may decide to expend more effort to reconnect if you have the ability to do so, but do not get caught in an endless loop of chasing.

Summing Up

Scheduling issues, communication habits, and blunders are some of the complexities that will inevitably arise as part of a study. The key to dealing with the unexpected is to do the best that you can. Support the participant, but end the session politely and firmly if needed.

Afterward, take the time to reflect about what happened with your team, so that others may handle something similar, without being hard on themselves.

Endnotes

1   Portigal, Steve. Interviewing Users. New York: Rosenfeld Media, 2013.
2   Steve Portigal has collected research "war stories" over the years. One of these stories, Cordy's War Story: A Crisis of Credibility is a good example of how difficult it is to recognize fabrications during a session. Cordy Swope, "Cordy's War Story: A Crisis of Credibility," War Stories (Portigal Consulting, January 15, 2013), https://portigal.com/cordys-war-story-a-crisis-of-credibility/.

NEXT STEPS:

DATA SYNTHESIS AND THINKING STYLES   **272**

CHAPTER 9

Next Steps: Data Synthesis

and Thinking Styles

I f you are doing deep listening to build relationships and understand your colleagues better, you probably won't be doing synthesis or strategy work. You'll be building your understanding internally. Your goal is to strengthen the connection between you and each of the people you are collaborating with. This is trust-building work. For that, you don't need this chapter.

There *is* a type of study where you listen to a set of stakeholders who are guiding a certain initiative at your organization, and you *do* conduct synthesis. You want to see where stakeholders have similar or differing intents and guiding principles with regard to the *purpose* of the initiative. The differences are good to get out in the open, for everyone to discuss and possibly clarify and resolve. You will want to understand the two-step synthesis I'll introduce in this chapter.

Lastly, for studies where you are building knowledge about a broader set of people you hope to support with your solutions, you will want all the steps I outline below. So, yes, if you are building an opportunity map for your organization's strategy, then there is more work to do. The rest of this chapter is intended to be a general, high-level overview of how the purpose-focused research process works. This overview might even give you ideas you can patch into your existing process.

Everything in the following pages is presented in summary, simplified because *this* book is about listening. And it's already long enough. Luckily, there are in-depth courses on all the steps of the purpose-focused method available at indiyoung.com … hopefully available for some decades to come, until the next people iterate the method and make it better.

The Purpose-Focused Method

The purpose-focused method is a transformation of how most organizations handle product strategy, basing it on people's purpose instead of the organization's solutions. The idea is to measure your progress in terms of how well you support different people's approaches to the purpose. This means becoming wary of your assumptions, paying attention to deeper nuances of interior cognition regarding the purpose, and inviting an understanding of people who have been ignored. The purpose-focused method is circular, and keeps building more knowledge to provide for more avenues of priority and opportunity as the years go by. It feeds into existing ideas and solutions methods, providing thicker, richer options to consider.

Here are the steps for the purpose-focused method. The bolded steps are covered in this book.

- Decide whether and when you want to build knowledge
- **Frame the study – what purpose to understand and who to learn from**
- **Build your understanding through listening sessions**
- Summarize interior cognition concepts from transcripts
- Cultivate patterns from these summaries, based on focus of mental attention
- Find differences in people's approaches to the purpose, to define thinking styles
- Lay out an opportunity map that shows gaps in how your solutions support these patterns and thinking styles
- Prioritize and track over the years the new support you can provide for the gaps, and how well you help different thinking styles accomplish their purpose
- Proceed with ideas, validation, design and development for a priority area (via existing solution space methods)
- Decide whether and when to add more knowledge to the opportunity map

The main steps are laid out in the illustration below:

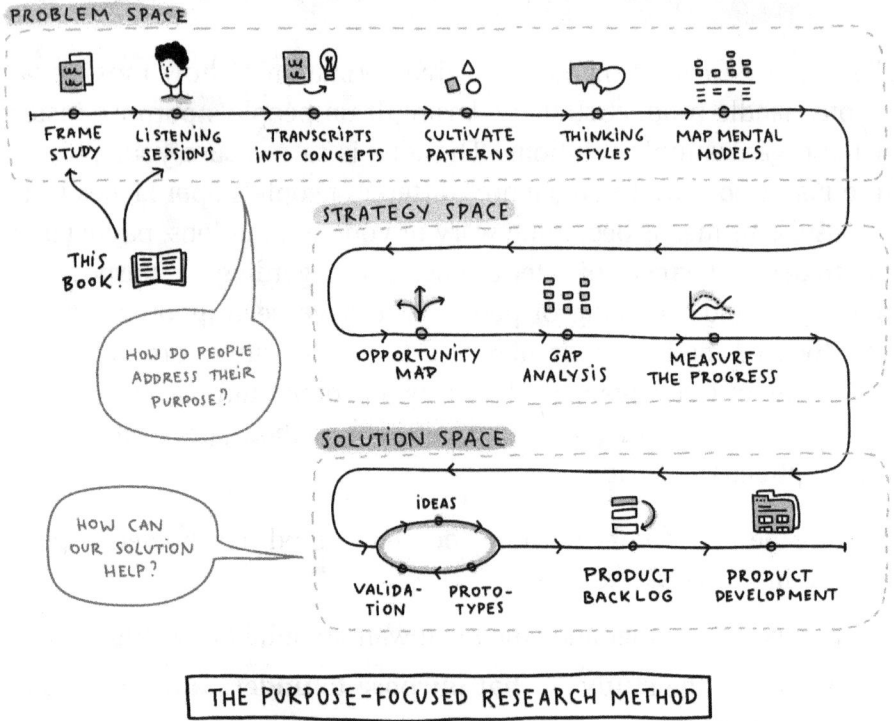

PROBLEM SPACE

FRAME STUDY — LISTENING SESSIONS — TRANSCRIPTS INTO CONCEPTS — CULTIVATE PATTERNS — THINKING STYLES — MAP MENTAL MODELS

THIS BOOK!

HOW DO PEOPLE ADDRESS THEIR PURPOSE?

STRATEGY SPACE

OPPORTUNITY MAP — GAP ANALYSIS — MEASURE THE PROGRESS

HOW CAN OUR SOLUTION HELP?

SOLUTION SPACE

IDEAS

VALIDATION — PROTOTYPES — PRODUCT BACKLOG — PRODUCT DEVELOPMENT

THE PURPOSE-FOCUSED RESEARCH METHOD

Over the next few pages, I'll briefly explain the process and some of the reasoning behind the steps in the problem space and strategy space.

Data Synthesis

After you finish your listening sessions, you will be sitting on a pile of raw information in the form of transcripts. But raw transcripts alone don't do you much good. So many organizations have mountains of transcripts, with no reliable, reproducible, and do-able way to turn them into knowledge. Here's how to harness those mountains—if the transcripts contain concepts at the core interior cognition layer.

First, though, is a challenge we all face, because we have human minds. Our challenge is to synthesize the data without imposing order based on our own assumptions. The human brain has evolved to be incredibly good at seeing patterns. The trouble is that we see patterns (and then act quickly on them) from our own perspective. If we are not careful, we overwrite what others are saying with our interpretation and assumptions, introducing layers of bias that warp the knowledge we build.

No Record of the Session?

There are situations where you cannot make a record of a listening session, like when it's an unscheduled chance to hear from a stakeholder. There are other times when a record gets lost or ruined. Not all is lost.

You can then capture the interior cognition concepts that came up and write them in the participant's voice. As soon after the session as possible, give yourself 15-20 minutes to write down the concepts. Write a summary for each concept, in first-person, present tense.

When you write from memory, you will not recall all the interior cognition concepts, but you'll be able to reconstruct about 30-40% of them. (You'll probably miss the ones that are not similar to your own perspective, and that's how bias creeps into data. Don't let this be your only way of preserving the person's interior cognition.) You can see some examples of concept summaries in the next few pages, written in first-person, present tense, from the perspective of the participant.

Letting Go of Your Own Perspective

One of the hardest skills for a researcher is to resist the temptation to impose meaning on the data. To accurately represent other people's perspectives, you try to let go of your own perspective and your instinct to see familiar patterns and leap to conclusions. You try to consciously enter a mindset where you cease to "make sense" of things and instead **"make space for patterns to surface."**

In the synthesis phases, just like in the listening sessions, you let go of your biases and preconceptions in order to understand what people are really telling you. You relinquish your need to "solve" and "make sense," and simply understand another human's perspective.

Likewise, when you're synthesizing, strive to accurately represent other people's thinking instead of "imposing order." Let the patterns build from the bottom-up, without pre-defined tags. Be aware that this approach can feel very uncontrolled and undirected, even to people accustomed to it. Feeling out to sea is normal. Of course you're going to feel out to sea when you try to understand and think like other people. But that's okay because that's the point: you go out to sea in order to understand the water you are swimming in.

Being willing to tolerate the discomfort is critical to getting past your bias and assumptions to find the opportunities that have been previously obscured. This is how your organization can stop ignoring people, stop giving them y*our* solution, and start giving them different solutions tailored for the way *they* think. These are the kind of solutions that people will gravitate toward and rely on.

Assumption-Wary Two-Step Data Synthesis

So how do you avoid this habit when dealing with your pile of listening session transcripts? You let each person's concepts lead, and you look for patterns across people based on *their* focus of mental attention.

Not yours.

This means there are two distinct steps to assumption-wary, purpose-focused data synthesis:

- **Concepts & Summaries:** Find and summarize each interior cognition concept
- **Cultivating Patterns:** For each summary, determine what the focus of the person's mental attention was, and find other summaries from other people within this focus of mental attention

Most people who are learning to synthesize a pile of transcripts are told to "find the affinities," without being told what to base the affinities on. So, a natural inclination is to base the similarities between concepts on nouns—parts or divisions or steps or features of the solution your organization produces. This re-introduces your own perspective. You are *curating* the concepts—tagging them with your own understanding of how they fit together, instead of how they came up for the people you listened to.

Taking the approach of *cultivating* the patterns instead—allowing space for the concepts to come together from the participants' point of view—avoids the problem of introducing your perspective. And it gives the researcher a solid guideline for dealing with the pile of transcripts.

Concepts & Summaries

Remember the jawbreaker candy metaphor from Chapter Three? Imagine a listening session as someone spilling a pile of jawbreaker candies of various topics on the table. Some topics will contain concepts at all four layers; some will only contain concepts at the outer layers, with no core, no interior cognition.

When you summarize concepts in the transcripts, you only will pay attention to the core, crystalline parts. You'll break apart each candy topic and pull out the core concepts. You will summarize each concept therein, and sweep the outer layers of the candies away. What you're left with are only interior cognition concepts: inner thinking, emotional reactions, and guiding principles. (You can actually use parts of the outer layers as supporting details for each summary.)

The summary of each concept is written according to a format so that it's easier to compare concepts in the second step, *cultivate patterns*. The format is: (first person, present tense) **verb + key point + supporting details**. This front-loads the most important information at the beginning of the summary.

Going through the whole transcript to crack open each topic jawbreaker candy and summarize the interior cognition is much more involved than the 20-minute scribbling I describe at the end of Chapter Six. That is an exercise in contemplating the listening session. These summaries are formal synthesis (similar to grounded theory and thematic analysis). It takes *a few hours* for each transcript, but the result is *three to four times* the number of concepts. You'll end up with 40 - 120 concepts.

You will also find concepts that are important to the participant which you didn't scribble down because they were outside your perspective. The result incorporates more nuance, as you untwist tangled concepts, pin down implied concepts, and merge repeated concepts. If you are building an opportunity map for your organization's strategy, you want all of these.

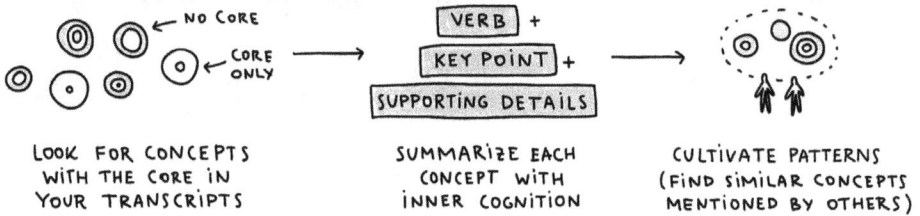

LOOK FOR CONCEPTS WITH THE CORE IN YOUR TRANSCRIPTS — SUMMARIZE EACH CONCEPT WITH INNER COGNITION — CULTIVATE PATTERNS (FIND SIMILAR CONCEPTS MENTIONED BY OTHERS)

Here are the summaries from the "awkward" example from Chapter Six. The summary itself starts with the verb representing the inner thinking, or the emotional reaction, or the guiding principle. The verb is followed by the key point—the thing the person was "verb"-ing. You can use some of the explanation, scene setting, or opinion as supporting details of these summaries.

You can also see in this example how a single concept might come from several different points in the transcript. Importantly, this example demonstrates how clarity about the person's thinking arises from the work of writing summaries, especially in the mental conflict between the last two concepts.

Summary	From the Transcript	Concept Type
Agree with the group that we are not staying to eat at the crowded restaurant	We're not going to go inside, are we? ... we knew, pretty much from the instant that we got there ... it was very clear, and I think to our whole group, that there's no possible way that we're staying here to eat. ... we are all on the same page immediately that that was not going to happen	*Inner thinking*

Agree with the group that we are not staying to eat at the crowded restaurant	... it's unfortunate. We went with the intention of having a meal outside on the patio and instead it was like, "Oh God, we're definitely not doing this." ... It was like a 15-mile boat ride, so it wasn't like a quick jaunt. ... okay, well we came all this way, but there's no possible chance that we're going to eat – we're not going to have the experience that we thought we were going to have.	*Emotional reaction*
Feel fatigued by constant risk assessment and maintaining a protective bubble against germs because I'm normally very friendly and not a germaphobe	... it sucks. It's unfortunate. There's this dichotomy between what we used to be able to do without a second thought and now everything feels riddled with risk assessment and thinking about germs. ... I am the opposite of a germaphobe so for me, this is like, "Oh God, I really don't even feel like thinking about this." There's just a fatigue that goes along with it. ... normally I'm very friendly, very open. I don't have problems talking with random people, and so for me, it's a little bit hard because all of a sudden, I need to have this like protective bubble around me because of COVID. And I don't like it. It sucks.	*Emotional reaction*
Feel affronted that the restaurant was not protecting the public and had the same capacity as pre-COVID	I was little bit judgmental that a business would run in a way that felt so risky ... a discord between what we would expect and what we were experiencing ... It just seems like, for the most part, people are reacting in a way that protects the public and this just felt like they weren't ... to have basically the same capacity that you would have pre-COVID, inside, just – yeah, I guess I was judging them.	*Emotional reaction*

Distrust the ventilation inside the restaurant to protect us as I eat with my mask off	you sit down and eat your food and take your mask off. You know we're all in the same room and it's the same ventilation system. I don't know.	*Emotional reaction*
Recognize that businesses can make their own decisions regarding money	it's ultimately their decision how they're going to run their business ... I get it. Like they need to make money	*Guiding principle*
Feel awkward that the difference of social norms are so visible about the pandemic—wearing or not wearing a mask—when differences of opinion did not used to be so outwardly evident	It feels awkward when – I feel like people are used to social norms and there have been occasions where it's like it's clear to me that somebody here doesn't agree with my level of conservativeness, and for that, that's awkward ... the difference between your opinions on this pandemic and mine are very evident, and that's awkward ... day-to-day you don't usually come across an interaction, pre-COVID, like where there's so much possibility of a discrepancy that big, that's that evident. Like you don't know if a dude sitting next to you is racist, but if he's not wearing a mask, he's probably – like he probably thinks COVID isn't real. It's kind of an outward social norm, and those normally aren't visible.	*Emotional reaction*
Believe I should not impose my pandemic conservativeness on anyone because each person can choose to deal with it in their own way	everyone has to deal with. They choose to deal with it in their own way ... I don't have to impose my conservativeness on everyone.	*Guiding principle*

Recognize that I have to impose my pandemic conservativeness on anyone coming within 6 feet of me without a mask, indoors, because I am pregnant	if you're dealing with it differently than someone else, unfortunately, that may mean that they're putting you at a higher risk ... they're willing to come within 6 feet of me, without a mask on, indoors, and I'm not comfortable with that ... "can you please back up." I need you to respect my decisions ... hey, I'm pregnant and I don't need you to come any closer right now, period. Like, just stop right there.	*Inner thinking*

Once you're finished pulling out the concepts and summarizing them, you'll have a collection of thoughts that represent this person's interior cognition about a purpose.

Cultivating Patterns

"Finding affinities" is allowing patterns to surface. Patterns, in qualitative research, are one form of evidence that the data has validity. In fact, if there are no patterns, you'll likely need to return to square one and reframe your study, then conduct more listening sessions.

Reproducible Patterns

Most researchers attempting to "find affinities" are concerned that they might not have done it reliably. Would another researcher looking at this same data come up with the same results? Usually, without explicit guidelines for finding affinities, the answer is no. Most traditional approaches create reproducibility by pre-determining tags.

The two-step method is reproducible because it also doesn't rely on affinities that spring from the researcher's mind. Rather, it relies on the person's focus of mental attention as they address their purpose. You can't predict these focuses of mental attention.

For example, if the purpose is getting to the airport on time to board a flight, then some focuses of attention you'll encounter might be find the gate, check for delays, pass the time, get food and drink for the flight, check off some easy to-do's, make progress on a work project, and make sure others with you are comfortable. That intense focus on the participants' thinking and way of approaching a purpose is what separates this method of data synthesis from others. Using this method, you can come up with patterns that another researcher trained in this kind of synthesis would reproduce from the same data.

Patterns Based on Focus of Mental Attention

Making space for patterns to surface in problem-space research is specific. You won't categorize and organize patterns based on the organization's goals or what sticks out to you as important. Instead, you sort patterns by the person's focus of mental attention.

What I mean by "focus of mental attention" is this: for each summary, consider the time when that particular inner thinking, emotional reaction, or guiding principle passed through the person's mind. The "focus of mental attention" is whatever is front-and-center in their mental landscape at that moment.

For example, maybe a person's stomach rumbles, and they think something like, "I'm hungry again already?! Wait, how long has it been since I ate something? Maybe I need to take a break and go eat. But I shouldn't be hungry. I just had lunch two hours ago. Am I just thinking about food in reaction to the stress of writing this book?" In this example, the focus of mental attention might seem obvious; this person is hungry. But that is a tag, not a verb. The verbs this person is thinking about include *decide* whether it's *time to eat. Calculate* how much time has passed since I ate. *Consider* how much I ate before and how much I need now. *Address* possible cravings.

You take a summary, hold the person's focus of mental attention in your mind, and look at each *other* person's list of summaries to see if anyone has a similar focus of mental attention. Another person might have a regular schedule of eating at certain times, so they may not have any focus of mental attention in common with the example above. Yet another participant might be pregnant and experiencing a whole new set of hunger urges, similar to *calculate* how much time has passed, but for a whole other reason. A fourth participant might be recovering from a marathon and have similar focuses of mental attention around *consider* how much I ate before and how much I need now. The summaries for each participant will be written differently, with different supporting details, but will have the focus of mental attention in common. This is how natural patterns between different people's thinking begin to emerge. Focus of mental attention is the key to reliable, reproducible patterns.

If you have difficulty finding a focus of mental attention in a concept you pulled from a transcript, that can be a clue that the concept or summary may need to be revisited and untangled, merged, or clarified.

Once a lot of smaller patterns emerge from the summaries, they will begin to reveal broader, more encompassing patterns—groups of groups. These groups ultimately build into a "city skyline", where there are towers representing each focus of mental attention with windows showing each summary. The towers build into city blocks, and those blocks build into neighborhoods or districts, all based on broader and broader focuses of mental attention. The city skyline is called a *mental model* diagram, and it forms the top half of the opportunity map. (If a visual helps, see the image of the city skyline under the section *The Opportunity Map* in a few more pages.)

Thinking Styles

Now that you've seen the patterns form into the mental model diagram, you can review each person involved in the research. You will notice that people tend to cluster around a small number of *ways* of approaching a given purpose. Even the most complex purpose will lead to a discrete number of these ways, which I call thinking styles.

A thinking style takes the format of a concise four-sentence description of a group of people. Thinking styles are a form of "archetypes" or "behavioral audience segments." You could call them "personas" in your organization if that works better for you, but they are very different than typical personas. In thinking styles, the people are not grouped by demographics; instead, the people in each group are associated because they keep two or three guiding principles or inner thinking top-of-mind as they address their purpose. The people may be incredibly different, but when they try to do this one thing, they think about the process from similar angles. The description of a thinking style is exactly those two or three top-of-mind guiding principles or inner thinking.

Importantly, people don't use the same thinking style all the time. The same person may approach the same purpose from different thinking styles at different times. Imagine the overarching approach of a passenger who is going on a business trip compared to that same person taking their toddler on a vacation. On the business trip, that person might follow a "keep myself moving (and working)" thinking style, while on the trip with the toddler, they might follow a "positive experience for everyone" thinking style.

On the mental model diagram—the city skyline—you can then mark up each window in each tower with the thinking style of that person at the time of that summary. This way, the mental model diagram depicts two things that go beyond what you already know about the "users" of your solution.

Because you used the focus of mental attention to find patterns and see towers, there are many new towers to consider. And second, you can see what thinking styles are involved for each tower. This gives you a way to design solutions that serve the specific ways people think about their purpose.

Instead of designing for the "average human" or for some demographic group of people who don't all have the same guiding principles and inner thinking, you can design for the approaches real people use when addressing their purpose.

You no longer are stuck with stretching one solution to fit a few more people. Nor do you face creating a bespoke solution for every human. Instead, you can design to 3-5 different thinking styles *and support a much wider range of people very well.*

The Opportunity Map

This example of a portion of an opportunity map shows how hiring managers and human resources folks at organizations in the U.S. approach the purpose of hiring and supporting employees with disabilities, in accordance with the Americans with Disabilities Act.

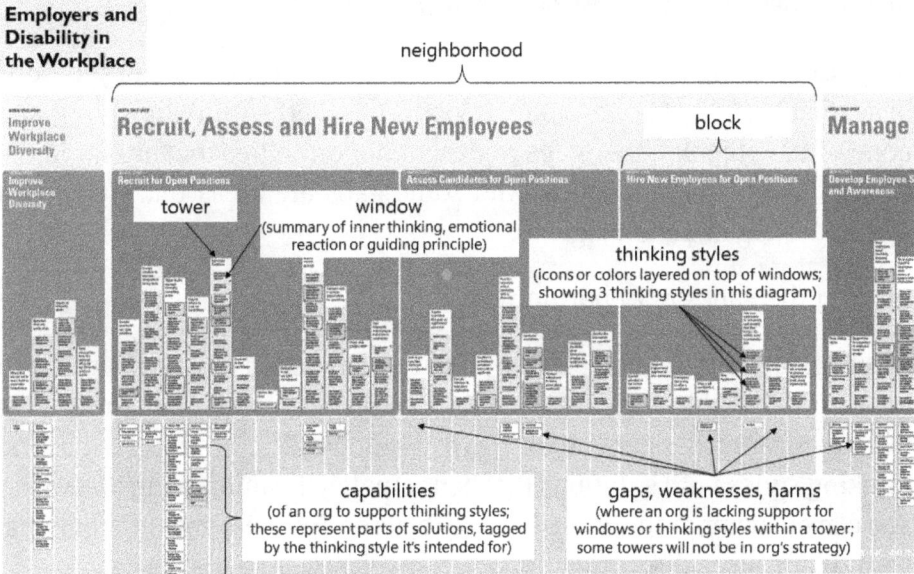

Employers and Disability in the Workplace

neighborhood

Improve Workplace Diversity

Recruit, Assess and Hire New Employees

block

Manage

Recruit for Open Positions | Assess Candidates for Open Positions | Hire New Employees for Open Positions | Develop Employee S and Awareness

tower

window
(summary of inner thinking, emotional reaction or guiding principle)

thinking styles
(icons or colors layered on top of windows; showing 3 thinking styles in this diagram)

capabilities
(of an org to support thinking styles; these represent parts of solutions, tagged by the thinking style it's intended for)

gaps, weaknesses, harms
(where an org is lacking support for windows or thinking styles within a tower; some towers will not be in org's strategy)

The city skyline (the towers on the upper half) represents employers' focuses of mental attention. The boxes below the towers represent what a federal agency might provide employers to support disability inclusion in the workplace. *(Thanks to Valerie Malzer, Sarah von Schrader, and Camille G. Lee at the Employment and Disability Institute, ILR School, Cornell University. You can view this map in detail at https://indiyoung.com/examples-employers-and-disability/)*

Once you have the thinking styles marked on the towers of a mental model diagram, you can arrange beneath each tower the capabilities of your solutions intended to support that tower. This simple act twists the conventional solution-first perspective and helps teams see how their solutions actually map to how people approach their purpose. In most instances, this is an eye-opening exercise.

There will be gaps.

The obvious gaps are where there are no capabilities beneath a tower at all.

Another kind of gap is where there is a capability beneath a tower, but it was not designed specifically for that tower. The capability will work in a pinch, but it is not an intentional design. It is just part of a capability that was designed for a different tower entirely.

Some of the gaps are harder to see—where seemingly abundant solutions beneath a tower turn out to only support one of the thinking styles, and none of the others. Other gaps represent opportunities that are far in the future for your organization. And some gaps are areas that just aren't within the organization's grasp.

Most of the gaps are opportunities.

Stakeholders get to decide the priority, depending on how each gap intersects with the strategic initiatives and other operational knowledge the organization has generated. You can support different approaches and thinking styles with solutions that better match the thinking in that tower. You can put demographic lenses on to focus on systemic and unintentional harm that causes discrimination and unwelcome experiences.

You can circle priority areas for your organization and take a measurement of how well or poorly you support each thinking style in each tower. Over time, once a quarter or once a year, you can also chart the improvement in how each capability helps people address their purpose in their way. You can map your competition's capabilities on the opportunity map, too, and measure them against the thinking styles in each tower, giving you insight into which path forward might play to your organization's strengths.

An opportunity map is also shareable. Show the priority areas, measurements, and plans for addressing the gaps present. People across the organization can clearly see new perspectives, existing harms, and opportunities. An opportunity map can be used to depict how your solutions are becoming less biased and more supportive.

The opportunity map is a strategic touchstone that your organization can add to over many decades with further research. It can act as a visual map to a broader data repository. The knowledge in an opportunity map is resilient. It is based on people's core thought patterns around a purpose, and those patterns are often timeless, or only change slowly. You can choose to deepen and extend that knowledge with new listening sessions.

It All Comes Back to Listening

An opportunity map is the result of listening to people and finding out how they approach the purpose you want to support. Listening sessions are the foundation of the purpose-focused method, and you can see why.

1. Deep listening gives you rare, first-hand understanding about how people think, react, and decide.

2. Deep listening challenges your assumptions about people and opens the door to perspectives you have ignored (and, therefore, opportunities you have missed).

The purpose-focused method is built around taking this first-hand data and using it to build a deep, long-lasting understanding. Big data gives you a picture of how people have interacted with the solutions and capabilities you have already thought of. Most business surveys ask respondents to choose from answers you have created, leaving no room for differing perspectives. Deep listening and opportunity maps add reality and humanity to the knowledge you can build for your organization. Mix the knowledge together.

Planting the Seed of Deep Listening

Even if you aren't in a position to steer your team or decide strategy, you can look for footholds in your organization where listening can be applied. In addition to big data or surveys, deep listening can give you a clearer view of people that those techniques tend to put into demographic groups. This helps your organization veer away from the peril of assuming those groups all think in the same, monolithic manner.

You can take the approach outlined in this book and mold it to fit within your organization.

Examine existing research techniques at your organization, such as usability testing, user interviews, or card sorting. Is there a chance for you to introduce more deep listening into any part of these? For example, can there be room within a user interview—can you frame it by the person's purpose and try to get to their interior cognition? Same for a card sort—can you ask about the person's reasoning as they address their purpose? There are a lot of different ways you can bring deep listening into your organization.

Above all, support your stakeholders. Find out which stakeholders at your organization you can develop relationships with, to help you see how and why product strategy is currently developed. Build relationships so that you respect where they are coming from, and so that they will trust you in return.

Planting the seed of listening deeply is not about teaching, demonstrating, or proving that this method is valuable and powerful. Stakeholders are not interested in how you produce the knowledge; they are interested in the impact of the knowledge itself:

- The gaps between how people think and how the solution supports them at each stage of the way they address their purpose
- The process of choosing which gaps to prioritize when making strategy and directing teams
- The value of intentionally focusing on the harms your solution causes people, and resolving them
- Adding knowledge from different sources inside and outside the organization to enrich the creativity of the solution

Over time you will build your tolerance for the "heavy hat" of listening. Questioning your assumptions will grow easier and easier. Listening deeply will expand your ability to experience the world from someone else's perspective. In this way, you can bring the practice of deep listening into your career, and it will enrich it in powerful ways.

Additional Resources

The following are essays about how people have molded this method to work at their organization.

Building Mental Model Diagrams, by Tiago Camacho and Leah Connolly

https://medium.com/seek-blog/building-mental-model-diagrams-72f30fc879f3

Designing with Mental Model Diagrams – *An Introduction*, by Tiago Camacho and Leah Connolly

https://medium.com/seek-blog/designing-with-mental-model-diagrams-an-introduction-5eadd21daf54

How I apply Indi Young's problem space research approach in coaching my mentees, by Pei Ling Chin

https://peilingchin.medium.com/how-i-use-indi-youngs-problem-space-research-approach-to-coach-my-mentees-55b31dc2c183

Opportunity Map Example: Indi assisted a team within Cornell University to support employers on workplace disability inclusion, who were working under contract to a federal agency:

https://indiyoung.com/examples-employers-and-disability/

These essays are also linked here:

https://indiyoung.com/explanations-articles/#featured

Conclusion

We are at another inflection point where, globally, we are realizing that designing for the "average user" harms those outside that narrow slice. Researchers and designers are understanding the impact of careless choices, and leadership at some organizations is finally listening.

Deep listening is the lever we can use to begin shifting away from the unintentional, yet very real harms that our solutions cause people, toward solutions that respect and embrace human complexity. We can use listening to discover perspectives we have ignored, notice different and valid approaches to the purpose, and find opportunities we didn't know existed. We can apply the deep listening techniques in this book to develop trust with leadership and stakeholders. Through supplying leadership with assumption-wary, purpose-focused knowledge, we can introduce a reliable method to counterbalance the rather de-humanized and simplified data produced by big data, surveys, and surface-level interviews. The solutions that organizations build in support of humans must take into account the complex systems that human agency and social interactions form.

Listening is the first step to creating long-term, actionable knowledge that builds broader support and equity into your solutions. When you know how people really think and really approach their purpose, you can enable them to accomplish their purpose in ways that work for their thinking style. And when you do that, more people will reach for your solution to accomplish that purpose.

The act of listening deeply by itself, however, isn't enough. *Who* you listen to and *how* you listen matters. Are you being intentional about including perspectives that have been ignored in your research studies?

Are you centering the person's purpose, and working hard to keep bias and assumptions out of your listening sessions and out of your synthesis? This book provides pointers and pathways for you to launch within your organization.

The choices *you* make influence the knowledge you build and the solutions you design.

By making solutions that support many ways of thinking and approaches to a purpose, not just the "average user," organizations will see more people using their solutions.

Yes, supporting people outside the middle of the bell-curve means more cost at first. But it also creates a much greater presence in the market, as well as sustainability and longevity for the organization. Taking the time to listen deeply will make business models more resilient in the long run, because people will return again and again to solutions that respect them. The result is greater resilience, a more trusting, respectful relationship with the people an organization supports, and significantly less harm to everyone.

Now is the time to listen.

Resource List

Design Justice Network Principles: https://designjustice.org/read-the-principles.

Disability Language Style Guide | National Center on Disability and Journalism - https://ncdj.org/style-guide/.

Empathy for Change: How to Create a More Empathetic World, Amy J. Wilson, January 2021. https://www.amyjwilson.com/empathy-forchange.

Empathy-Driven Software Development, Andrea Goulet and Carmen Shirkey Collins (coming mid-2022 through Pearson/Addison-Wesley) https://empathyintech.com.

Freakonomics Radio, Episode 481, "Is the U.S. Really Less Corrupt Than China?" with guest Yuen Yuen Ang, 03-Nov-2021 (includes a part about how research is often driven by "how easy it is to get the data").

HmntyCntrd https://hmntycntrd.com – an award-winning organization focused on supporting people in their personal and professional growth.

Inclusive Design Principles: https://inclusivedesignprinciples.org.

Interviewing Users, Steve Portigal, New York: Rosenfeld Media, 2013.

Listen Like You Mean It: Reclaiming the Lost Art of True Connection, Ximena Vengoechea, March 2021.

Mixed Methods: A Short Guide to Applied Mixed Methods Research, Sam Ladner, PhD.

Qualitative Research Practice: A Guide for Social Science Students & Researchers, by Jane Ritchie, Jane Lewis, Carol McNaughton Nicholls, and Rachel Ormston.

The following are essays about how people have molded this method to work at their organization.

Building Mental Model Diagrams, by Tiago Camacho and Leah Connolly

https://medium.com/seek-blog/building-mental-model-diagrams-72f30fc879f3

Designing with Mental Model Diagrams *– An Introduction*, by Tiago Camacho and Leah Connolly

https://medium.com/seek-blog/designing-with-mental-model-diagrams-an-introduction-5eadd21daf54

How I apply Indi Young's problem space research approach in coaching my mentees, by Pei Ling Chin

https://peilingchin.medium.com/how-i-use-indi-youngs-problem-space-research-approach-to-coach-my-mentees-55b31dc2c183

Opportunity Map Example: Indi assisted a team within Cornell University to support employers on workplace disability inclusion, who were working under contract to a federal agency:

https://indiyoung.com/examples-employers-and-disability/

These essays are also linked here:
https://indiyoung.com/explanations-articles/#featured

Vocabulary List

Address: (in this context) a more inclusive verb to use to describe how a person does their purpose, since it's possible to actively "not do" (postpone) it.

Approach: how a person does the thing that they are occupied with (their purpose), which is often different than how another person does that same thing, and is also defined by people's different guiding principles.

Centering: (in this context) to focus on peoples' purposes rather than focusing on your organization's solution and features.

Closing question: to make it easy for the person, guide them back to what they were thinking as they anticipated the listening session, and what they expected to bring up: "Is there anything else you expected to cover today?"

Concept: the various discrete ideas or notions that a participant brings up about a topic (e.g. deciding to stop grocery delivery because I'm retired and have time to shop now; feeling joy to restart grocery delivery during COVID).

Concept type: a way of categorizing concepts.

Concept layers:

   Description layer: contains these concept types:
   + Explanation
   + Scene setting
   + Fact

Expression layer: contains the concept types that the person uses to summarize how they see something or how they show up in relation to it:

+ Opinion
+ Preference
+ POBA (perceptions, opinions, beliefs, attitudes)

Almost cognition layer: contains these concept types:

+ Generalized (about description, expression, or interior cognition concepts)
+ Implied (about interior cognition concepts)
+ Future (about description, expression, or interior cognition concepts)

Interior cognition core: contains these concept types:

+ Inner thinking
+ Emotional reaction
+ Guiding principle

Conjecture: a question about a person's future actions, expression, or interior cognition, which causes them to guess (avoid in all but market research, co-creation).

Memory mode: the second mode of the listening session is where the person is focused on relating a memory of theirs.

Description-layer question: asking for more detail about an explanation, scene, or fact that the person mentioned, which usually results in more of the same (avoid for deep listening, except for clarification).

Expression-layer question: asking about a person's opinion, preference, perception, behavior, or attitude, which will usually not bring up interior cognition (avoid for deep listening, except as support).

Fill in the blank: encouraging the person to go into detail by saying "and …" followed by a pause; similar words like "because …" will also work.

Find the roots: help the person return to the time when an opinion, preference, perception, behavior, or attitude initially formed, to understand their interior cognition back then.

Framing: defining or setting the scope of a study based on an existing purpose people are addressing.

Germinal question: the one question that a listener poses to the person at the beginning of a listening session; basically, "what went through your mind the last few times you were addressing your purpose?"

Leading question: a question worded in a way that suggests you know what the answer is, guiding the person in the direction you indicate (avoid universally).

Micro-reflection: mentioning a pull-tab the person brought up, but not as a complete sentence, to encourage the person to unfold more details about a topic.

More about that: broadly asking a person to give more details, in hopes of understanding their interior cognition.

Pin to a past place & time: help the participant more easily talk about their interior cognition by connecting it to a particular event in the past.

Pull-tab: words that indicate there might be interior cognition that the person hasn't unfolded yet; phrases, hints, emotional shading, assumed understanding, "of course".

Purpose: a purpose can be anything a person is addressing, doing, pursuing, making progress on, deciding, planning, or even putting off. It's their aim, intent, objective, what they want to accomplish or achieve.

Session mode: there are two mental focuses for the participant of the listening session; session mode is where the person is focused on the listener and their current session together.

Topic: the subject a person is communicating about (e.g. grocery delivery); each topic is like a jawbreaker candy, with four layers and several concepts mentioned at different layers.

Turn passive into active: passive action happens to a person, and you can help them more easily speak of their interior cognition by asking about their intentional actions and reactions.

What went through your mind: specifically asking about a person's interior cognition.

Thank You

Thank You For Being My Partner:

Alex Hughes Capell, for being an amazing editor and asker-of-hard-questions.

Andrea Villa, for helping me think through complicated topics, to "make space for meaning to arise."

Anna Iurchenko, for expanding the visual representations beyond my wildest dreams.

Kunyi Mangalam, for making me better at this craft.

Jaime Levy, for being my consulting partner.

Lad Decker, for applying the craft with better nuance.

Lucy Simon, who urges me to take care of myself.

Nathan Boole, for brilliance at the website, code, social media, word-smithing, editing—all while keeping me chuckling.

Philip Ramsey, who models non-demographic language for me.

T. Lovetree, for book layout ideas that support information-finding, and for having fun at it.

Yousef Kazerooni, for the Indi Young Books imprint design, helping me evolve concepts, doing visual exploration, and writing on behalf of problem-space research.

Zulaikha Rahman, for writing the foreword.

Thank You For What to Call Things:

Bibiana Nunes, for awareness that I tended to write negatives.

Charissa Ramirez, for advice regarding the word "listen" and "partner."

Community on Twitter and LinkedIn, feedback on title and subtitle ideas, again and again.

Jane Hellendag, for advice regarding the word "listen."

Kunyi Mangalam, for opening my eyes to the fact that "surface" and "true" sound judgmental.
Pam Mayer, for the sub-title.
Stephanie Noble, for the series title.
Steve Grieshaber, for asking me to look more carefully at the perspective of a colorblind person.
Svetlana Kouznetkova, for advice regarding the word "listen."
Thesaurus.com, for being there with the word I want.

Thank You For Examples to Show:

Alexandra Jacoby
Andrea Villa
Andrew Herndon
Jazmyn Latimer
Jess Wainer
Katrina Grigo-McMahon
Pei Ling Chin
Valerie Malzer
William Miller

Thank You For Reviewing Chapters:

Anja Maerz
Augusto Bianchi
Bibiana Nunes
Cecilia Gonzalez
Francesca Barrientos
Gerry Wunsch
Jess Sand
Natalia Harzu
Pei Ling Chin
Yousef Kazerooni

Thank You For Urging Me:

Ameila Cole, to create better online learning.
Andrea Goulet, to develop the courses.
Christina Wodtke, to self-publish.
Dawn Ahukanna, to write the next book in the series.

Also by Indi Young

Books:

Mental Models: Aligning Design Strategy with Human Behavior (published by Rosenfeld Media)

Practical Empathy: For Collaboration and Creativity in Your Work (published by Rosenfeld Media) (audiobook available from Audible)

Online Courses:

1. Listening Deeply
2. Concepts & Summaries (Synthesis Part One)
3. Cultivating Patterns (Synthesis Part Two)
4. Thinking Styles
5. Mental Model Diagrams as Opportunity Maps
6. Framing Your Study

find links to these and other resources at *indiyoung.com*

Indi
Young

About the Author

I began my career as a naïve young woman who believed gender equity had been achieved, who believed in meritocracy and individualism, and knew that the company I had joined planned to keep me employed forever. It took four years for me to recognize that a career on the company ladder wasn't for me. I left full-time employment still believing in meritocracy, individualism, and gender equity as reality. It took fifteen more years for these beliefs to erode. I still have a tendency toward individualism at my core, and am always learning how to see past it.

Race and gender orientations are for me so closely connected to my extended family of friends and partners that I only recognized and began to study their history in the past decade. With this added awareness, I am finding ways to contribute to the shift toward equity. This book is intended to be helpful in this regard.

—Indi